Rethinking World Politics

Series Editor: Professor Michael Cox

In an age of increased academic specialization where more and more books about smaller and smaller topics are becoming the norm, this major new series is designed to provide a forum and stimulus for leading scholars to address big issues in world politics in an accessible but original manner. A key aim is to transcend the intellectual and disciplinary boundaries which have so often served to limit rather than enhance our understanding of the modern world. In the best tradition of engaged scholarship, it aims to provide clear new perspectives to help make sense of a world in flux.

Each book addresses a major issue or event that has had a formative influence on the twentieth-century or the twenty-first-century world which is now emerging. Each makes its own distinctive contribution as well as providing an original but accessible guide to competing lines of interpretation.

Taken as a whole, the series will rethink contemporary international politics in ways that are lively, informed and – above all – provocative.

Published

Nick Bisley
Rethinking Globalization

Adrian Guelke
Rethinking the Rise and Fall of Apartheid

Richard Stubbs
Rethinking Asia's Economic Miracle

Forthcoming

Mark T. Berger and Heloise Weber
Rethinking the Third World

John Dumbrell
Rethinking the Vietnam War

David H. Dunn
Rethinking Transatlanticism

Peter Shearman
Rethinking Soviet Communism

In preparation

Rethinking European Integration

Rethinking Global Governance

Rethinking the Twentieth Century

Rethinking the Cold War

Rethinking the Emergence of a Global Economy

Rethinking the Post-Cold War World Order

Rethinking the Rise of Islam

Rethinking the First World War

Rethinking the Second World War

Rethinking the Twenty Years Crisis: 1919–39

Rethinking US Hegemony

Rethinking Globalization

Nick Bisley

First published 2007 by
PALGRAVE MACMILLAN
Houndmills, Basingstoke, Hampshire RG21 6XS and
175 Fifth Avenue, New York, N.Y. 10010
Companies and representatives throughout the world

PALGRAVE MACMILLAN is the global academic imprint of the Palgrave
Macmillan division of St. Martin's Press, LLC and of Palgrave Macmillan
Ltd. Macmillan is a registered trademark in the United States, United
Kingdom and other countries. Palgrave is a registered trademark in the
European Union and other countries.

ISBN-13: 978–1–4039–8694–8   hardback
ISBN-10: 1–4039–8694–0   hardback
ISBN-13: 978–1–4039–8695–5   paperback
ISBN-10: 1–4039–8695–9   paperback

This book is printed on paper suitable for recycling and made from
fully managed and sustained forest sources. Logging, pulping and
manufacturing processes are expected to conform to the environmental
regulations of the country of origin.

A catalogue record for this book is available from the British Library.

A catalog record for this book is available from the Library of Congress.

10   9   8   7   6   5   4   3   2   1
16   15   14   13   12   11   10   09   08   07

Printed and bound in China

Contents

Contents

Foreword

The purpose of the *Rethinking World Politics* series is to allow original scholars with something worth saying a space within which to reflect broadly on big international problems in a form accessible to the general reader as well as the student and specialist. The series was always animated by an underlying aspiration: to insert new ideas into old debates, to stimulate discussion, and hopefully move it onto a higher, and more interesting, plane.

In this outstanding *tour d'horizon*, Nick Bisley makes the strongest case possible for rethinking the character of globalization without either sinking into the stale polemic or apologetics that have marked much debate about this most confusing and important of phenomena. With a sharp eye for detail and a rare ability to distinguish the essential from the inessential, the momentary from the enduring, Bisley shows that one cannot talk about globalization in general. The quest for the perfect definition is impossible; in fact, almost beside the point. As he points out, the answer to the question 'what does globalization actually mean' depends not only on 'one's basic visions of its constituent elements', but also 'on the sphere of human life in which one is interested'.

But Bisley does far more than simply establish a coherent framework for thinking about globalization. He shows in a most distinctive manner the interplay between globalization and the workings of the international system and the ways in which globalization is working not just to transform the fundamentals of the system but actually changing 'the relative balance of influence among the actors in world politics'. His study is certain to become one of the defining texts in the contemporary analysis of International Relations.

In common with the previously published texts in the series, Bisley's book shows that the ambitious task I set is not an unrealistic one given the right authors. Like Adrian Guelke and Richard Stubbs, he makes a strong case – and provides a mass of evidence – to show that, while all politics may be fought out within the boundaries of regions or states, in the end any analysis that privileges the local over the global is bound to be wanting.

PROFESSOR MICHAEL COX
*Department of International Relations
and Cold War Studies Centre
London School of Economics
December 2006*

Preface

Globalization has caused a huge proliferation of books offering a vast array of interpretations of this complex phenomenon. My justification for adding to this expanding literature is that relatively few books on the topic provide a balanced, concise and accessible overview. The intention here is to stand back from the heated debates about the nature, and very existence, of globalization and to critically examine some of the key issues and claims made about one of the most important and controversial topics in the social sciences. The other justification is that the book provides a systematic assessment of what globalization means for the structures and institutions of world politics. In short, it comprises a succinct overview and an accessible analysis of globalization that is geared to students and general readers, as well as those with a particular interest in globalization's implications for the international system.

This book began life as a lecture given to the senior staff college of the Australian Defence Force, the Centre for Defence and Strategic Studies (CDSS). I was asked to give a lecture on globalization and the myth of the powerless state to a group of fifty senior military officers from Australia and other states in the Asia-Pacific. Such a request focuses the mind. One does not need to try too hard to convince someone who has spent time as part of INTERFET or in Afghanistan that globalization has not rendered state power obsolete. But it was clear to me that globalization, and its attendant transformations, mattered considerably for the kind of strategic work that the course members were going to undertake, and yet there was a dearth of literature that could provide an accessible and systematic assessment of globalization for people with their interests and needs. The editor of the *Rethinking World Politics* series, Mick Cox, was in the audience that day and as we discussed these matters, in his typical fashion, he suggested that I write such a book. The book, therefore, owes its existence, such as it is, to CDSS in Canberra and most particularly to Mick. I would like to thank Gary Smith and David Lowe of Deakin University, who ran the programme at CDSS, for the opportunity to get my thoughts moving in this direction. Also, many colleagues have generously given me their advice and thoughts on the dreaded g-word and I would particularly like to thank for their help, both direct and indirect: Steven Slaughter, Richard Tanter, Allen Gyngell, Fred Halliday, John Wiseman and Peter Hayes. My publisher at Palgrave Macmillan, the indefatigable Steven Kennedy, provided just the right balance of enthusiasm and critical advice during the planning, writing and editing of the book, for which I am especially grateful. I would also like to thank Palgrave Macmillan's two anonymous reviewers whose perceptive comments were of great use. Usually writing is interrupted by a move between universities, but in my case relocation to the very welcoming environment of the Department of Management at Monash University has had quite the opposite effect. This has been largely thanks to Chris Nyland and particularly to my comrades on the sixth floor, especially Vivek Chaudhri, Nell Kimberley, Gaby Ramia and Peter Gahan. Finally, Catherine Button has done far more to ensure the completion of this book than anyone else; as always, many thanks.

NICK BISLEY
Melbourne

List of Abbreviations

ADB	Asian Development Bank
APEC	Asia Pacific Economic Cooperation
ASEAN	Association of Southeast Asian Nations
BIS	Bank for International Settlements
CCP	Chinese Communist Party
DRC	Democratic Republic of Congo
ECOWAS	Economic Community of West African States
EU	European Union
FDI	Foreign Direct Investment
FSF	Financial Stability Forum
GATT	General Agreement on Tariffs and Trade
GCC	Gulf Cooperation Council
GDP	Gross Domestic Product
IATA	International Air Travel Association
IFI	International Financial Institution
IMF	International Monetary Fund
INTERFET	International Force in East Timor
IO	International Organization
IR	International Relations (the academic discipline of)
LDC	Less Developed Country
MERCOSUR	*Mercado Comùn del Sur* (Southern Common Market)
MNC	Multinational Corporation
NAFTA	North American Free Trade Agreement
NATO	North Atlantic Treaty Organization
NGO	Non-governmental Organization
NYSE	New York Stock Exchange
OAU	Organization of African Unity
OECD	Organization for Economic Cooperation and Development
PMA	Private Military Actor

PRC	People's Republic of China
PSA	Private Security Actor
PTA	Preferential Trade Agreement
SAARC	South Asian Association for Regional Cooperation
SADC	Southern African Development Community
SARS	Severe Acute Respiratory Syndrome
TNC	Transnational Corporation
UK	United Kingdom
UN	United Nations
UNCTAD	United Nations Conference on Trade and Development
UNDP	United Nations Development Programme
US	United States of America
USSR	Union of Soviet Socialist Republics
WAEMU	West African Economic and Monetary Union
WIPO	World Intellectual Property Organization
WTO	World Trade Organization

Introduction

The sense that globalization was everywhere and changing everything appeared to develop as a collective common wisdom in the
1980s and 1990s. Academics, politicians, and business people all
seemed susceptible to the beguiling charms of this evidently pervasive
and transformative social phenomenon. It is hard to find a university
that has not established a centre for the study of globalization or
some variation on the theme, nor a government that has not invoked
reform in its name. Of course not everyone thought that globalization
was an unalloyed Good Thing. The well organised protests at Seattle
in 1999, and subsequently in Washington, Quebec and Genoa
reflected strong anti-globalization sentiment. Regardless of whether
you liked it or detested it, whether you thought it was changing
everything or changing nothing, it was extraordinarily hard to avoid.
In academia, some scholars attributed it with almost transcendental
importance arguing that we were living through a fundamental
transformation of human existence. Outside the ivory tower, the idea
of globalization had resonance because it was so clearly tangible in
people's everyday lives. For those in East Asia whose savings were
wiped out by the financial crisis of 1997–98, the volatility of global
financial markets was all too apparent. The international outsour-
cing of telephone support services has meant that a woman in Sydney
now speaks to a telephone operator in Mumbai to renew her car
insurance. In that most material element of life – food – the daily
experiences of globalization are particularly evident. From the
adoption of sushi as a lunchtime staple in Chicago, Manchester
and Paris to the year-round global markets in fresh fruit and
vegetables, people's quotidian consumption, and its relative afford-
ability, is a function of palpably global forces. When one bites into a
South African or Chilean Pink Lady apple, in some small way, one is
tasting the process of globalization.

There appears to be hardly a sphere of social life which globalization has left untouched – from food to freedoms, rights to royalty –

1

globalization has left its mark across the spectrum of cultural, economic and political life. Phenomena as diverse as the spread of McDonald's and Starbucks across the world and the emergence of the World Trade Organization (WTO) are thought to be products of the power and pervasiveness of globalization. It is said to be undermining national environmental and labour standards in the developed world, further exacerbating the poverty of the poor and, at the same time, boosting national wealth through market expansion in Botswana and Brazil. Clearly something is going on. The small number of academic writings that announced the onset of globalization has rapidly expanded into a massive and diverse literature on what it is and how significant it is going to be. Yet the expansive nature of the debates about globalization, as well as the extraordinarily vast terrain that the phenomenon is said to be influencing, means that the debate often creates more confusion than it resolves. The late political economist Susan Strange bemoaned the concept's woolliness, declaring that it is 'a term which can refer to anything from the Internet to a hamburger' (Strange, 1996: xiii). Yet there is an enduring sense that it captures developments of significance. Recent years have brought about an increase in the rate and volume of interactions between states and societies. This has been facilitated by a considerable reduction in the barriers – political, economic and cultural – which had previously constrained these actions. The shifts, in some spheres, are very real: the internationalization of production, the rise of global financial markets and the global spread of the sovereign state system cannot be denied. The problem, however, is that it is particularly challenging to determine the significance of historical change without the necessary perspective. Moreover, it is easy to lose one's bearings when much of the work which has tried to do just that is larded with grandiloquent hype.

So what does globalization actually mean? The answer ultimately depends not only on one's basic vision of its constituent elements but also on the sphere of human life in which one is interested. The dimensions of globalization that affect cultural practices in North America are of a different form and magnitude than those that influence changing perceptions of security threats in Southeast Asia. This makes it very difficult to talk about globalization in general terms. In consideration of globalization, context is all. This book offers a reflection on globalization viewed from the empirical and theoretical perspective of world politics and has two distinct aims. First, it is an attempt to make sense of a debate characterized by dramatic claims, a vast terrain and a bewildering range of sources. In this sense, the argument presented here attempts to digest what globalization means for world politics and through this provide a fresh perspective on a broad-ranging social phenomenon. Second, it is an effort to determine the nature and impact of the changes associated with globalization on the structures, norms and institutions of the contemporary international system.

How does this book differ from the many other studies of globalization that already exist? It does so in three ways. First, I have not found a book-length study which reflects on the interplay between globalization and the workings of the international system and provides a systematic assessment of how globalization is and is not influencing key facets of world politics. Second, as a result of this analysis, it provides a unique vantage point to reflect on the current state of globalization, as both an empirical and discursive phenomenon. Third, it emphasizes the ways in which globalization is working not so much to transform the fundamental features of the system as to change the relative balance of influence among actors in world politics and thus influence their modes of behaviour. For those interested in world politics, it provides a clear means to make sense of how globalization is influencing the field, and for those who are more concerned with globalization itself, the argument provides important institutional and theoretical depth of field.

For the student of world politics making sense of globalization is a task of considerable importance. At the most obvious level claims about globalization are assertions about the character of the social world and its fundamental structures and processes. All students and scholars of world politics need to take such claims seriously as part of their participation in a broader social science. To be more specific, it is clear that the world has changed in important ways – the nature of economic interaction, the relationships between political communities that are geographically distant, and the character of modern warfare are only the most obvious examples – and that these changes are associated with the forces of globalization. Areas that are the core business of the study of world politics are a key part of the process and are, if some are to be believed, undergoing fundamental transformation. If we are to make sense of the underlying character of world politics, it is imperative that we have a clear sense of the forces that are of significance and those which are not, and how these affect the structure, and institutions as well as the behaviour of actors in the international system.

What kind of rethinking of globalization is on offer here? The renowned historian John Lukacs observes that, in its most straightforward sense, rethinking is a process of digestion (Lukacs, 2005). He makes this reference in a foreword to a book on the bloodiest battle of the Second World War, the Siege of Budapest, and to the way in which the population of that city has not really come to terms with the horrors inflicted during the Second World War. For Lukacs, the citizens of Budapest have not yet rethought the war or the battle. What it means to rethink in this basic, and yet quite profound, sense is the process by which one makes sense of the world given time and space for adequate reflection. It is in this sense that this book offers a rethinking of globalization. This work does not set out an iconoclastic interpretation of the changes in the world nor does it try to show how everyone else is wrong. Rather, it seeks to take advantage of a certain amount of perspective which is afforded by the time that has passed since the globalization debate began to help clarify our understanding of this complex and important phenomenon. Moreover it seeks to provide a systematic assessment of globalization for those – students, policy-makers and analysts – who have to try to make sense of globalization as it affects the structures and dynamics of the international system.

World Politics and Globalization

As a field which lies at the intersection of sociology, diplomatic history, political science, economics and political philosophy, International Relations (IR) is well placed to make sense of globalization. As with many other fields, globalization made its presence felt in priority research funding and new degree courses as scholars scrambled to apply some rigorous thinking to the general sentiment that there were significant changes afoot relating to the increased rate and speed of transnational flows. Yet despite this popularity, there have been few attempts to analyze the way in which globalization is influencing the workings of contemporary world politics. This book seeks to rectify this shortcoming.

Although the term world politics has come to be increasingly used, some may be uncertain as to just what it refers. In a book on globalization it is hardly enough to assert that world politics means simply the system of relations among sovereign states, nor is it adequate to vaguely invoke the name as being sufficient to describe the focal point of concern. Traditionally understood, international relations or international politics refers to studies that examine the conduct of states in their interactions with one another and its primary concern has been the business of war and peace. In more recent years, the terrain has been opened to include aspects of international economic relations and the inter-state cooperation that has arisen to facilitate these processes. This widening of the analytic aperture has generally not involved a move away from a primary focus on the relations within and between states. For example, studies of international economic affairs within international politics might examine the ways in which states have individually or collectively set the rules of international trade. The traditional label lays a particular emphasis on the role and function of the state in its dealings in international society. As opposed to this statist focus, 'world politics' is a useful way of conveying a conception of the subject matter that is somewhat broader than this orthodox approach. While it has become relatively fashionable of late, the term has been in use for some time. One of IR's leading scholarly journals takes the label as its name. *World Politics* was founded in 1948, and its first issue includes articles by Jacob Viner, Gabriel Almond and Hans Morgenthau. One of the earliest references to globalization appeared in Modelski's 1972 study *The Principles of World Politics* and Bull's seminal 1977 work on international society is subtitled 'A Study of Order in World Politics'. Using the term to refer to the broad field of international relations has a longer-run history than we often realise, as do concerns with the intellectual limits of a narrowly statist conception of the field.

World politics thus refers to the broad field of studies that is concerned with the organization, structure and social processes of the modern international system. The international system itself is hardly a self-evident label and here describes the system of social relations that derive from the division of the world into a series of legally equal, territorially defined political organizations. This does not mean that we are only interested in the relations between these entities, rather we are concerned with the political, economic and ethical consequences of dividing social space up in this way. The concern of this book is with the way in which globalization is influencing the institutions, norms and modes of behaviour across this system. Its scale is so vast, and the issues which can be reasonably said to shape world politics are so diverse, that there is simply not room to consider every interaction. To that end the book focuses on six central elements of the system which have been chosen for two reasons. First, they are fundamental parts of the contemporary order in the sense that they play a vital role in structuring its shape, determining the dominant actors and influencing the pattern and form of their relations. Second, they have been identified in the literature as sites of the most discernible and important influence of globalization. The elements of the system which receive detailed scrutiny are: the state, the global economy, international institutions, nationalism, war and the structure of international order. Consideration of how globalization interacts with these features of world politics provides the means through which the broader reflection on globalization occurs.

A Short Overview

The assessment of globalization offered here is set out in eight chapters. The first chapter examines the nature and evolution of the globalization debate and provides an assessment of the competing economic, sociological and political interpretations of globalization. The chapter also sets out a basic conception of globalization on which the ongoing discussion is based. Globalization is defined as the set of social consequences which derive from the increasing rate and speed of interactions of knowledge, people, goods and capital between states and societies. Chapter 2 examines globalization's past and discusses the ways in which the contemporary phenomenon is a continuation of longer-run historical processes as well as being a distinctive socio-economic development. While globalization shares characteristics with previous 'global eras', such as the *belle époque* or the Indian Ocean world economy of the first millennium, the scale, speed and universality of central elements of contemporary globalization mark it off as historically distinct. Following these two introductory chapters, Chapter 3 examines globalization's interaction with the most important social institution in world politics: the state. It argues against the declinist literature and emphasizes that rather than doing away with the state as the key actor in world politics, globalization is changing the environment in which it operates and thus causing some shifts in domestic and international behaviour.

Chapter 4 examines the political economy of globalization and assesses the current state of the world economy with a particular focus on the changing balance of power that exists between states and markets under conditions of globalization. One of the more notable developments in world politics during the 20th century was the rise in prominence of international institutions. Chapter 5 examines this phenomenon and the ways in which international institutions are thought to be enhancing their power and position due to globalization. It argues that while institutions have had their structural opportunities enhanced by globalization they have not been able to capitalize on this and become markedly more important. Indeed, some are finding life under globalization surprisingly challenging. Chapter 6 argues that while globalization has changed elements of the character of war, its fundamental nature, as a means by which political ends are advanced through the organized use of violence, is much as it has always been. But new developments do mean that the context in which force is used to achieve political aims is undergoing important change. One of the reasons for the rise in prominence of questions of culture and identity within IR is thought to be the way in which globalization is recasting these forms in dangerous and destabilizing ways. Chapter 7 examines the extent to which globalization is influencing identity politics and particularly the way in which it is transforming nationalism, the dominant form of collective identity in the international system. It argues that, rather than undermining nationalism or diluting its power, globalization is strengthening its political capacity, although it is driving new strategies and approaches to this powerful means for mobilizing collective identity. The final substantive chapter examines the interaction of globalization with the institutions and principles of international order. The focus is on order understood as the system which structures relations between states. The chapter shows that globalization is not recasting the key structures of order – indeed it is enhancing the power of some traditional aspects – but it is revealing the growing disjuncture between the norms and institutions of the international system and the social reality of world politics.

Ultimately, this book argues that globalization is not about to cast the state into the abyss, nor is it ushering in a novel post-Westphalian political and economic order: world politics is still a state-centred social system. But globalization makes clear that state-centred conceptions of politics and economics have distinct problems, whether viewed from a moral or an efficiency point of view. Yet globalization provides insufficient incentive to make any meaningful reconfiguration of the structural underpinnings of the current system at all likely. Indeed one plausible interpretation is to see that while globalization shows the limitations of existing organizations its social dislocation acts to constrain the possible room available for man-oeuvre and the necessary transformation by states and peoples. The book finishes with a reflection on what the intersection of globaliza-tion and world politics means for our understanding of globalization. The conclusion argues that globalization is not yet bringing about fundamental transformation either to the system or to the nature of the key actors, but it is changing the relative influence, forms of behaviour and strategies of states and peoples. Moreover, it empha-sizes that although globalization is generally associated with eco-nomic and cultural phenomenon, globalization is a deeply political process. Finally, the experiences of world politics make clear that globalization is not a singular, homogenizing force, rather it has a deeply uneven, contradictory and unpredictable character. Many liberals feel that globalization has unleashed forces which will empower a cosmopolitan sensibility and drive policy-making to more appropriate and efficient levels. Yet the experiences thus far should dampen such enthusiasm. The most straightforward sum-mary of the argument contained in this book is as follows: globalization is changing world politics, but not nearly so much as its enthusiasts may claim nor in the ways in which we might have expected even five years ago. Before we can explore this, however, it is important to provide some introductory comments about globa-lization and the debate which it has presaged.

1
Parameters of the Globalization Debate

In the opening chapter of one of the most influential International Relations (IR) textbooks readers discover that globalization is producing a 'fundamental shift in the constitution of world politics' (McGrew, 2005: 38). Its force is so profound, the author asserts, that, if we are to make sense of the transformations it is bringing about, we must rethink the very nature of politics itself. From the institutions of government to the most basic duties that we owe to others, all is being transformed by this pervasive social force. Yet in a leading scholarly journal published just months after the textbook, we are told, with no less certainty, that 'the "age of globalization" is over' (Rosenberg, 2005: 3). The philosophical and sociological arguments about globalization were, it seems, an intellectual optical illusion. The much trumpeted world of global governance has failed to materialize, atavistic nationalism is rife, and the actions of the US, Russia and China glaringly fly in the face of all the prescriptions of the globalization prophets. Rosenberg argues that the claims made about globalization have been shown to have little to offer the serious scholar of social life.

What are we to make of this? Is globalization so thoroughly debunked that the only real puzzle that we have left is to work out why so many bright people thought it was so important? Or are the self-styled 'transformationalists' right to assert that the economic, social and cultural links created over the past twenty years are driving human society into a distinctly novel phase? Beyond having some pity for the undergraduate presented with such contradictory messages, we must recognize that the globalization debate is far from settled. But this is not necessarily a bad thing. It is such a broad

9

term, it relates to such a diversity of social experience and touches on so many politically sensitive elements of human existence that it would be surprising if there were a happy consensus. The challenge, of course, lies in working out how to make sense of the various lines of debate, and determining on what basis to evaluate the differing conceptions which derive from diverging assessments of its character and dynamics. The purpose of this first chapter is provide some guidance in this regard. It presents an overview of the ways in which globalization has been used so as to provide a means to make sense of what is a vast and unwieldy literature and to clarify the conception of globalization that is used in the book.

The lack of consensus as to what globalization actually involves is due to many factors – analytic weakness, intellectual fashion and stark differences over the relative weight of empirical evidence are just some of the reasons – but the heat of the argument that was the hallmark of much of the literature in the 1980s and 1990s has cooled in recent years, although some feel that the reduction in intensity has served to mask globalization's acceleration (Friedman, 2005). As shown by the contrasting views mentioned at the outset, the various positions have begun to talk past one another. The true-believers cling to their position that the transformation of space and time is recasting the rules of social life and the sceptics find ever more confident tones to express their doubt. Also, the strategic and psychological consequences of terrorism, from the seismic events of September 11 to the bombings in Bali, Madrid and London, as well as America's more muscular approach to its global role, has reduced globalization's centrality in academic debate. This allows an opportunity to take stock of the range of debates that emerged over globalization and to cast a critical eye over the competing assertions. Whatever one's thoughts about the character of globalization, even if one is of the most sceptical frame of mind, the sheer volume of writing across a vast array of sectors – from academic to activist, policy-maker to management consultant – demands our attention.

The wide range and disciplinary diversity of these writings has made the globalization debate especially confusing. Considerable disputes exist over its origins, nature, dynamics, novelty and its implications for economic and political institutions. Indeed we cannot be sure that it is even an 'it'. As this quite influential definition shows, globalization is generally defined in anything but a parsimonious fashion:

[globalization is] a process (or set of processes) which embodies a transformation in the spatial organization of social relations and transactions – assessed in terms of their extensity, intensity, velocity and impact – generating transcontinental or interregional flows and networks of activity, interaction, and the exercise of power (Held *et al.*, 1999: 16).

It is not clear whether it is a singular process or a set of processes – is it one thing or is it plural? If so, how can we tell when it is singular and when multiple? One way is to view this as not especially problematic. Globalization varies in time and place: sometimes it is singular and at others it is a multi-dimensional force. The problem is that a lack of clarity can breed inconsistent analysis and a vagueness which can be the source of exasperation. Although there are problems with seeking a certain parsimony – complexity is all in such a broad-ranging topic – how can one provide some clarity and analytic precision given the protean nature of globalization processes? Scholte argues that globalization can be more effectively defined as 'the spread of transplanetary – and in recent times also more particularly supraterritorial – connections between people' (Scholte, 2005: 59). This provides some specificity but the difference between these two very influential definitions points at the challenges the student of globalization faces simply at the point of conceptualization.

Central to the broader rethinking on offer here is an effort to make some analytic sense of the divergent concepts that debate has thrown up. This is done by sketching out the evolution of the arguments about globalization as they emerged through the late 1980s and 1990s. Following this, the chapter considers the competing visions of the essential character of globalization and categorizes the ways in which scholars have conceived of globalization's core elements. The chapter then sets out the definition of globalization that forms the basis of the analysis in the subsequent chapters.

A Short History of the Globalization Debate

Arguments about globalization appeared to flower rather suddenly in the early 1990s. To be sure, the issues that argument began to crystallize around – such as the decreasing salience of national forms of power and the increasing importance of international economic relations to domestic social and political life – had surfaced earlier in important work about interdependence (Keohane and Nye, 1972; 1977) and world systems (Wallerstein, 1974). George Modelski even used the term globalization to refer to what he perceived to be the key developments in world politics in the early 1970s (Modelski, 1972). Such was the resonance of these non-traditional issues emerging in the 1970s and early 1980s that IR appeared to be on the cusp of another of the 'great debates' that supposedly define its development (Maghroori and Ramberg, 1982). While globalism did not quite catch on in the way that one might have expected (due in part to the second Cold War), the explosion of work in the late 1980s and early 1990s was not the first time that transnational, economic and cultural forces had been flagged. Of course, while the subject matter that came to be central to the story of globalization had antecedents, the forcefulness with which it gripped the social scientific, as well as the policy, imagination in the 1990s was remarkable. Such was the enthusiasm for globalization that it can be hard to distinguish patterns of argument, but looking back over these years one is able to discern five distinct phases of the debate (summarized in Table 1.1, p. 17).

The first bloom of globalization writing emerged in the late 1980s and involved assertions that globalization was reorganizing the patterns of social life. While earlier work had identified developments that we now associate with globalization – for example transnational relations in IR and international production in political economy – this group was the first to argue that something distinctive was going on. Some of the more notable works are Giddens (1990) in sociology, Harvey (1989) in geography, Luard (1990) and Rosenau (1990) in IR, Appadurai (1990) and Featherstone (1990) in cultural theory and Ohmae (1990) in business studies. While from a diverse disciplinary background, they share some important characteristics. First, they all argued that significant changes to existing social structures were occurring, and that both the pattern of social relations and the means with which we approach these relations (in policy and theoretical terms) needed significant change. Second, they explicitly used globalization as the label to identify this or their depiction was so close to that which came to be called globalization that they belong to this grouping (e.g. Rosenau, 1990: 7). Third, they gave quite expansive accounts of the scope and consequences of this new phenomenon.

The second phase gathered pace in the early 1990s and amplified the claims made about globalization and their consequences for existing practices, both theoretical and policy-related. This expansion of the literature saw not only a fleshing out of the more ambitious claims made about the phenomenon, but also the acceptance of globalization as an increasingly mainstream line of inquiry. No longer a subject for the prophets alone, this phase brought globalization to orthodox academia and it began to figure in public policy debates across the developed world. Work here involved the pioneers substantiating their initial claims about globalization, such as Ohmae (1995) and Giddens (1994), as well as others who seized the initiative and advanced their own versions of globalization and its consequences. For example, Camilleri and Falk's (1992) argument about the end of sovereignty substantiated the ideas set out by Rosenau (1990). Albrow's grand sociological work, followed lines forged by Giddens, and argued that modernity was in the process of being replaced by 'globality' (1996: 4).

This phase also saw a crystallization of several propositions that became central to debate about globalization. First, it involved an upsurge in economic interpretations of globalization (e.g. Casson, 1992; Dicken, 1992; Dunning, 1993; Ohmae, 1995; Reich, 1991) and cemented the idea of a truly global economic system that influences the success of the world's states and societies in the popular imagination. Second, the claim that the state and its attendant norms and institutions (such as sovereignty and nationalism) were being undermined or outmoded by the changing circumstances received more nuanced attention (e.g. Horsman and Marshall, 1994; McGrew and Lewis, 1992). Third, the further elaboration of macro socio-logical claims about globalization reinforced the proposition that the social realm was in the midst of a broad-ranging transformation (e.g. Albrow, 1996; Axford, 1995; Featherstone *et al.*, 1995; Scholte, 1993).

The second phase gave globalization wings in the academic realm leading to the establishment of institutions for its study and courses of learning devoted to unravelling its threads. It also set in train important debates in core areas of concern (for example, integration in economics, sovereignty and the state in IR and modernity in sociology) and globalization began to appear more frequently in the world of policy and politics.

Globalization swiftly moved from being a concept advanced by a narrow band of specialists to becoming a watch-word of almost all social science and was increasingly a part of public policy-making across the developed world. It became hard to avoid this suddenly fashionable concept. Whether at the summit meeting, in the class room or in the mass media, globalization was everywhere. For a growing band of scholars, analysts and policy-makers, something of great significance was going on. Yet while almost everyone could agree that life was not going to be just as it had in the past, doubt began to emerge about the claims made in the first phases of globalization writing.

The mid to late 1990s saw the publication of a range of critical reactions to many of the arguments advanced by globalization advocates and claims about the end of the state and the death of sovereignty came in for particular criticism. Scholars argued that such claims misunderstood sovereignty (Gelber, 1997), that they underestimated the continuing power and competence of states (Weiss, 1998) and that they lacked the subtlety to understand where and how change mattered (Cerny, 1997). Their point was not that social life was continuing unchanged, rather that it was undergoing a more subtle transformation than had previously been claimed (Mann, 1997). Political economists argued that far from constraining states and their autonomy, globalization was enhancing state power and choice (Garrett, 1998). In the economic sphere, many doubted the extent of global economic integration (Boyer and Drache, 1996) and the reach of ostensibly 'global' economic activities (Hirst and Thompson, 1996). They further argued that change was being over-hyped and that globalization was little more than a repackaging of internationalization and interdependence (Krasner, 1993; Ruigrok and van Tulder, 1995). In their landmark study, Held *et al.* describe much of the writing that appeared in this phase as typical of what they call the 'sceptic' position (Held *et al.*, 1999: 5–7). Their view – which has become the most influential study of globalization – groups these writers somewhat unfairly. On the one hand some are very doubtful about the grander claims made about the world – not an unreasonable position given some of the rather ambitious things that had been said – but on the other hand, many of these writers accepted that things had changed in important ways. Their point was that the language used and concepts advanced by many earlier writings had undermined efforts to understand what was actually going on.

The other element of the globalization debate which began to appear at this stage, but which became more significant in the following phase, was the emergence of an anti-globalization position. In the main, writing about globalization had been of a largely analytic hue. In this phase, activists and scholars began to associate it with malign forces and to question the motives of those advocating it. They highlighted the negative costs of economic, social and political integration (e.g. Gray, 1998; Hoogvelt, 1997; Rodrik, 1997) and saw policy-makers embracing liberalization with undue enthusiasm, lured by the sirens of multinational corporations and their accomplices in academia. Beyond providing balance to some of the more extreme claims that had hitherto been made, this phase was significant because it consolidated globalization as a central area of academic and policy contestation. More importantly, this phase provoked reaction among the globalization adherents and was, in many respects, the impetus for the fourth phase.

The subsequent element of the globalization debate involved the appearance of a number of broad-ranging studies which sought to provide some shape to conceptions of globalization. This phase was particularly successful in solidifying contemporary understandings of globalization. The best known and most influential of these studies is Held *et al.*'s *Global Transformations* (1999). The work is well known for its characterization of the globalization debate as between 'hyper-globalizers' and 'sceptics' and sets out its own position – the 'transformationalist' – as a middle road which argues that globalization is transforming the character of global economics, politics, and culture due to shifts in spatial dimensions of social relations. Other important examples of this kind of writing are Scholte's work on 'supra-territoriality' (2000), Castells' landmark series on the network society (1996; 1997; 1998), Giddens' discussion of globalization presented in the BBC's annual Reith Lectures (1999) – an example of the widespread acceptance of these ideas outside of academia – and Beck's dissection of 'globality' (1999; 2000). This period also saw a number of slightly less ambitious studies containing self-styled 'level-headed' assessments of the phenomenon (e.g. Cable, 1999; Clark, 1999; Jones 2000).

The fourth phase also witnessed the emergence of a more activist literature that was critical of globalization and which coincided with a series of high-profile and, at times, violent demonstrations at meetings of the WTO, the World Economic Forum, the European

Union (EU) and North Atlantic Treaty Organization (NATO). The concerns voiced by both demonstrators and writers – a group Martin Wolf derides as 'new millennium collectivists' (2004: 3) – include the belief that globalization is increasing global inequality, eroding democratic control of states and societies, destroying workers' rights, damaging the environment and allowing global corporations to ride rough-shod over the world (e.g. Forrester, 1999; Greider, 1997; Hertz, 2001; Klein, 2000). Such arguments were not only the preserve of the usual left-wing suspects; Joseph Stiglitz, a mainstream economist and one-time adviser to President Bill Clinton, joined the fray with a searing critique of global economic institutions (2002). The fourth phase consolidated the intellectual framework of globalization and catalyzed groups concerned with the consequences of globalization on states and societies.

The fifth and latest phase is characterized by two developments. First, the various positions increasingly talk past one another thus leading to the situation depicted at the start of this chapter. Second, recent years have seen a tranche of works which have sought to sell globalization in the face of its critics. To a certain extent those supportive of the changes associated with globalization – which they generally see as involving increasingly open markets, more fluid capital movements, the emergence of a global production process and with it a global division of labour – had been somewhat complacent in the earlier phases. They had assumed that many in the world felt as they did and that the benefits would accrue rapidly and woo the doubters. Clearly they were wrong. As such, economists (Bhagwati, 2004), journalists (Friedman, 2005; Legrain, 2002; Wolf, 2004), and consultants (Leadbetter, 2002) have come out to defend their vision of the benefits of globalization.

The supporters of a largely economic version of globalization, and those who present it as a positive and universal force are, at present, in the ascendancy. The positions have firmed and debate currently focuses more on reform of existing structures than on the fundamental issues at stake (e.g. Held *et al.*, 2005; Stiglitz, 2006). Competing parties are less inclined to engage substantively with one another and the lines of enquiry appear more fixed. Within the social sciences, although excluding economics, the 'transformationalist' position articulated by Held *et al.* (1999) is more influential than any other, but it is far from hegemonic and no position reflects a consensus on the matter.

Table 1.1   Evolution of the globalization debate

Phase of debate	Characteristics	Examples
1. Late 1980s	Globalization identified as a process driving radical change in the social realm	Giddens (1990), Harvey (1989), Featherstone (1990), Luard (1990)
2. Early to mid 1990s	Claims about globalization amplified, they become increasingly mainstream and key lines of contestation emerge	Ohmae (1995), Giddens (1994), Camilleri and Falk (1992), Albrow (1996), McGrew and Lewis (1992), Scholte (1993)
3. Late 1990s	Central claims about globalization are theoretically, empirically and politically challenged	Weiss (1998), Garrett (1998), Hirst and Thompson (1996), Rodrik (1997), Hoogvelt (1997)
4. Early 2000s	Consolidation of globalization through parameter setting studies and as a site of political contestation	Held *et al.* (1999), Scholte (2000), Castells (1996, 1997, 1998), Klein (2000), Stiglitz (2002)
5. Mid 2000s	Merits of globalization overtly defended in the face of the critics	Bhagwati (2004), Wolf (2004), Legrain (2002), Friedman (2005)

Competing Visions of Globalization

There is an extraordinary diversity of views about the essential character of globalization. The most influential typology of this sprawling literature is the sceptic–transformationalist–hyperglobalizer continuum set out by Held *et al.* (1999). They argue that on the one hand there are 'hyperglobalizers', those who tend to overstate the character and impact of globalization, and on the other 'sceptics' who deny that it is anything more than epiphenomena. In between these two poles lies their own middle road, the 'transformationalist' position. They argue that globalization is a real phenomenon that is transforming fundamental social structures through changes in spatial relations in ways whose end-state we cannot yet grasp.

Yet this depiction of the debate has limitations. For one thing, it puts the analyst's belief in globalization as the central line of distinction. More importantly, it blurs the lines between scholars' assessments of the nature of globalization, the causes of change and their effects; for Held *et al.* all of this is clumped together as 'globalization'. Such an approach is unfair to many writers; while some studies fit neatly into this three-way typology, many do not. For example, they are right to say that Ohmae (1990) is a hyper-globalizer whereas Hirst and Thompson (1996) are sceptics, however, for the bulk of the literature, globalization involves not only an assertion which can be placed along a sceptic–believer continuum, but also a set of claims about origins, dynamics, causation and social impact (see for example, Scholte, 2005: 15–23). To make sense of the range of debate a clearer analytic path can be found by assessing the different ways in which scholars have conceived of globalization's essential character. Once one is clear about what social forces have been identified as underpinning the phenomenon, analysis of the claims of cause and consequence can be more effectively undertaken.

Classifying Globalization: A Many Splendour'd Thing

All assessments of globalization recognize that it is not a narrow phenomenon whose impact can be isolated in one sphere. Most studies consider that it has political, economic, military, cultural, social and even ideological aspects. This variety in impact should not be down-played, but it can obscure the fact that, in spite of this diversity, conceptions of globalization tend to subscribe to three broad conceptions of its core character. Core character refers to the way in which scholars have identified the central causal dynamics of a complex phenomenon. Most assessments tend to group the funda-mental character of globalization as being primarily about either economic, sociological or political phenomena, and from these underlying traits flow the raft of changes that are said to embody globalization.

Economic Interpretations

Economic assessments of globalization are among the most influen-tial and tend to have the most positive assessments of its impact (e.g. Krueger, 2000; Micklethwait and Wooldridge, 2000; Wolf, 2004). The majority of these tend to come from a liberal point of view and see the global spread of a capitalist system of economic relations as a good thing. Bhagwati's definition is typical of this approach: globalization involves 'the integration of national economies into the international economy through trade, direct foreign investment, short term capital flows, international flows of workers and humanity generally and flows of technology' (2004: 3). Wolf's concept follows this premise in a more succinct fashion. For the *Financial Times*' senior economics editor, globalization is the 'integration of economic activities, via markets' (2004: 19). While the emphasis on economic features tends to be dominated by liberals, Marxists also place economics at the centre but interpret its broader dynamics in a more critical fashion (e.g. Amin, 1997; Callinicos *et al.*, 1994). These interpretations see the rise in trade, investment and financial flows, which are increasingly drawing geographically disparate markets together, as a new form of imperialism in which states, especially the United States, are playing a major, if concealed, role (e.g. Harvey, 2003).

The economic understanding of globalization sees process as an essential feature. The term is associated with the activity of integration and transformation. An interesting, though unresolved, question is the extent to which there is a global end-point, where the process of change ends and a truly global economic system exists. Economic interpretations see globalization as a process that involves the integration of once-discreet markets into a broader system of relations where geographic and political constraints have diminishing significance for the allocation of resources. Under globalization, resources are distributed through the exchange of goods and services, the movement of capital in search of return, and the relocation of people pursuing employment and material advancement, all eased by the rapid flow of knowledge and information.

The anti-globalization movement also shares this view of its basic character. While a broad church, these protesters are primarily concerned with what they perceive to be the negative aspects of the economic integration. They are critical of globalization because they believe that power has been leeched by states and societies to heartless corporations. Whether one is supportive of the kinds of change which bring mobile phones to Rwanda, McDonald's to Moscow and build Volkswagens in Shanghai, the economic conception sees globalization as a process that is integrating national markets into a properly global capitalist economy. Of course, ascribing economic matters an analytic centrality in the process does not exclude political or social questions. It sees these dimensions as deriving from the transformation of economic exchange whereby the constraints of geography, both physical and political, matter less and less to the global allocation of resources.

Sociological Transformation

In contrast, the second strand argues that while economic integration is significant, it is only one part of a much broader-based transformation of the character of social life. Heavily influenced by social theory and with a tendency to make somewhat grandiose declarations about the scale of its significance, these writers argue for new ways of thinking to come to terms with globalization. One of the earliest of these approaches was set out by Anthony Giddens who argued that globalization is '[t]he intensification of worldwide social relations which link distant localities in such a way that local happenings are shaped by events occurring many miles away and vice versa' (1990: 64). Similarly, Martin Albrow argues that globalization 'involves the supplanting of modernity with globality and this means an overall change in the basis of action and social organization for individuals and groups' (1996: 4). He argues that the ontological underpinnings of social thought are ill-equipped to cope with the kind of world that is emerging in the 'global age'.

This group is characterized by a number of common themes. Most importantly, they argue that the reduction in the significance of geography and geographic constraints to human interaction is fundamentally changing the structures of social interaction. For example, Waters notes that globalization is 'a social process in which the constraints of geography on social and cultural arrangements recede and in which people become increasingly aware that they are receding' (1995: 3) Whether this is due to 'space/time compression' (Bauman, 1998), 'supraterritoriality' (Scholte, 2000; 2005) or the reorganization of social life around space-flows and a collapse of time (Castells, 1996), the hallmark of globalization for this group of writers is the collapse of distance and the rapid acceleration of communication that shows little regard for geographic constraints (e.g. Harvey, 1989; Robertson, 1992). The second common theme is the shared belief in the breadth of social forces and fields which intersect to produce globalization. Beck's definition is typical: globalization 'denotes the processes through which sovereign national states are criss-crossed and undermined by transnational actors with varying prospects of power, orientations, identities and networks' (2000: 11). Globalization is caused by diverse forces and its influence can be discerned in fields as varied as the military, family life, class relations, and democratic politics, to name but a few.

The third common point is a belief in the transformative power of globalization. The most influential work from within this group makes this abundantly clear. Held *et al.* argue that the 'historically unprecedented levels of global interconnectedness' are fundamentally transforming all aspects of social life; from the economy to the environment, the military to the state, all sectors are being recast (1999: 7–28). Social transformation – albeit of varying hues – is globalization's central characteristic. Akin to the more economic understandings, the sociological strand also emphasizes process as central to the dynamics of globalization. Though authors may not all agree as to what shape things are being recast into, nor indeed do they all set out a firm view on how things are changing, they concur that globalization is the most important social process of contemporary times and that it is causing a revolution in the structures and institutions of social life.

These sociological understandings of globalization focus on the way in which the compression of social space is reconfiguring fundamental human relationships. As some critics point out, this involves a significant departure from classical social theory (e.g. Rosenberg, 2005). Unlike other modes of social theory, these writers argue that the determining aspects of life are the geographic dimensions of social space and their collapse is restructuring social relations. In summary, globalization is characterized by change in political, economic, military and environmental life due to the reorganization of spatial relationships in which geography and territory no longer play the kind of determinative role that they played in the past.

Political Conceptions

The first two strands are the most influential and widely discussed interpretations of globalization. One can, however, identify a smaller third classificatory strand which conceives globalization's central feature as being political. This group sees political phenomena at the heart of globalization and not all those who attribute it with some political dimensions. For this group, globalization is not a verifiable empirical phenomenon, but is a means of understanding what is going on in the world. Globalization is not the creation of foreign exchange markets, the death of sovereignty or time–space compression, it is a way of thinking about the world, and as such is an inherently political phenomenon. The discourse of globalization is, from this perspective, the function of a particular political project and its central dynamic is the way in which it is used to advance specific interests or ambitions. For example, if a head of government declares that globalization makes reform of welfare or public services necessary, this perspective argues that we are not witnessing an elected representative responding to changes in productive processes but the playing out of a political project that drives a particular conception of policy determination.

While generally associated with Marxist inspired critics of neo-liberal economic policies (e.g. Hoogvelt, 1997), there are two camps within this strand. The first takes a more instrumental view and sees the vague and often woolly depiction of globalization as a means through which politicians can sell complex or unpopular domestic reform (e.g. Gray, 1998). Political elites are able to tap into the idea of globalization as a powerful and elemental force which demands privatization or taxation reform because it is said to leave elites with no alternative. Globalization allows elites to mobilize support for policy choices in a way that they otherwise may not be able to do.

The second camp adheres to a more structural view whereby globalization is a means not only to legitimate or sell a political project but to reorganize how we conceive of politics (Kofman and Youngs, 1996). For example, Germain emphasizes that there is a need to ensure that globalization is not assumed to exist in the world, rather, he argues that there are sets of experiences of the world which have come to be associated with globalization and that the process by which these experiences are understood is the political programme of globalization (2000: xiv).

This group is not the only one to discuss the political dimensions of globalization, but it is distinct because it puts politics at the heart of the conceptualization. The political understanding of globalization is thus not one associated with debates about the death of the state, the demise of sovereignty or the fusion of political ideologies, but is concerned with the way in which the idea serves a distinctly political purpose, both instrumental and structural.

Table 1.2   Classifications of globalization's core features

Conception	Key features	Examples
Economic	Globalization is essentially about economics. The integration of markets and productive processes is reducing the influence of geography in the distribution of resources. This process drives subsequent changes, for example, in practices of governance, statehood and sovereignty.	Bhagwati (2004), Wolf (2004), Amin (1997), Callinicos *et al.* (1994), Luard (1990), Strange (1996)
Sociological	Globalization is changing the fundamental structures of social life by recasting the role that territory plays in organizing social structures, such as political institutions or sovereignty. The central feature is produced by a complex interaction of changes in economic, political, and cultural relations.	Giddens (1990), Camilleri and Falk (1992), Albrow, (1996), Held *et al.* (1999), Scholte (2005), Waters (1995), Castells (1996, 1997, 1998), Beck (2000)
Political	Globalization is not a phenomenon but a means of (a) advancing a political project; and (b) changing the way people think about the world.	Hoogvelt (1997), Gray (1998), Kofman and Youngs (1996), Germain (2000)

The Extent of Globalization

The foregoing discussion is the first step in organizing the different ways in which globalization has been classified. The second requires a consideration of the differing degrees to which globalization is said to influence social life. One can identify three broad groups. The first argues that globalization is not especially extensive and that many overstate its impact (e.g. Gilpin, 2001; 2002; Hirst and Thompson, 1996). These are not globalization deniers (a rare breed today), rather they note that many of the empirical claims made about globalization are exaggerated and its impact on state power, political systems and domestic social structures is not particularly significant. Of course, these writers note that the emergence of global financial markets, containerization of shipping and the internet all make a clear difference, but assessments of their consequences need to be tempered with a dose of reality. For them, states still hold the whip hand over firms, openness is contingent on favourable political circumstances and levels of economic integration are not nearly so great, nor so new, as the prophets tell us.

The second group argues that globalization is relatively widespread and of considerable and growing importance to the modern world (e.g. Hay and Marsh, 2000; Keohane, 2002; Legrain 2002; Wolf, 2004). These writers argue that although it may not be completely global in its geographic reach nor ubiquitous as a social phenomenon, it is still something which demands careful attention. The changes of globalization may not be epoch making in themselves, but they are transforming the character of contemporary economic, political and social life. These changes can be uneven and partial but they are serious and of growing significance. Finally, there are those who contend that globalization is deeply rooted and of overwhelming importance (e.g. Albrow, 1996; Appadurai, 1990; Giddens, 1990, 1999; Ohmae, 1995;). While these writers clearly have different claims about the kinds of changes and their consequences, they share a belief that globalization is extensive in its manifestations and, because of this, is a force which is fundamentally recasting business practice, patterns of consumption and forms of identity, and destabilising political institutions.

This depiction of three broad levels of degree is not flawless. For one thing it is far from clear how precise one may be in determining the extent of globalization. The categories are necessarily rough and are more gradations of distinction than absolute lines of differentiation. One could tune things more finely by considering both its intensity (the level of effect) and its extensity (the breadth of social experience shaped by globalization). Globalization could therefore be considered as a function of how widespread, in spatial terms, are experiences of change and how much change penetrates existing social institutions.

Classifications of Globalization

In much of the literature, globalization is seen as involving almost all aspects of social life, from patterns of media consumption to the production of cars, from the ubiquity of mobile phones to revolutions in gender relations. In spite of this, it is possible to identify different basic conceptions of its core features and the character of its extent. More directly, even among the different approaches set out above, one can discern a number of common themes. First, virtually all work on globalization sees it as a social process. It is an ongoing set of changes – we may disagree about the nature, dimensions and extent of these – but almost no one denies that there is *something* going on. Second, the character of globalization is shaped by the interaction of technological, political and economic forces. It is unusual to come across the determinist who feels that globalization is driven purely by one dimension, whether technological or economic. Third, the 'global' aspect of the term is somewhat misleading. Few who write about globalization make simplistic one-worldist arguments that see it as an evenly distributed force that is drawing the planet's population ever closer. Although critics of globalization point this out, the reality is that few actually make such claims. While the underlying purpose of the term is to emphasize the way in which disparate actions around the world have consequences a long way from where they are undertaken, few see globalization as properly global in scope and even in impact.

The competing visions of globalization beg the question of singularity. Many see it as a set of uneven processes intersecting in often unpredictable ways. Globalization appears to be used more as a shorthand for a range of, at times, quite disparate phenomena, some interrelated (for example, the liberalization of trade policy and domestic economic reforms such as privatization) and others quite distinct (such as internationalization of production and the rise of cosmopolitan norms and global democratic institutions) which appear to be moving social life in a 'globalized' direction. Others argue that it has a clear presence and a singularity that is more than analytic convenience. Given that it is such a variable and multi-dimensional process any analysis of its interaction with the structures and institutions of world politics is particularly fraught. In essence, there are two problems. First, globalization appears to consist of a huge range of sub-phenomena which make any attempt to analyze its role as a singular force problematic. Second, not only is there a vast array of aspects which constitute the process, the term is used to refer to causes, consequences, explanations and indeed normative aspirations. To be able to make some analytic sense of all this, therefore, it is necessary to narrow the aperture and exclude many of the more expansive claims. One useful way of doing this is to make a distinction between globalization as cause and globalization as consequence. This is not to say globalization must only ever be one or the other, clearly it can be both, but the focus here is on the latter. Prior to establishing the definition, it is useful to consider the debate which has emerged over this aspect of globalization.

Globalization as Consequence

For some, globalization is a force for positive change that provides opportunities for societies to lift themselves out of poverty. It is argued that globalization not only facilitates rapid economic growth, but also creates the possibility of enhancing human freedom through the expansion of choice and democracy (Bhagwati, 2004; Norberg, 2001; World Bank, 2002). As Martin Wolf writes: '[i]t has brought benefits to hundreds of millions of people and helped secure the biggest ever falls in the proportion of humanity in extreme poverty' (2004: ix). Writing with some concern about threats to globalization *The Economist* bemoans 'despite the spectacular rise in living standards that has occurred as barriers between nations have fallen, and despite the resulting escape from poverty by hundreds of millions of people ... it is still hard to convince publics and politicians of the merits of openness' (2005b: 9). According to others, the growing inter-connectedness of globalization is fostering a cosmopolitan sensibility and a global civil society (see Keane, 2003). The collapse of the constraints of geography are said to be ushering in an era in which states are no longer able to exercize the governance functions that they had hitherto undertaken and that humanity is on the cusp of an era of multilateral global governance (Rosenau, 1997), where democracy and human rights will be advanced on a global scale (e.g. Held *et al.*, 1999; 45–86).

On the other hand globalization is thought to be further exacerbating inequality in the world – both between and within states (Fieldhouse, 1999; Sassen, 1998) – and increasing poverty and deprivation across the globe (e.g. Chussodovsky, 1997; Owen-Vandersluis and Yeros, 2000). Rather than distributing efficiency gains brought by integration across a wide population, these writers argue, globalization concentrates wealth in ever fewer hands, allows MNCs to overwhelm states, impoverish workers and ultimately subvert democracy itself (e.g. Hertz, 2001; Klein, 2000; Monbiot, 2003). From a less alarmist perspective, globalization is said to have altered the balance of power in favour of firms and that their size, scope and influence means that states trying to bargain with MNCs have an ever harder task (Held *et al.*, 1999: 236–82; Moran, 1999). Others see globalization as damaging the environment, emasculating workers' rights and more generally stymieing those who attempt to advance social justice. From a more structural point of view, globalization is thought to be producing a new form of empire (Hardt and Negri, 2000), homogenizing culture and wiping out the distinctive markers of social life from language to dress, food to music. Globalization is also purported to be undermining state autonomy and capacity (e.g. Ohmae, 1995; Scholte, 1997). For example, it has led to the destruction of the welfare apparatus that many states had erected after 1945 (Falk, 1999).

Globalization is also said to be having important cultural consequences. Many think of it as little more than a synonym for Americanization. Evidence for this is found in things like the popularity of the *Star Wars* movies, the ubiquity of McDonald's and Levi jeans. On the other hand, rather than creating a bland homogenized world, for others globalization is causing people to place greater weight on perceived points of cultural, ethnic and religious diversity. The narcissism of small differences has an ever greater meaning in a world increasingly aware of them.

These are only some of the more notable consequences which have been linked to various conceptions of globalization. When trying to adjudicate between these claims the challenge lies not only in assessing the evidence in support of the arguments, but also the concepts which underpin them. In some cases, determination about consequence is muddled by a causation–consequence elision. Take, for example, arguments by Albrow or Giddens among others that globalization is the reduction in the influence of geographic distance social relations. Such claims imply a single process but really refer to (at least) three distinct things: (1) changes which reduce the relevance of distance; (2) the collapse of distance itself; and (3) the consequences of this compression for existing social institutions and practices. The analytic confusion which stems from this trio of meanings – each distinct though clearly related – makes determining the veracity of claims particularly challenging. Analytically speaking, it is vital to be clear about the difference between the causes of change in social institutions and the effects that these changes are having, both specific and in the aggregate. Instead of trying to disentangle which changes cause globalization and which changes derive from it, at the same time it can be more effective to deal with these aspects separately. There is nothing inherently wrong with portmanteau terms provided that we are aware of the various elements of which they are constituted. In this case, globalization, as generally used, involves both causal and consequential dimensions. Given the problems that this can cause and the ambitions of this book, it makes sense, therefore, to deal with only one element of globalization. Here the focus is on the consequential.

Globalization: A Definition

To start with, one must emphasize that the consequential understanding of globalization used here is not predicated on a moral or an empirical judgement about the way in which globalization is being played out. Rather we are interested in the way in which changes in social practices produce a set of consequences – which we call globalization – and how these in turn influence the structures and institutions of world politics. Further, any attempt to determine these consequences is going to depend on what part of human existence one is considering. If one is trying to make sense of globalization for supply chain management one is going to use a different set of concepts than if one is trying to determine its impact on democratic politics. The reason is that the ways in which the interrelated phenomena that drive globalization play themselves out varies enormously from sector to sector. The central task of this book is to consider how globalization and world politics interact. This requires a delineated and analytically manageable definition of globalization and one which takes seriously the warnings that others have made in relation to using this particularly over-burdened term. First, we need to ensure that the definition is not simply repackaging existing ideas in a fashionable new cover. As Scholte rightly points out, too often claims about globalization have not really gone much beyond pre-existing notions of interdependence, liberalization or westernization (2000: 44–6). Keohane and Nye show one way of getting around this problem. They argue that globalization is not a state of affairs – not a description of things as they are – instead, the term globalism should be used to describe the state of affairs (which, unsurprisingly, is seen to be a kind of complex interdependence) and that globalization should be used to describe the process through which globalism is increasing its scope and impact (Keohane and Nye, 2000). To make the distinction between globalism and globalization, while analytically useful, still does not satisfy Scholte's objections; globalization is little more than a version of interdependence.

Anyone who uses the term must recognize that she makes several important implicit points. First, one conveys a notion that involves something that goes beyond terms such as international, interdependent or transnational and that there is some 'global' dimension to the proposition, whether ideological or geographic. Second, as the 'ization' suffix implies, one is referring to an ongoing process. The suffix of global*ism* is inappropriate both because it implies a relatively stable state of affairs and because of its ideological overtones (though, given the sentiments of many on both sides of the debate, the ideological strain is not entirely out of place). Third, one is choosing to be part of the broader discourse of globalization and thus associated, however critically, with the existing framework of debate.

The starting point of this book is that plainly the world has undergone a series of quite rapid changes across a broad range of important spheres of human life. One need only enter a supermarket in the developed world, use a mobile phone to call someone on the other side of the planet or log on to the internet to get a sense of the kind of very real shifts in human experience which the past twenty years has witnessed. But it is one thing to recognize that there has been change, quite another to conclude that everything is being recast. Yes, there has been remarkable technological development in communication, media, production, finance and so on, but it is less clear whether these changes have provided, or are going to provide, the kind of radical shift in the institutions of human existence – social structures, class relations, political systems, states, legal systems and international institutions – that globalization is alleged to have wrought. The changes associated with globalization have not yet engendered the radical transformation in the basic patterns of human life that one might have expected to see given the nature of the claims made by the more enthusiastic. For example, for the vast bulk of humanity, the geographic pattern of life is much as it has been for the past fifty years. To be sure, in countries like China and India economic growth has driven large-scale urbanization, but this is hardly flying in the face of patterns established in the first industrial age. For the small chunk of humanity that spends more time in airport lounges and business class seats than anywhere else, the geography of life may have changed. But for the rest of us, the fundamental patterns of human interaction in social space are not vastly different.

To try to provide a certain degree of analytic precision globalization is defined for our purposes here as a set of related social, political and economic consequences of a series of transformations in the social world, though the causal character of the relationships is uneven and often very unclear. Globalization refers to the aggregate social consequences that derive from the dramatic increase in both the rate and speed with which people, goods and services, capital and knowledge are able to move around the globe. This increase is the product of reductions in the transportation costs (both fiscal and ideational) associated with movement and the reduction of barriers that prevent or constrain these exchanges from taking place. The notion of cost and barriers includes both the economic and non-economic spheres.

To be clear, globalization refers not to specific changes in the way trade is conducted, or to a particular firm's reliance on global markets for inputs and sales, but to the broader consequences that derive from the increase in speed and rate with which goods, services, people, capital and knowledge moves around the world. There have been a vast array of often interconnected changes in the economic, political, and cultural spheres facilitated by shifts in technology, government policy and individual choice, among other things. Our concern here is with the way in which changes to patterns of trade, investment and the like have aggregate flow-on consequences for the institutions and social structures that govern human life. The point is that we are not interested in any one instance of a trade relationship or a capital flow, rather we are concerned with the effects on human behaviour that come from sufficient volumes of these flows, and the institutions we have created to govern this behaviour. The purpose of this definition is to be clear about what aspect of globalization we will be focusing on, as well as the way in which it is a product not only of changes to economic practices but also of political, cultural and ideological forces. Like concepts such as modernity, class or culture, the nature of globalization makes it impossible to form a precise determination as to its exact identity. However, the discussion in subsequent chapters will flesh out the empirical dimensions of globalization as it is conceived here.

Concluding Thoughts

The globalization debate crashed almost without warning on the social sciences and policy world in the 1990s. While far too much was made of the phenomenon, there appears to be some consensus that there has been a range of transformations in key spheres of human existence which, when taken together, have produced a dynamic and transformative context for world politics in the 21st century. This book is an attempt to think this through and to determine the extent to which globalization has changed the character of world politics. The survey of the debate has made clear that there are a number of important changes with which we need to grapple. The proposed definition emphasizes that globalization is a set of consequences deriving from the reduced costs and increased speed of transporting goods, knowledge, people and capital around the world. Having defined globalization, it is necessary also to consider the ways in which it has been previously experienced and the extent to which we can say that the contemporary phase is distinct from that which came before.

2

Globalization Past and Present

Those sceptical of the more extravagant claims made about globalization often point out that the level of international trade and investment in the *belle époque* of the late 19th and early 20th centuries was at least as high as it is today (e.g. Hirst and Thompson, 1996). Others point out that networks of military, social and economic relations which allow actions in one place to have significant consequences across vast distances, are hardly new (Holton, 1998). Europeans brought their diseases to the New World in the 16th century with catastrophic results. In economic terms, prior to the First World War, Great Britain exported 7% of its gross domestic product (GDP) in capital, a level no state since 1945 has yet achieved (James, 2001: 12). As historians point out, we have seen a lot of the sorts of things we associate with globalization before; indeed they remind us that we tend to forget that things came badly unstuck last time around when openness led on to cataclysmic war in 1914 (e.g. Ferguson, 2005). How new is globalization? To what extent do the levels of integration we have today differ from levels achieved in previous global or universal eras? Questions about novelty are important because they provide some welcome perspective to cool the ardour of the more enthusiastic globalizers, but they are significant in themselves because they force us to think about the nature of the phenomenon as well as its historical trajectory.

Too often it is assumed that globalization is inevitable and almost irreversible; borders that are opened to capital and trade will forever remain thus. Many think that because the apparent costs of closing things down are high, such action has become effectively unthinkable; thus globalization is here to stay. While it appears as if the globalization genie is out of the bottle, the forces which facilitate the high-speed linkages so typical of the current era – airline travel, email and the internet, cheap long-distance telephone calls, open markets and global trade – can also be reversed. States can close borders, ramp up barriers to trade and investment, isolate phone lines and freeze capital markets. Although states are not likely to do this any time soon, nor would they be capable of entirely turning back the clock, a significant curtailing of the current freedoms of movement for capital, people and goods alike is both plausible and possible. While unlikely in the short term, its possibility needs to be taken seriously. The openness of European economies and their interdependence in the early years of the 20th century came to an abrupt and disastrous end. The openness which is the lifeblood of globalization is contingent on circumstances which are fluid and subject to significant change. An awareness of the previous experiences with globalization and the sources of the contemporary phase is thus necessary to understand the evolution of the forces on which the character of the current era depends.

Globalization's Past

Analysis of globalization is especially prone to a fixation on the contemporary. With the notable exception of the unfashionable discipline of economic history – which has produced the best comparisons between the present era and previous periods – a sensitivity to globalization's past is too often lacking. In reading the enthusiasms of the prophets one could be forgiven for thinking that humanity had never before experienced life when events on the far side of the planet shaped local conditions.

Globalization has a past in two obvious senses. First, human society has seen previous periods in which the international, even global, movements of people, goods, capital and knowledge was of great significance (see generally Hopkins, 2002). The most recent example of a previous global era, of course, did not foster peace but produced decades of warfare and violence (Ferguson, 2006). What some refer to as the golden age of globalization began to unravel in 1914 and was smashed by the Great Depression and the policy responses which exacerbated its effects. Equally, the spread of Islam across the Middle East, Africa and Asia in the 7th and 8th centuries, and the reformation ideas of Martin Luther in 16th century Europe, show that the rapid transnational spread of ideas is contingent not only on the telegraph or the internet.

Second, the contemporary conditions are the product of specific forces of historical development. The connections of global production and finance networks, the social and cultural diffusion made possible by communications technology such as satellites and the internet, and the global spread of the political system of sovereign states are not only the creation of recent developments, they are also products of the 18th and 19th centuries. The expansion of European power through colonialism was central to this process. It brought the idea of a distinctly *international* politics to parts of the world that had practised rather different approaches to authority and government (see generally Buzan and Little, 2000). The financial systems which facilitated the adventures of empire laid the foundations for the post-war monetary system which led to the global financial networks that have become central to the processes of contemporary globalization (Eichengreen, 1996). In many parts of the world, the map of states and nations are direct legacies of empire. The unusual patchwork of sub-Saharan Africa is typical. The Caprivi Strip, the narrow protrusion of Namibia which juts out over most of Botswana's northern border was created so that the Germans, who had colonized this part of the continent, could ensure their access to Victoria Falls. In Southeast Asia, colonialism froze the ethnic make-up of the territories that have become sovereign states. Prior to the parcelling up of authority by Europeans, traders and labourers could move relatively freely to take advantage of opportunities that locational change afforded. Traders from Hainan moved to archipelagic Southeast Asia, and Arab merchants settled in Aceh. Once European attitudes to territory and authority were imposed, the ethnic mix was frozen for the longer run (Yahuda, 1996: 8–9). The linkages of globalization are part of a much longer run set of developments which have linked disparate human communities for thousands of years.

There is a tendency to think that the modern world's development is best understood as a function of the expansion of European systems of politics and economics, through the brutalism of empire and colonialism, to separate parts of the globe. This view implies that the parts of the world that European forces dragged into modern international society were living in splendid isolation. While imperialism was central to the creation of the modern world, and played an important foundational role in globalization, the reality is that parts of the globe have been connected in political, economic and social relationships for as long as human communities have been aware that there were other groups to trade with and to compete against (e.g. Abu-Lughod, 1989; McNeil, 1963). But the point is not just the existence of a thriving long distance trade network in pre-colonial Meso-America or a Chinese tributary system involving a complex web of political protection and symbolic exchange. These interactions were important to the communities that partook in them, but many of them also had effects that can be felt to this day. For example, the diseases that the Spanish brought with them to Latin America caused not only massive 'action at a distance', they caused a precipitous demographic collapse among the indigenous population which made conquest more straightforward and has influenced the political and social make-up of post-colonial societies since the Spanish departure.

Perhaps more notable was the Asian 'world economy' whereby complex trade and social interactions dominated global productive processes and linked geographically disparate communities (Chaud-huri, 1990). This world economy was established by the Islamic caliphate between the 8th and 13th centuries, and spanned the conquered territories of North Africa, parts of Europe and the Middle East, and the trade networks of Eastern Africa and Central and Eastern Asia. It was made possible by the economic rules which the Caliphate imposed, especially the creation of a unified currency, and a loose political structure. The location of power gave oppor-tunities to benefit from links between the distinct worlds of Asia, dominated by the Chinese empire, and the European Mediterranean. The legacy of this previous globalization process can still be seen today. For example, it was the central force behind the rapid transformation of the religious map of the Indian Ocean littoral as the new religion of Islam spread across the networks created by this vibrant Asian economy. Had trade networks not linked archipelagic Southeast Asia, with the sub-continent, the Middle East and Eastern Africa, then the political dimensions of today's 'war on terror' would be entirely different.

The current globalization period is not utterly unique. The world has experienced previous periods in which an increase in the rate and impact of inter-continental linkages of trade, investment, conquest and exploration has shaped vital elements of human existence. Of course not all inter-continental linkages are equally significant and while communities have always interacted, it is not right to say that these have always been of particular importance. That said, we can point to a number of periods and processes of what some have called proto-globalization. Some of the more important examples include: the expansion of the Mongol Empire; the age of European exploration in the 15th and 16th centuries; the slave trade; and the previously mentioned Asian world economy which stretched from modern Spain to Indonesia (see generally Buzan and Little, 2000; Pomeranz and Topik, 2006). Indeed a prominent historian has argued that globalization – understood as a broader process knitting the fates of disparate human communities together – can be seen as having four previous forms: archaic, proto, modern and post-colonial (Hopkins, 2002: 3–9). This view draws attention to the fact that globalization is not a linear process of Western modernity expanding and other forms of political and economic organization capitulating in front of these superior forces. Earlier forms of globalization were decidedly non-Western (Abu-Lughod, 1989; Chaudhuri, 1990), and have always involved an interaction of global processes with local manifestations to create novel formations. The post-colonial states of Southeast Asia, and their conceptions of nationalism and identity, are only the most obvious examples of this hybridity (see generally Anderson, 1998). More generally, the differing forms and phases of globalization have been shaped by a complex array of forces and ideas. Technology facilitated European imperialism, but it was propelled by motives of both economic advancement and expansion of 'civilization'. Geopolitics and religious fervour also played their part, as they have in other phases of globalization (see for example, Bennison, 2002).

The current preference for generally liberal attitudes to trade and investment – as well as an openness to ideas and some cultural difference – at least among the rich countries, has a particular history which needs to be considered. It is too easy to assume that the broadly liberal consensus among the developed states is a natural state which 'reasonable' policy-makers have rationally determined as an optimal strategy. The preference for a generally open approach, to trade, investment, tourism, cultural flows and the like (although, with the exception of the member states of the European Union, notably *not* the movement of labour or people) is the product of specific political, economic and military developments. Without the guarantees provided by American military power and American markets the economic and ideological foundations of the current era would never have been constructed (see generally, Keohane, 1984). The creation of a liberal order out of the ashes of the Second World War was a deliberate choice intended to avoid the mistakes of isolationism, nationalism and protectionism of the interwar period (Latham, 1997).

Is Everything New, Old?

How new is globalization? There are generally three ways in which the novelty question is answered in the literature. The first argues that contemporary globalization is qualitatively and quantitatively different from previous forms of global interconnectedness (e.g. Held *et al.*, 1999; Yergin and Stanislaw, 1998). This view argues that although it builds on lessons of the past, such as the negative political consequences of protectionism, it is a distinctive form of global interaction. Rates of trade and investment, the movement of ideas and people, and the speed with which people, information and capital move around the planet together produce a dynamic environment that represents a manifest break with the past. Levels of social, economic and cultural integration have produced, and are continuing to expand and entrench, a kind of interaction that is inducing new forms of behaviour and new social institutions and norms to meet the demands of a changing world. In short, globalization today is demonstrably different from previous eras and the nature and extent of the connections that are creating a 'global world' are far more important than they were in earlier periods.

The second view sees the current phase of globalization as not especially new nor particularly distinctive (e.g. Rodrik, 1998; Sachs and Warner, 1995). It argues that the current circumstances of global interconnectedness, especially related to economic integration, are merely a return to the integration of the *belle époque* of the late 19th and early 20th century (e.g. Schwartz, 2000). From this point of view, international capital flows and intercontinental trade are a return to the time when European capital spread out around the world on the back of opportunities opened up by colonization. Just as Volkswagen and ExxonMobil invest in China and Singapore, Europeans invested in railways, mines, and agriculture in Australia, Argentina, and Africa seeking returns not available at home. Figures to support this position include the observation that the value of world trade in the mid 1870s was roughly comparable to trade in the 1990s and that US exports in the late 1990s were 8% of GDP while in the late 1870s the figure was 7% (Bordo *et al.*, 1999). Also, they point out that the global financial system then was more stable and more integrated courtesy of the gold standard. This monetary standard meant that the currency risks for international investors and traders were minimized by adherence to a set of rigid international rules (Zevin, 1992). On the political and military front, the 19th century saw vast tracts of the planet, and their populations, dragged into a global economic and political system by European colonialism. The linkages between Sydney and London, Hanoi and Paris, Windhoek and Berlin were more important to their inhabitants than such inter-continental connections are today. From this perspective, while the internet and satellite communications may have sped things up somewhat, they have not created anything substantively new. When one strips away the superficial differences, so this position argues, what we have today is not especially different from what came before.

The third view argues that today's globalization is a continuation of the *longue dûrée* of capitalist economic development. Associated with the world systems theory of Immanuel Wallerstein and Andre Gunder Frank, and influenced by the *annales* school of historical analysis pioneered by Ferdinand Braudel, this view argues that capitalist economic development has always been globally oriented (e.g. Denemark *et al.*, 2000; Frank and Gills, 1993; Wallerstein, 1974). The contemporary phase is a continuation of the longer-run emergence of a capitalist world economy with social, political and cultural institutions emerging to further its advance. The unfolding of this system, they emphasize, has been uneven and punctuated by crises and contractions and globalization, from this perspective, is merely the latest – and most complete – phase of this longer-run process. The growing integration of markets, the rapid movement of capital around the world, the emergence of a global political system of sovereign states are all elements which strengthen the chains of economic relations whereby surplus value is extracted from periph-eral economies and transmitted to the core.

Each view has something to say about the nature of present-day integration. The first emphasizes the distinctive way in which contemporary trade, investment, finance and knowledge movements are shaping social life. This approach draws attention to the fact that, however similar economic integration may be, the world looks very different today than it did 100 years ago. Not only are trade and investment significant, but the speed with which ideas, people and goods move has far reaching consequences for economic and political life. The second view highlights the similarities between the current period and the economic and military dynamics of European colonialism. While the political framework may be different, the interdependence of distant lands was significant then, and in some places even more so than it is today. As economic historians point out, the vulnerabilities that openness induced then have not necessarily gone away, indeed, the increase in speed of movement makes us more susceptible to these forces. The third view underlines the degree of continuity that exists among apparently different eras. While the ruptures brought about by the upheavals between the two world wars may have been great, the contemporary system has been importantly influenced by the political and economic systems created by European empires which were forged between the 16th and 19th centuries.

Globalization's Belle Époque

It is useful, at this stage, to consider the modern world's previous experience of globalization, that is the period of the late 19th and early 20th centuries. There are two main reasons for examining this period of globalization's past. First, the foundations of the current era were laid at this time. The European state system, and its rules and norms, was taken to the world and the foundations of contemporary global capitalism were created during this phase. This includes the expansion of the capitalist structures, systems of banking and finance, as well as the creation of an urban infrastructure that is largely intact today. Second, it is not only our most recent experience with a form of globalization but it consisted of a range of processes similar to those which are presently influential. A brief consideration of this period allows us to better comprehend the current phase and to have a sense of how distinct it is.

Measured in any terms, volumes of trade, movement of capital, the spread of ideas and peoples, and the consequent transformation of social life, the 19th century and early 20th century's experiences certainly qualify as a version of the globalization that is so keenly written about today (e.g. O'Rourke and Williamson, 1999). One of the more commonly cited passages in works on the economic history of globalization comes from the opening pages of Keynes' famous indictment of the Treaty of Versailles. In *The Economic Consequences of the Peace*, Keynes analyzes the setting of the world economy prior to the First World War and describes a world remarkably similar to the present. The passage notes that a Londoner (of suitable means) could order 'the various products of the whole earth, in such quantity as he might see fit, and reasonably expect their early delivery upon his doorstep', he could invest anywhere in the world, he could swiftly travel the world without let, hindrance, or even a passport (Keynes, 1920). It is unsurprising that such a passage has become a staple for those who remind us that current circumstances are not as novel we may think.

Although one may point at previous 'universal' eras and phases of global interconnectedness such as the Mongol empire, the Ottoman dominance of Europe and the Middle East or the Asian economy of the first millennium which have resonance with current experiences – what Scholte refers to as 'intimations of globality' (2005: 87–91) – none really come close to the character of the 19th century experience of globalization. For in many of the spheres of human life that are perceived to have become more closely connected during the contemporary phase, during the 19th century they were at least as integrated and, in some sectors, they experienced more significant linkages than exist today.

The 19th century was the first truly universal era in human society. As a function of technological developments and an expansionary mindset the world was linked by relatively rapid flows of goods, capital and people. Primary products such as wool from Australia, cotton from India and America, gold from Africa and South America moved at hitherto unimagined speeds and finished goods, such as textiles and railway parts, just as swiftly traversed vast distances. The great migrations of the 19th century saw Europeans depart for all corners of the globe. The global era of the *belle époque* was not only a product of economic integration: 19th century globalization was a product of political, social and technological change which, alongside economic integration, created a global system.

The similarities between the circumstances of the 19th century and those of today can most clearly be seen in the economic sphere. The economic well-being of communities in Britain and France were dependent on weather patterns and harvest conditions in South

Carolina and Danang (see generally, Frieden, 2006, Chs 1–5). More specifically, it was the high volumes of international trade and capital movement, facilitated by a relatively stable and robust international financial system, which prompted some to note that 'the world economy at the end of the 20th century looks much like the world economy at the end of the 19th' (Sachs and Warner, 1995: 61).

The relative significance of international trade is particularly striking. The volume of international trade, expressed as a proportion of the world's aggregate GDP, was as great in the late 19th century as it is today (Baldwin and Martin, 1999:15; Feenstra, 1998: 33). In aggregate terms, international trade played as important a role in the world economy as it does today. More remarkable still was that a number of the dominant countries were *more* dependent on trade than their equivalents today (Krugman, 1995). Great Britain relied on trade for its economic well-being – both imports and exports – to a much greater degree than the USA does today. It is well known that Britain relied on its surplus trade with India to balance its payments, particularly to fund its military. It is less well known that in turn India paid for this surplus trade through exporting goods to China. Chinese imports from India were in turn funded by remittances from Chinese living in Southeast Asia and elsewhere (see Latham, 1978 and more generally Harley, 1996). Not only was international trade of considerable significance to the world economy – and to the key player it was absolutely vital – the dynamics of interdependence and knock-on vulnerabilities and linkages that are so characteristic of today's economy were evident then. The idea that discrete economies only traded items of economic insignificance until the emergence of jet planes and containerized shipping is simply wrong.

The second important arm of this world economy was investment. Given our fascination with international banking and its attendant crises, one could be forgiven for thinking that international investment is a recent development, yet the 19th century saw high volumes of mobile capital flitting about the world with remarkable ease. Understood in relation to GDP, capital flows were as high, and in some cases higher, than anything seen since (James, 2001). For a group of relatively well-off states, net capital flows had dropped from a late 19th century average of 3.9% of GDP to 2.3% by the mid 1990s (Obstfeld, 1998: 12; see also Frankel 1993: 45–9). In proportion to total wealth, as much investment capital moved around the world then as now. While these flows did not lead to the emergence of the global financial markets we have today, capital mobility was high, and embryonic international capital markets had begun to emerge (see generally Obstfeld and Taylor, 2003). This integration was facilitated by the gold standard and the rise of financial institutions based mainly in London (see generally Frieden, 2006: 17–19). To illustrate, international capital flows in the 1988–1996 period were similar to those of the late 1890s (Taylor, 1996). Indeed in the case of the UK, Argentina, Australia, Canada, and France capital flows in the period 1988–1996 were lower than they were in the last years of the 19th century. Without the stability created by linking currencies to gold then international trade and investment in the 19th century would have been significantly constrained. The stability of money, which promoted economic integration, was not only a function of convertibility but also of the creation of modern central banks. Although some states had central banks prior to this period, they did not become institutions intended to manage the currency conse-quences of economies subject to the vagaries of international trade and investment until this time (Goodhart, 1988; James, 2001; 17–20).

It is tempting to assume that, in the *belle époque*, the emergence of a global economy was the essence of the universal age. One can easily forget that its creation was not simply the product of market forces working their magic. In studies of the historical evolution of globalization and previous experiences with the international inte-gration of markets and societies, most scholars tend to focus on the development of a global economy. This predilection reflects the relative ease of access to the relevant data, but is also the product of a general belief that globalization, in whatever era, is primarily about market integration. Such a view neglects some of the more important aspects of globalization, both then and now. The emergence and development of a global economy, as well as its consequential social transformations, in the 19th century were fundamentally shaped by political forces. Without the administrative infrastructure provided by the leading states, especially the major imperial powers, then trade, investment and migration would not have expanded as they did (see generally Bayly, 2004: 121–69 and 199–244). Three political factors were of particular importance: imperialism, state policy choice and ideology.

The most important force in this earlier phase was European imperialism. While some insist that imperialism is a function of economic conditions – a position most famously associated with Lenin's theory – the rise of an imperial ethos, the pursuit of empire and the conduct of colonial administration were, in the first instance, political impulses. While influenced by economic considerations – and the success of imperial adventures was dependent on their prosperity – imperialism was, at its core, a political project. The expansion of territorial control across the world by the major European powers, joined at the turn of the century by Japan, was driven by geopolitical calculation, strategic considerations, ambition and ideology. It was about profit as well, but the character of empire was far more influenced by these decidedly non-economic forces. Imperialism is ultimately about the political control of territory and peoples by an alien power. The benefits that accrue from this control, whether economic or strategic, are a function of this fundamental aspect. Political processes in many respects brought modernity to the world on the back of European imperialism (Ferguson, 2002).

It is hardly surprising that empires were the engines of 19th century globalization. Between the late 19th century and the start of the Second World War, European powers (and latterly Japan) governed large swathes of territory and huge populations. In 1914, the UK, France, Belgium and Holland alone ruled about one-third of the world's territory and a little under 30% of its population (Townsend, 1941: 19). Their resources began to be traded globally and lives in these colonies began to be heavily influenced by events in the metropolitan centre. Developments in Paris, London and Berlin mattered deeply to social, economic and political well-being in Saigon, Sydney and Tsingtao. The emergence of international trade in commodities, the global spread of capital and the mass movement of people all occurred on the back of imperial developments. British naval hegemony ensured the security of trade on the high seas and the gold standard itself was a product of imperial expansion. The imposition of European systems of law and administration provided the necessary framework for traders to spread their technology, invest and trade in these remote places. The emergence of a global economy was the product of the political globalization of European imperialism.

Beyond the broader role played by imperialism, the *belle époque* was also produced by the policy choices of key powers. The 19th century is often described as a 'golden age for free trade' (Bairoch,

1993). Governments chose to be open to trade, migration, and to adopt monetary standards and the consequent institutional arrangements that these demanded (Bairoch and Kozul-Wright, 1998). Then, as now, states chose to participate in the international economy. States reduced tariff barriers and, when they felt threatened and challenged, they ramped them back up again (see generally Kitson and Michie, 1995). They constructed institutions such as central banks to help mediate the domestic consequences of international trade and investment and, in the case of Britain, underwrote the functioning of the international economy through the provision of public goods, the most obvious of which was the security of sea lanes of trade and communication. Policy choice, state power and state capacity were central to the 19th century experience of globalization.

While figures of trade–GDP ratios and the construction of stable international monetary regimes give a sense of the extent of integration, recognition should be given to the ideology of internationalization which underwrote the development and consolidation of the 19th century version of globalization. These ideas involve two elements. The first relates to the more obvious ideology of empire. During this phase empire was seen as a measure of power: successful states expand their territory as a mark of their success and as a means to further their position. The second involves the way in which elites believed that internationalization was a good thing. It was beneficial not only in terms of the advantages that accrued from gaining strategically important ports such as Hong Kong, Cape Town or Singapore, but also because elites saw that such interactions brought about broader-ranging benefits (see generally Foreman-Peck, 1998). Here we see remarkable parallels with the present era. For example, elites felt that free trade would harmonize interests and reduce the likelihood of conflict between states. After the signing of the Franco–British Cobden-Chevalier free trade treaty of 1860, it is reported that the Prussian ambassador declared that war between Britain and France had been made 'impossible' (James, 2001: 13).

Economics and politics were vital ingredients of 19th century globalization, but technological advance, and its application in infrastructure investment, had an important part to play in the spectacular growth in international trade. The dramatic reduction in the cost of transportation by sea, which occurred alongside rapid increases in speed as shipping turned to steam power and adopted metal hulls, was perhaps the most obvious (see Aghion and William-son, 1998). But at least as important as this was the widespread adoption of railroads, in Europe and the colonies, which radically reduced land transportation costs and times (Baldwin and Martin, 1999; Clark and Feenstra, 2003). Not only could goods cross from New York to Liverpool or Cape Town to Cherbourg more rapidly and more cheaply than ever before they could also be moved from Liverpool to London or from New York to Chicago without prohibitive cost consequences. O'Rourke and Williamson argue that virtually all market integration after the 1860s was due to the fall in transport costs and not because of liberal trade policies (1999: 29–56). The other important advance was the invention and commercial application of the telegraph cable. In 1866 London and New York were connected and rapidly the rest of the world followed. By 1888 Australia and Britain were connected by telegraph cable. Within a generation communication times between govern-ment officials in Melbourne and London had dropped from six months to a matter of minutes.

The mass migrations of people were made possible by imperialism and by the globalization of economic relations. Opportunities deriving from the massive flows of capital in turn fostered large export flows providing the economic opportunities sought by many (see O'Rourke and Williamson, 1999). Migrants moved from the poorest parts of Europe as well as parts of Asia to the most dynamic regions of the 'New World', most notably the United States, Canada, Australia and South Africa. Migration peaked between 1870 and 1910 and played an important role in driving the globalization process (Potts, 1990; Segal, 1993). Once again, politics played a vital role in the story of this globalization. First, few states had any controls on movement. Travel was expensive but open, something which stands in stark contrast to the current era's deep mistrust of population movement. Second, large numbers of the population moved and established new and lasting political communities, which spread ideas of globalization and internationalization but also created hostile reactions (see generally Castles and Miller, 1998; Wang, 1997). Indeed migration was a key factor which prompted the global backlash that ended the previous era of global openness (see Williamson, 1998).

Globalization Today

From migration to trade and investment to political systems, the expansions of the global economy and a European system of international relations, the 19th century experience was very much a process of globalization. The world of the 19th century, when viewed through the abstract lens of trade–GDP ratios, looks remarkably similar to the one we have today. Beyond these raw economic figures, it is clear that disparate parts of the globe were linked and these connections drove new developments in politics, culture and the economy and were tangible in the ways they affected everyday life. Diseases spread rapidly (the pandemic following the First World War killed far more people than the war), the profits from whales slaughtered in the south Pacific came home to Nantucket, grapevines were transplanted to Australia, and European great power politics began to be played out on a properly global stage. It is tempting, therefore, to assume that contemporary globalization is essentially a return to the past. Yet the world we have today is different in many important ways. From political systems to the mechanisms of production, gender roles to the character of the international system, the world in the early years of the 21st century is quite different from the age of empire. While there are similarities – and continuities – with the previous era it is important to distinguish how the world today is distinctly different from what came before.

Similar Processes – Important Differences

As Baldwin and Martin point out, the integration of markets and people that began with the first industrial revolution started in vastly different circumstances from the current phase. During the late 18th century, when the foundations for 19th century globalization were laid, virtually the entire world was relatively poor and agrarian. It was industrialization and globalization in the 19th century which led to an absolute and relative reduction in wealth and power among those outside the West (Baldwin and Martin, 1999: 2–5). When the globalization process began again in earnest in the 20th century, some were rich and some were still very poor. A second point to emphasize is that, just as in the 20th century, the conditions which facilitated 19th century integration were heavily shaped by state policy choices. Trade and economic policy and, indeed, the broader context of the 19th century – in which European powers lived in relative peace under the Congress System between 1815 and 1872 – favoured integration and openness, however unevenly it was experienced (see for example O'Brien, 1984). It was as much the collapse of an international consensus on appropriate policy choices as it was rivalry and the rise of nationalism that brought this phase of globalization to an end. At the time, no one in New York, Paris or London could foresee an end to the prosperity brought about by this period of globalization. Yet it came badly unstuck, and it did so, primarily, because of the weakness of the institutions that had emerged to try to manage the system and the backlash against all things foreign that manifested itself in damaging policies of protectionism, ideologies of nationalism and ultimately total war.

The international economy is usually considered the element of contemporary globalization that is most similar to the previous period. How does it differ from the international economy of the late 19th and early 20th century? Although the absolute value of trade is similar, on closer inspection there are some important qualitative differences. As a number of economists have pointed out, the character of international trade has changed and, because of this, the effects of market integration across borders are said to be much more widely experienced. First, international trade is largely conducted among industrialized economies with similar productive and industrial capacities (what is called intra-industry trade). Around 90% of world trade is conducted among OECD economies (WTO, 2005: 19–20). In the past, trade was primarily between differently endowed economies. Even though the relative value of trade in terms of GDP–trade ratios may be similar, the nature of what is being traded has changed. The most obvious demonstration of this is the massive growth in merchandise trade, expressed in terms of GDP, given the relatively small increase in volumes of trade (Maddison, 2001: 127). Trade in merchandise goods and in components for further production are significantly higher than in the 19th century which means that international trade matters more for traders than it did previously and that developed states trade more with one another than with developing states. Second, a much wider range of domestic economic affairs are influenced by international forces including such services as banking, retail and insurance. Third, multinational firms (MNCs) play a much more important role in transmitting trade

(Rugman, 2000). Of course MNCs have been around for a while, but the scale of activity, their scope and economic influence today far outstrip the relatively modest economic influence of their antecedents. Fourth, the barriers to trade are significantly lower today than they were in the past. The success of the General Agreement on Trade and Tariffs (GATT) and the WTO and the emergence of preferential trade agreements, such as the EU, which produce zero tariff areas have significantly reduced the legal barriers to international trade as compared with the previous era (see generally Hoekman and Kostecki, 2001). Finally, while transportation costs dropped significantly in both periods, international trade today benefits from the significant reduction in communication costs which has been brought about by technological developments which have facilitated a huge reduction in the costs of telephony and international travel. This means that the movement of ideas, of managers, instructions, methods of production and so on can be far more rapid, and thus influence economic life much more easily, than previously. In the past, economic decision-making was as hindered by the costs of transport as by those that derived from the difficulty of determining information about investments or trade.

Contemporary international investment also appears, in aggregate statistical terms, to be similar to the past. Yet it too has some significant new dimensions. In the 19th century, investment was almost entirely of the long-term capital variety intended to develop primary products, such as money ploughed into railways in Africa and farms in Australia and New Zealand. Today investment helps to expose the complete range of economic activity to international market pressures, involving everything from banking and other professional services to petrochemical plants and automobile factories (UNCTAD, 2005: 260–1). International investment in productive facilities aims not only to expand market opportunities but is also intended to take advantage of genuinely international production systems. Firms now not only sell their products on an international market, they seek to take advantage of locational advantages in production to facilitate a global or at least inter-continental strategy (Dunning, 1993; Rugman, 2005). A wider range of sectors and a greater proportion of economic activity is influenced by international markets and forces than in previous times.

Second, in the past capital investment went from the imperial centres to the periphery. For example, investors in London and Paris invested in railways and agriculture in Australia, Indochina and Southern Africa. Today, investment capital flows primarily among the wealthy OECD states (UNCTAD, 2005). The other difference is the emergence of short-term capital. Today investment in short-term speculative ventures is a massive and very volatile business and unstable markets in foreign exchange have grown tremendously. For example, the UNDP notes that between 1973 and 1998 the daily turnover of global foreign exchange markets grew from USD 15 billion to USD 1.5 trillion, dwarfing the total value of annual global trade (UNDP, 1999: 30–31). This speculative financial capital which roams the globe in search of tiny differences in currency value or bond yields is an entirely new development. Finally, in monetary terms, the world is a very different place. Gone are currencies pegged to precious metals. All major economies have free floating currencies, even the only major exception to this, China, appears to be moving in this direction. International financial markets are also now more integrated than anything that has come before. The key to this has been the opening of almost all major economies to free capital movement.

In some respects, economic globalization in the 19th century is similar to the integration of markets today, but in a range of very important ways it is vitally different. In trade, investment, production, finance, the role of MNCs, the speed and ease with which information can move, as well as the broader geopolitical and policy circumstances in which the global economy exists, the current era is fundamentally different. In the words of an influential study: 'the globalization of commodity and financial markets is historically unprecedented. Facile comparisons with the late 19th century notwithstanding, the international integration of capital and commodity markets goes further and runs deeper than ever before' (Bordo *et al.*, 1999: 56–7).

In the political sphere the differences between the two periods are even more stark. Imperialism, understood in the classical sense, has gone. More importantly, it is no longer seen as morally acceptable and its basic underlying method – territorial expansion to augment the power of the metropole – is deemed to be an unacceptable form of behaviour. In its stead we see the most remarkable and complete form of globalization: the universal adoption and acceptance of the sovereign state as the pre-eminent form of political and moral authority. This political system is defined by sovereignty, which, understood in its classical sense, is a principle stating that final authority for a specific territory and people lies in the hands of the state *and nowhere else*. The two central norms of modern international politics – (i) the legal equality of states and (ii) non-interference in the affairs of others – stem from this principle. We often forget that prior to decolonization, the international system was not structured by the singular rule of sovereignty, rather it was a system involving two distinct practices. Between the European powers there was an adherence to the rule of non-interference, but in European relations with non-Europeans then the rule was not held to apply. The crude justification for this was the 'standards of civilization' whereby Europeans did not extend the privilege of the norms of their Westphalian system, such as respect of sovereignty, non-interference and the respect of territorial integrity, to those political communities which they felt did not meet their standards (although they did believe the system to be universal) (see Gong, 1984).

The universal acceptance of the territorial sovereign state as the foundation of the global system, while revolutionary, is not the only political difference between these global eras. In the post-1945 period international institutions have emerged to play a role that had not really existed in international politics previously. In a range of issue areas, from economics to peace and security, sovereign states have clubbed together to establish institutions to regulate their affairs, mitigate the effects of anarchy inherent in a system with universal acceptance of the principles of sovereignty, and to further their individual and collective interests. Institutions such as the United Nations, the Bank of International Settlements or the World Trade Organization are only some of the best known examples. Their significance for our concerns lies not only in their functional roles but also in their near universal subscription. For many, membership of the UN and the WTO is important, not only because it provides the benefits of political cooperation or the gains from trade, but also because of the symbolic significance that membership of these bodies brings. It bestows legitimacy on the states and prestige on the political elites, and is a badge representing the state's membership of the distinctive club of international society.

A further important difference between globalization in the 19th century and its contemporary experience lies in the character of the international norms which guide state behaviour. Although the principle of sovereignty means that domestic political differences are ostensibly irrelevant, the 20th century witnessed the evolution of several key principles which mark a decisive transformation from the classical understanding of sovereignty. The first is the idea of self-determination. Although not a part of the UN Charter (as it lies uneasily alongside sovereignty) it has become increasingly accepted internationally that people have a right to participate in the determination of their political fate (see generally, Moore, 1998). The second, and related, development is democratization. At the turn of the 20th century there were few, if any, genuine democracies. The primary limitation for states like America and Britain at this time was the failure to extend the franchise to women and ethnic minorities. Today, democracy, while still young in many states, is becoming the norm and not the exception to political governance. More importantly, it has become a properly global norm. A third development is the acceptance of the illegitimacy of the use of force in foreign policy except under tightly circumscribed conditions (see Finnemore, 2003).

Finally, a hallmark of the previous era of globalization was the ease with which people could move around the world. Whether as migrants seeking to create a new life in America, Canada or South Africa free from the burdens of Old Europe, or as traders and labourers seeking opportunities from colonial trade and investment in Hong Kong, Singapore or the Philippines that were unavailable in Hainan or Fujian, one could move with few restrictions. At least this was so up until the backlash against this openness that began to emerge in the late 1890s (Zolberg, 1997). Today, population movement is far more restricted even though the means with which people can move is cheaper and more accessible (Castles and Miller, 1998). Of the societies which accepted mass migration from Europe and elsewhere in the 19th century, only the United States and Australia maintain anything like the degree of openness that they once did. Even in America the long-term political support for this appears to be on the wane. Anti-immigration sentiment is popular across the developed world and, while borders are open to movements of trade and capital, the flow of people is far more restricted.

The other sphere in which there are marked differences is technology. Satellite technology has facilitated cheap long-distance telecommunication. Although the internet and email have not yet presented the kind of economic advance promised in the 1990s, computer technology has produced large efficiency gains in productive processes around the world. The emergence of relatively cheap long distance air travel has also made a very real difference to economic and political life. In six days in June 2005, the US Secretary of State, Condoleeza Rice, held meetings in Jordan, Egypt, Saudi Arabia, Belgium and London. This gives a sense of the way in which intercontinental aircraft travel has changed the conduct of modern diplomacy, to say nothing of the cultural shift which has allowed a black woman to hold the premier diplomatic post of the world's most powerful country. But these technological developments need to be put in some perspective. While aircraft can move people across the globe at previously unimaginable speeds, they only move a tiny proportion of the world's population. Equally, air freight is still far too expensive for most goods that are traded internationally; the vast majority of merchandise trade travels by ship (Levinson, 2006). The most significant difference between the current and earlier phases of globalization is the massive reduction in the cost and speed of the movement of information (Castells, 1996). Other changes, such as air travel and air freight, do matter but they are not as important to the broader patterns of world politics as they may appear to be in our day-to-day lives.

Overall, there are four broad ways in which contemporary globalization is distinct from previous experiences with global interconnectedness. The most notable is the scale of contemporary globalization. The globe today is both much bigger and much smaller than before. The networks and linkages cover much wider terrain, technology allows the costs of distance to be much more easily borne and thus globalization's impact can be felt more widely than in previous times. In this sense the globe is being made more compact. But the population of the planet is at its greatest and globalization thus influences far more people than ever before. A second distinction is the universality of key parts of contemporary globalization. Globalization is more widely experienced by states and societies than previously but also the central ideas and institutions – such as states, international organizations, currencies and markets – are universally accepted as legitimate. For example, previous eras of globalization have involved the interaction of very different political systems – such as European empires and indigenous tribes – each with different conceptions of basic ideas such as appropriate conduct, property rights, and mutual recognition. This did not mean that interaction was impossible, but the interactions of the current era are structured around universally supported notions and are therefore quite distinct. Third, there is a broad ranging consensus on the basic ideas and ideals of economic management. This does not mean that neo-liberalism holds all in its sway; rather that there is a basic global consensus about private property, the right to make profit and the appropriateness of markets to resolve most questions of resource distribution. Of course there is still a vast range of different approaches to the detail, such as the rights of labour, the nature of market regulation and the precise balance of state participation in the economy, but the basic principles of the global capitalist economy are uncontested. Finally, the speed of so many of today's globalization processes distinguishes the current period from earlier forms. It is not only that more of the world is better linked than ever before, but many of these linkages occur at a much higher rate than we have seen previously. This involves not only the ability to transfer vast sums of money across the world at the press of a button but also the capacity to move people, goods and knowledge faster than ever before. That said, one should temper the enthusiasm slightly. Most goods are shipped by sea and the speed of sea transportation has not increased markedly since the 1970s. However, in most other areas, such as the movement of capital, information and ideas, the speeds of contemporary globalization are truly unique.

The Current State of Globalization

The contemporary era is more integrated, connections are more speedily made and international order is based on more universal principles than ever before. In Chapter 1, globalization was given a consequentialist definition. That is, globalization was defined as being the consequences that derive from increases in both the rate and speed with which people, goods, labour, capital and knowledge move around in the world. From this view, globalization is not coterminous with, for example, reduced tariff barriers. The changes themselves are said to induce transformations (the consequences of change) which is the process we are concerned with. Even those of the most sceptical frame of mind would be hard pressed to refute some of the more remarkable developments in the transmission of goods, services, capital and ideas around the world. Global financial markets that allow 24-hour trading of currencies, equities, bonds and commodities are both new and of great significance to people's lives. Equally, the movement of goods and ideas across borders and vast oceans at high speed cannot be ignored. The sceptics are on stronger ground in their doubts about the consequences of these changes on social structures and institutions.

To summarize, how has the world changed so that there is, or at least appears to be, significant transformation in vital political, economic and social structures associated with globalization? The most significant changes relate to:

(i)   the international trade of goods and services, and specifically, the increased importance of trade to a wider range of sectors;

(ii) international movements of capital, and most particularly to the wider distribution, more diverse and dynamic sectors receiving global investment and, of course, the rise of high volume short-term speculative capital movements;

(iii) the huge increase in the ability of knowledge and ideas to move rapidly around the world;

(iv) the consolidation of the political spread of the sovereign state.

All of these spheres, with the exception of the last, have increased not only volumes and rates of movement, but, most importantly, their speed and impact has increased as well.

The most important aspect of contemporary globalization is its level of openness and a broad-ranging political consensus in support of this state of affairs. Never before has so much of the world been so open to the movement of goods, services, investment and ideas. This is not to say that the world is a free marketeer's Utopia, nor that all governments support all aspects of openness. In trade the unwilling-ness of the developed economies to liberalize agriculture and textiles trade and the desire to apply tight border controls by most states are the most obvious exceptions. But viewed in the aggregate, the openness to trade, investment, and ideas is remarkably high. Equally important is the general consensus that openness is a virtue and holds the key to prosperity and human fulfilment. Whether this consensus is justified is another matter. It is beyond dispute that there is general support among rich, as well as many poor, states for what could be described as an ideology of openness. The circumstances that have produced this include the perceived success of international institu-tions such as the GATT, the collapse of communism which killed off an attempt to structure economic relations along closed lines and the experiences of Japan, Taiwan and South Korea, as well as the more recent experiences of China and India which demonstrate the economic success that stems from embracing the international economy.

The second central feature of contemporary globalization is the significance of information. While some sociologists and economists may over-sell this, the huge distances over which information can move, the speed and the low cost are important. The investor can make infinitely better informed decisions about markets, costs and relative prices (although of course this does not mean that all decisions are good). The activist has a raft of opportunities for organization and influence (see generally Williams, 2005), while for the diplomat on-line news services and the increased use of summits have transformed the work (and influence) of the foreign service officer, though not necessarily enhancing her influence (Talbott, 1997). While the flow of ideas across borders and continents has been with us forever, the speed with which ideas can cover vast distances is perhaps the most distinctive aspect of contemporary globalization.

Finally, although the environment of openness is facilitated by states, the current era is notable in that private organizations are particularly important in the broader process of international integration. For example, the massive flows of financial capital and speculative foreign exchanges are undertaken primarily by private actors. Currency collapses such as the British experience in 1992 or the Thai crisis of 1997 were brought about by, among other causes, the inability of governments to compete with market forces. MNCs, seen by some as the heavy bombers of globalization, play the most important role in international investment, production and consumption patterns.

The hallmark of contemporary globalization is the rapid movement of information that is made possible by ideas and policies supportive of openness and which thus allows a considerable increase in the capacity of private actors to influence world politics. More broadly, the social consequences of the speedy flows of goods, knowledge, capital and people are playing themselves out in complex ways. That these flows exist, and are relatively new in both form and intensity, is reasonably clear. It is less clear, however, quite what consequences the increasing ease with which these flows can zip across the planet are for the international system. This is the focus of the remainder of this book.

3

Globalization and the State: Leviathan Under Threat?

Since globalization first emerged the argument that contemporary economic and political circumstances are undermining the power and efficacy of the state has been never far from sight. As far back as the late 1960s, Charles Kindleberger famously declared that the nation state was 'just about through as an economic unit' (Kindleberger, 1969: 207). Unsurprisingly, the proposition that globalization is hollowing out the state has become one of the central arguments in the globalization debate. Footloose capital, global money markets and muscular MNCs are thought to be reducing states to little more than pawns in the game of global capitalism. States are said to have virtually no control over their economies and must follow the dictates and interests of global economic forces. Beyond the economic sphere, it is said, the state is caught in a pincer movement as the power and pervasiveness of international organizations suck political authority and regulatory power up and away from states while ethnic groups, regions and local networks grab what remains for themselves. As borders become ever more porous, this anachronistic institution, so the argument goes, can do little to stem the tide. Given the nature, scale and speed of change it is unsurprising that analysts and scholars might come to the conclusion that a social institution that has its origins in Europe's 17th century wars of religion is not particularly well suited to deal with the gamut of economic, political and social challenges that human societies face in the 21st century.

Chapter 3 firstly considers the argument of state decline and the various strands of the argument that global forces are pushing the state into history's ever-present dustbin. This assessment shows that interpretations of the globalization–state relationship depend on the conception of the state that is used, and one of the problems of many state-decline arguments is a general misunderstanding about the character and role of the modern state. This chapter tries to clarify matters by setting out a clearer understanding of what the state is. The primary focus here is with statehood as experienced in the developed world. However, the conclusions have relevance to the broader practice of statehood in the whole contemporary world. Rather than killing off the state, the chapter concludes that globalization is changing the environment in which it operates, both domestically and internationally, and is thus contributing to a shift in the role that states play in the domestic and international spheres. States are a product of the political, cultural, economic and military circumstances of their times. Just as they were changed by industrialization, so they are subject to change today. The challenge is to determine the extent and character of the shifts in state behaviour and the role played by global forces in these transformations.

Globalization and the State: Manufactured Obsolescence?

For most writers who argue that the state is in decline, it appears that the problems posed by globalization are in-built. It is precisely the state's territoriality, the absolutism of its credo of sovereignty and the firmness with which its borders must be marked and patrolled which, so the critics say, make it unsuited to the trials of globalization. The modern state emerged as a function of changes in the geographic patterns of moral authority, the changing character of modern warfare and the emergence of modern capitalism (Tilly, 1990). It centralized authority over a territory, expanded its capacity so as to ensure its military security and constructed this on the moral foundation of sovereignty. What made the state distinctive was its exclusivity and its territoriality: only the state had the right and power to determine events within its jurisdiction. The nature of the institution allowed for considerable variation among entities. Provided the basic instrumental and moral aspects could be maintained, it did not matter if one was democratic or absolutist, socialist or *laissez-faire*, domestic structural questions were entirely in one's own hands. Yet contemporary circumstances are said to fundamentally challenge the exclusivity of states. Many argue that they lack both the capacity and the moral authority to back up traditional doctrines of sovereignty in the face of globalization.

The essence of this argument is that a wide array of pressures is shifting both power and authority away from states and toward a motley assortment of markets, firms, international organizations and social groups. In the third phase of the globalization debate many of these propositions were written off as the delusions of a disconnected few. Yet one must give this literature its due and recognize that the arguments of state decline have themselves been subject to over-statement and misrepresentation (see Hammarlund, 2005: 175–7). Instead of simplistic, Chicken Little-style prognostications, this literature depicts a range of symptoms of weakness and possible anachronism which are thought to be indicative of change. Among this group, one can identify four general sources of pressure which are identified as undermining the autonomy, capacity and authority of the state: economic factors, international organizations, social forces and a loose category of transnational challenges.

Economic Forces

Due variously to the internationalization of production, the huge growth in international trade and the rise of global financial markets, writers such as Ohmae (1990; 1995), Luard (1990) and Strange (1996) determine that there is a serious challenge to the traditional role of the state in matters economic. The argument has a number of dimensions, the first of which is the challenge posed by the heightened mobility of capital. The ease and speed with which capital is able to move, as well as its sheer volume, makes any state's core business of managing the economy increasingly problematic (Wriston, 1992). If markets disapprove of state behaviour – if taxes are too high, the budget deficit too large or regulations too onerous – then, so the argument goes, capital will flee (e.g. Gray, 1998). State dependence on international markets to finance spending means that states are especially vulnerable to the judgments of financial markets. Rather than determining their economic policy based on strictly domestic criteria, states now operate within the strictures of what markets deem to be acceptable policy. The perception of deviation from appropriate policy by markets is said to draw severe punish-ment and this acts to control what states do.

Market discipline is said to have dramatically reduced the range and character of economic policy-making. Gone are the Keynesian and corporatist policy tools of demand management, industry policy and ownership of strategic industries. In their place we now find that only monetary and fiscal policies are available for states to influence their economic well-being. There is perceived to be a single model of acceptable economic policy which sets very narrow parameters within which states may operate. Its core is a deregulated, open economy in which tight fiscal policy is the order of the day, social welfare spending is kept to a minimum, the taxation regime is firm-friendly, non-progressive and structured around indirect mechanisms, such as consumption taxes, the labour market must be flexible and monetary policy is run by an independent central bank fixed on a low-inflation target. Attempts to deviate from this minimalist model will result in global markets imposing severe penalties (e.g. Reich, 1991).

The second area in which change can be seen is in the state–firm relationship. States and firms have always had a bargaining relationship – firms offer injections of capital, employment, skills and technology, in return states provide markets, labour, infrastructure and the like – and the relationship is negotiated with these common interests underpinning action (see Stopford and Strange, 1991). However, because of globalization, so this thinking goes, the balance has tipped in favour of firms (e.g. Hertz, 2001). MNCs are able to play states, labour and other groups off against each other. In the bargain between states and firms, the economic might of ExxonMobil, GlaxoSmithKline and Matsui overwhelms the state's ability to act even as an equal. This also brings about a purported race to the bottom where firm's dominance of bargaining produces competition among states for the most business-friendly environment (e.g. Korten, 2001). For example, where Malaysia offers tax breaks, Singapore offers non-union labour and softer regulation. Not wanting to miss out on the investment opportunity, Indonesia offers both these enticements as well as lax environmental regulations. States compete to outdo one another to remove costly regulations on labour, environment and taxation and this drives the broader international market of standards ever lower.

This view perceives the global economy to be so powerful that the state is increasingly unable to determine questions of domestic economic welfare. All it can do is nudge things around the fringes, but to do more than that is to risk the ire of the market. For some, this unwillingness or inability to lead economic matters at home brings into question the very purpose of modern statehood (e.g. Guéhenno, 1995; Luard, 1990).

International Organizations

The growth and expansion of international organizations (IOs) has been one of the more notable developments in 20th century world politics. But for some the expansion of IOs is an institutional reflection of state weakness and incapacity in the face of global pressures, while for others it involves a more sinister element. Democratic states are handing over policy powers to unelected and opaque international bureaucracies who are able to determine the fate of millions without accountability and scrutiny.

This view is predicated on the perception that membership of many IOs requires states to give up specific policies or to hand them over to the organization. This visibly constrains state policy choice and, in the eyes of some, reduces member states to being little more than conduits for an international bureaucracy (see the discussion in Zürn, 2004). There is a huge range of IOs in world politics, from the Association of Southeast Asian Nations (ASEAN) to the Bank for International Settlements (BIS), from the African Union to the World Bank. The most advanced – some might argue, most extreme – example of an IO undermining the state is the European Union (EU). As a condition of joining the EU member states sign up to a comprehensive set of administrative commitments, known as the *acquis communautaire*, which describes in considerable detail the legal obligations of membership. The most important element is that EU law trumps member-state law in the event of a conflict (Craig and de Búrca, 2003). Moreover, the EU provides legal scope for redress if member states fail to comply with the centrally determined directives. Equally, the adoption of single market provisions, which allow for the free movement of goods, capital, labour and people, has also created substantial levels of legal harmonization.

The EU is unique. Its extensive administrative reach, legal personality and political structures make it the most far-reaching IO in existence. Such is its scope and scale that it is well beyond the intergovernmentalism of most IOs. The WTO is a different type of IO, but one which represents the kind of erosion of state capacity that many associate with globalization. The WTO is a technically focused organization that is intended to promote and regulate a liberal international trading system (Hoekman and Kostecki, 2001). It has a very wide and diverse membership with its 149 members ranging from the wealthiest to some of the least developed. The WTO's essential remit is to oversee a range of international agreements on trade with the purpose of providing a binding and one-way path to a global liberal trading system. Although there is some scope for states to protect themselves temporarily from health threats or short-term economic shocks, the intention is to provide a mechanism that reduces barriers to trade and keeps them permanently down. It is a good example of an organization designed to remove specific policy options from the hands of states; in this case to limit the ways states can establish barriers to trade.

Social Factors

As IOs take aspects of state capacity from above, emerging social forces are said to be stripping state institutions of power and purpose from below. The rise of ethnic- and identity-based political move-ments through the 1980s and 1990s is thought to be the most tangible evidence of this. Around the world groups and territories below state level pushed for enhanced autonomy, or even separation, from existing institutions. Not satisfied with Spanish, British or Ethiopian governance, Catalans, Scots and Eritreans sought enhanced auton-omy and freedoms (Guibernau, 1999). Governance and state-like functions were said to be better suited, under conditions of globaliza-tion, to IOs and more local forms, leaving the traditional state little clear purpose.

The rise of populism across the developed world in the 1990s has also been attributed to this broader process. Demagogic outsiders in many states presented themselves to disillusioned voters as alter-natives to 'politics as usual'. While often at quite some remove from the ordinary electors for whom they claimed to speak, they packaged themselves as 'non-politicians' who would speak unpalatable truths to the entrenched political elites. Ross Perot and Pat Buchanan in the US were the harbingers of a phenomenon which also saw some political success for Jean-Marie Le Pen in France, Jorg Haider in Austria, Pym Fortuyn in the Netherlands, Stockwell Day in Canada, and Pauline Hanson in Australia. Populism is said to be a symptom of the lack of fit between existing political structures and the social conditions created by globalization. Globalization undermines the capacity of traditional political elites and appears to be responsible for a considerable degree of alienation among the citizenry, both of which open a space for the populists (Mudde, 2004: 555–6).

Globalization is also making state borders increasingly porous to ideas. On the one hand this was manifest in the dominance of neoliberal ideas about the role of the state and the economy. States were complicit in the dismantling of important areas of competence as privatization, deregulation and liberalization became the watchwords of government policy around the world. Of course there was some room for minor variations – America's farmers could receive protection, some social welfare could be retained in Germany and banks were bailed out in Japan – but from a macro point of view, globalization was said to foster a dominance of ideas about the state and economy which promoted the kind of minimalism which the declinists determined was a key feature of statehood under conditions of globalization. At a more basic level globalization made the prevention of the spread of ideas around the world ever more challenging. If states were traditionally thought to be the economic and political gatekeepers then globalization was thought to have made this role virtually impossible. How can one keep out unwanted thoughts when confronted with the internet, email, mobile phones and satellite television?

Transnational Challenges

Most of the literature diagnoses state decline in terms of function: states are prevented from taking action by global financial markets or their hands are tied by IOs. But the final strand of the declinist argument relates to the inappropriateness of the state rather than a drop in its power. States had emerged to resolve problems of security and economy, and this fourth line argues that the environment of globalization brings issues with which the territorial state is ill-equipped to cope. There is a wide range of transnational challenges which threaten people, societies and economies, whose effects are magnified by globalization, and which states cannot resolve.

Whether it is pollution, global warming, the narcotics trade, piracy, SARS or pandemic influenza, globalization is said to be enhancing the effects, scope and scale of the problems these pose to peoples, states and systems of economic relations (for example, Dupont, 2001; Lipschutz, 1995; Sandler, 1997). Moreover some organizations positively prey on the political and legal gaps which are inherent in the territorially-based sovereign state system. The international system has jurisdictional problems which allow pirates to act with a degree of impunity, and state rivalries to get in the way of adequate coordination, to solve problems relating, for example, to the environment. Not only do microbes not respect human borders, it is said that they thrive on the opportunities to spread provided by globalization. The connections among states and societies that are rapidly enhanced by globalization present a set of problems which, many scholars argue, states cannot solve on their own. In this view, globalization reveals the practical limitations of territorially determined political entities. In days gone by, states could, with good policy, virtually wipe out the threat of diseases, increase standards of education and ensure economic goals such as full employment. Appropriate responses are transnational or global in scale and, the literature argues, provide not only evidence of the inappropriateness of states in a global era but also the momentum to further rob the state of capacity and authority.

In summary, declinists argue that globalization presents the traditional territorial state with a set of profound challenges which seriously question that institution's appropriateness to contemporary circumstances. Economic forces are said to render the state unable to act except for slight manoeuvres around the fringes. Forces from above and below are challenging its monopoly on authority; they limit its capacity and transnational threats reveal its manifest inadequacies. The declinist argument involves three core propositions: (1) state autonomy has been undermined because global forces impose punishingly high costs on states that deviate from the basic neoliberal model; (2) in key sectors the state no longer has the power and authority to alter outcomes; and (3) the state lacks the resources and structures to resolve the kinds of security and social problems it had in the past.

Death, Decline or Adaptation?

Are those who set out this declinist interpretation of globalization right? Many of these assertions were contested in the third phase of the globalization debate (e.g. Gelber, 1997, Hirst and Thompson, 1996; Weiss, 1998). On the whole the evidence that the state is on its way out is not compelling. However, there is a case to be made that the changes associated with globalization are inducing a more subtle, though not unimportant, transformation in the conditions of modern statehood. Before discussing these, we will briefly consider some of the particular shortcomings of the declinist literature which feed into the interpretation of the state–globalization interaction fleshed out below.

The most basic problem with the globalization literature is that global economic processes and flows are not as extensive as many argue and thus, critics claim, its effect on states is not great (e.g. Gilpin, 2001). While some recognize that the internationalization of production, global finance and the rise of IOs are real and of importance, critics emphasize that the state has been, and continues to be, the key player in the globalization process. The picture that the declinists paint, of globalization as an inexorable force of nature external to states, is not only misplaced, it ignores the very real ways that states created and continue to perpetuate globalization. For it was states opening up their economies to investment and trade, and their creation of an infrastructure supportive of global forces (from legal systems to telecommunications), that allowed globalization to occur. Even in the most sophisticated of such institutions, the EU, the state retains a primacy and significance that is often overlooked. In spite of the considerable levels of legal and economic integration among members, the EU is still primarily an organization of member states. While it might look legally strong it is administratively weak. The relatively puny size of the EU's budget makes this plain. It consists of just over 1.2% of member states' GDP and its total is presently capped at a maximum of 1.27% of member states' GDP (European Commission, 2000a: 8). Ultimately, it is the states themselves that carry out the practical enforcement of European decisions and make the EU, as a legal entity, happen.

Critics also rightly point out that declinists have an unrealistic view of what states used to be able to do. Never has a state had the degree of control or dominance that it has been said to have lost due to globalization. International factors, such as the availability of gold, the whim of international finance and the actions of other states have always significantly constrained the domestic policy-making autonomy of states, to say nothing of domestic interests and pressures which have always constrained state autonomy. To think that there was once a period of absolute autonomy and sovereignty that is now on the precipice is to get the historical development of states very wrong.

As both Mann (1997) and Weiss (1998) point out, among the declinist literature there is a rather muddled understanding of just what the modern state actually is. It is true that modern sovereign statehood is a dominant political form and that it is not unreasonable to speak in general terms about its strengths and weaknesses. The problem, however, is that much of the declinist literature seems not to grasp the complexity of states and the way this particular political system relates to broader social forces. The modern state consists of a range of institutions which provide final functional rule-making over a specific territory and population and which is distinguished from other institutions by its claim to provide the highest legitimate moral authority within its territory (Bisley, 2004: 32–3). It exists in a political and economic system that is structured around its claim to embody the pinnacle of authority, that is the modern international system. This particular set of traits – its authority, its centrality, its territoriality and its international character – mean that the state has three distinct modes of existence. It is the predominant force within its territory, it is a participant in the international system and it is the link between these two spheres. The state exists as a complex multiplicity of institutions and principles. Moreover, the diversity of functions that institutions play means that they can give up considerable functional tasks without necessarily undermining their broader dominance or purpose. No longer practising a traditional policy (such as trade protection) should not be confused with a broader weakening of the structural significance of statehood in domestic and international society. Changing function, or indeed a net reduction of function, does not logically equal overall decline unless one takes a narrow and strictly functional definition of the state. Such a view misunderstands the contemporary character of the modern state which embodies not only functions but also norms, values, ideals and principles, all of which need to be severely undermined to warrant a conclusion of decline.

A further error that many commit when confronting the state–globalization issue is to think of the relationship as zero sum (on this see Shaw, 1997; Weiss, 2003a). The idea that states have a fixed quantity of power and authority that is being leeched away by globalization misunderstands not only the nature of state power but also the fact that the practice of statehood is constantly changing in response to political, economic, cultural and strategic circumstances. State power is a function of social interactions and not merely the product of some static repository of coercion and authority that can be bled away. The state is able to capitalize on the way in which its actions, such as the provision of security, education or health care, not only ensure its functional dominance but embody the idea of final authority. It is the interactive quality of state power and authority – what might be described as a positive-sum theory of state power – which declinists neglect. If state power were zero sum it would be extremely hard to explain why states have been so keen to adopt policies which would do them out of a job. From the reduction of barriers to policies of neoliberalism, state policy choice has been vital in establishing the context of globalization precisely because states see in these choices a means to advance their objectives in domestic and international society. Moreover, even in some of the most tangible cases where states have voluntarily ceded certain powers or policies to IOs, or have unified a set of currencies, it does not follow that these states have become less powerful or less relevant. To be sure, states are not behaving as they have in the past and the locus of authority is a more complex matter than it has been, but states are a long way from finished.

Not only are there conceptual problems with the state decline argument, there is little empirical evidence to support the position. Policy-makers around the world do not feel that their work is pointless and their perceptions about policy options, and the competing payoffs that these entail, provide a basic indicator that the state is very much alive. The most clear evidence of state decline would be visible in a number of statistics; particularly in a reduction in state spending as a ratio of GDP, a reduction in state capacity to establish and enforce laws, and in the numbers employed by the state, decreasing allegiances to state forms of identity and, as economists have emphasized, a convergence of prices. For economists, states inhibit markets and the differential prices among countries are thought to be a function of market distortions created by taxes, tariffs and regulations. If globalization is diminishing state capacity then it ought to be observable in some basic fashion.

Yet, there is little economic evidence to support claims of a reduction in state role of influence or even that trends are tending in that direction. Since the mid 1960s OECD states have continued to increase government expenditure as a share of GDP and increase the percentage of the workforce that they employ (Hay, 2004; Tanzi and Schuknect, 2000). The work of Prime Minister Thatcher and President Reagan did not prevent the increase of the size and scope of their states (although it changed *what* they did). States are not having their capacity to raise revenue through taxation limited by globalization nor their propensity to increase their size and role (Hobson, 2003). As for questions of convergence, the much-touted race to the bottom, whereby states are 'waging a war of competitive deregulation, forced on them by the global free market' (Gray, 1998: 78) has not occurred. There is no evidence to back up the claim that foreign direct investment (FDI) shops around for the best tax rates (Wilensky, 2002). Even in finance, the sector which even the most committed sceptic agrees is more integrated than ever before, interest rates continue to run along separate and decidedly statist paths (OECD, 2006). In fact it is interest rate and bond yield differentials which drive much of the foreign currency speculation in global markets.

Globalization is said to discipline states and force them to adhere to a singular model of economic behaviour. Yet if one looks at the fiscal policy of the richest states – those most heavily influenced by globalization – there is little evidence to support the claims that globalization has tied their policy hands. At the time of writing (2007), the UK, France, Germany, the US, Japan and Italy are running significant budget deficits and have done so for a number of years. While some developed economies run surpluses (such as Canada and Australia), loose fiscal policy is the order of the day for the United States. Between 1980 and 2005 the US ran a deficit in all but four years between 1998 and 2001 (OMB, 2005). Indeed, if anything, globalization has meant that the consequences of deficits appear not to be as ruinous as some had once thought because it allows states greater capacity to access and manage debt. Beyond fiscal policy, Garrett shows clearly that there is no policy convergence among OECD states on government spending, deficits or capital tax rates nor that capital flees at the sight of interventionist states (1998: 812–19). In short, the economic integration which has undoubtedly occurred in the world has not undermined state policy choice and has not created a drive for a homogenous approach to economic policy.

In the realm of politics there is not much to support the ardent declinist. While much is made of secessionist movements, such as the Quebecois or the Kurds, on closer inspection one does not see a rejection of the idea of statehood or a belief that states are of declining relevance. On the contrary, the Palestinians, Kurds and Chechens feel that the states to which they belong do them harm. For them the state is not in decline, it is far too prominent. These groups seek not to reject the state *per se* but the state of which they are a part. In the realm of the military and matters strategic the proposition of decline is most fanciful. Of course on 11 September 2001 al Qa'eda scored a clear psychological victory for a section of the transnational and the under-resourced, but states retain the overwhelming predominance not only of the resources and materials of war but also the moral authority to act.

Just because globalization has not pushed the state from centre stage it does not follow that globalization is of no relevance to the practice of modern statehood. Instead of killing off the state, it is argued here, globalization is doing two things. Firstly, it is constraining the range and effectiveness of certain forms of state action and, secondly, it is providing opportunities for states to advance their interests and prompting new forms of behaviour. Globalization provides new means for states to interact with global capitalism which can work to their advantage, such as through cheaper debt, access to efficiency gains and new sources of labour. Globalization limits certain choices but also enables others. Globalization does not present a fundamental challenge to the political and moral dominance of the practice of modern statehood, rather it provides circumstances which contribute to a slight strengthening of the international position of the state. But, states are clearly facing a different environment from that of even 25 years ago, and they must respond to it. Around the world we see different approaches, but at the heart of national reform programmes such as Oman's Vision 2020, the transformation of Australian trade policy and the reform of education programmes in Britain, one sees direct and indirect national responses to the challenges of globalization.

Globalization and the State: At Home

Globalization involves a set of changes in the social realm which subtly shifts the context in which states find themselves. States have always reconfigured their relations, both to society below and the international community above, based on changes in their circumstances. Just as states shifted their forms in response to developments in defence technology and industrialization, the increase in movement of goods, people, knowledge and capital is having an influence on state preferences, behaviour and policy.

Before considering these, however, it is useful to reflect on the role the state plays so as to have some framework for assessing any changes. The most basic purpose of states is to achieve three goals:

1. to ensure institutional survival;
2. to maximize the aggregate welfare of state and society, however conceived;
3. to minimize insecurity to state and society.

This focuses primarily on developed state experience but relates to the broader practice of statehood. These goals are not all evenly advanced by all states, and in some circumstances they can be contradictory. The achievement of these aims, or at least their advancement, involves action in both domestic and international realms. Even though globalization has made the formal distinction between these two somewhat less clear cut, there is little evidence to show that globalization has changed the state's basic aims (Thompson, 2006). Globalization does, however, involve some changes to the environment in which states seek to achieve these goals and to the means with which they go about protecting themselves and advancing their interests. How states maximize welfare and minimize insecurity is influenced by the reduction in costs of the movement of goods, capital and knowledge.

The modern state first emerged as a territorially defined political entity in reaction to changes in the character of war and the social and economic structures of human society in the late Middle Ages in Europe (Hall, 1986; Tilly, 1990). As industrialization developed, and particularly as industrial warfare transformed the use of force in international relations, so states began to change not only their domestic economic functions but also the normative expectations of the kind of role, both economic and social, that they were expected to play at home. The rise of corporatist states and the growth of the welfare state did not necessarily entail a fundamental rethinking of the basic purposes of the state. Rather, they reflected an important shift in the character of state action designed to advance the fundamental ends. As, for example, the British state moved away from a *laissez-faire* approach to domestic society and began to embrace a distinct social purpose to its actions (to redistribute resources from the wealthy to the poor and to provide some basic insurance against large-scale poverty), one saw a change in how states sought to maximize domestic welfare, as well as a shift in the social expectations of what welfare meant. The changes brought about by globalization in state role and behaviour are at this level; shifts in the kind of roles states play, the sorts of policies they adopt to advance these ends and in the way statesmen and women think about the means through which the basic goals of welfare and security maximization are understood. In the EU one sees an interesting development whereby states have agreed to reduce their autonomy so as to strengthen their institutional mechanisms and advance their economic and social goals (see generally Moravscik, 1998). The story is not one of a straight-line strengthening–weakening trade-off, but of innovative developments in state practice prompted by changing circumstances (see Sørenson, 2003). One can identify both economic and political aspects to the changes in the state's domestic behaviour in response to global pressure and these involve changing approaches to both appropriate policy and broader aspects of the role of the state in domestic social relations.

Perhaps the most obvious shift that has been brought about by globalization has been the demise of traditional statist approaches to economic policy. While the move away from state owned enterprises, guided industry policy and the like has a longer-run trajectory, globalization has made the economic policy that was dominant in the 30 years after the Second World War both practically and politically unworkable. Across the OECD it is electoral suicide to advance such approaches. Moreover, in the developing world policy-makers are moving in this direction as well. Make no mistake, we are not living in a neoliberal paradise, rather the general trend in economic policy among the vast majority of the world's states is to move away from large-scale statist projects. This reflects not only the changing economic circumstances of the modern international system but also a shift in attitudes about the role that many feel the state should play in economic affairs. During the high tide of Keynesianism the state was expected to play a significant economic role; for example, through the ownership of key activities and intervention in the market-place to achieve full employment and redistributive social goals. The openness associated with globalization and the dynamism that generally goes with it, plus the enhanced competitive pressure experienced by markets and firms, has pushed the state away from this once dominant approach to its relationship to markets. Today, markets are seen as better providers of economic outcomes and it is a strongly held belief by many across the globe that state participation in the economic sphere, at least as an owner of industry or director of resources, can be positively detrimental to patterns of economic distribution.

The general trend is not for states to wring their hands in the face of globalization and allow markets free rein, nor is it to retreat behind protectionist walls and nationalized industry, rather we appear to be witnessing the emergence of a form of state behaviour that Weiss calls 'governed interdependence' (2003b). Instead of fostering a minimalist state, globalization is prompting states to adopt strategies to try to advance their basic aims using novel policy approaches. This involves, for example, creative attitudes to industrial policy, to education and training, to taxation regimes and to fiscal policy. While traditional industrial policy may be dead, states across the OECD are finding new ways to advance their national economic priorities through creative approaches to high technology industry support, export finance programmes, infrastructure support for market access and investment support (Weiss, 2005). As noted above the mechanisms of globalization rely in many respects on states, but, conversely, states cannot act in any way that they choose. States attempt to negotiate, as they have always done, the balance between the domestic and the international and globalization appears to have made this a somewhat more complex game. For Weiss, a state's success in maximizing its basic interests is contingent on the character of the state, its policy-making strength and its capacity to respond quickly to changing circumstances (2003b). While it is too early to determine whether this proposition is entirely correct, she is right to emphasize that, in the economic realm, state capacity is central to determining how the changes associated with globalization are played out. This complements the arguments contained in the literature on different national institutional settings and their impact on economic success, which shows that these are crucial to social development (see generally Hall and Soskice, 2001). The literature shows clearly that globalization is not driving a homogenization in approaches to economic policy – quite the opposite, it is prompting considerable institutional diversity (see Berger and Dore, 1996; Cerny, 1995; Hall and Soskice, 2001: 54–66).

Although shifts in political structures are less clear-cut than in the economic sphere, one can discern a subtle change in the character of politics, shifts in the normative underpinnings of the political role of the state and some clear moves in domestic security policy driven by the new threats and vulnerabilities associated with globalization.

The tableau of domestic politics cannot remain immune to changes in economic or social life in any state. Whether the rejection of Soviet communism by a generation of Eastern Europeans or the failure of the Shah to recognize the social dislocation being caused by widespread urbanization in Iran, states and political elites ignore changes in domestic social structure at their peril. Globalization has altered the landscape of domestic political systems for modern states. With the exception of North Korea, Burma and a handful of African states, all states are exposed, in differing degrees, to the international economic and political system. The impact of this on the character of domestic politics varies considerably. In part this is a function of differing degrees of openness and in part a result of different political institutions and cultures. Broadly speaking, there are four ways in which globalization influences domestic political systems. First, in democracies, it has been associated with the homogenization of political parties. As the consensus around a broadly liberal conception of the fundamental economic structures of society has been reinforced, political parties in democracies which had hitherto taken distinctive approaches to these fundamental questions are becoming increasingly hard to distinguish, at least in terms of macro-economic policy. Second, globalization has prompted, and in some cases facilitated, a wide ranging set of reforms. Most states have seen politicians declaring that some reform programme is necessary, no matter how painful it may appear, to cope with perceived global challenges. Whether in the US, Australia, Spain, Italy, Japan or elsewhere, reform efforts are almost the norm of government and not the exception. Third, political elites have been prompted to respond to the domestic consequences of globalization. Global forces have created unemployment in areas that have become uncompetitive, as well as economic and demographic growth in areas that have benefited from its changes. Political elites must respond to these, either to capitalize on positive developments or to ameliorate detrimental effects. Finally, globalization has contributed to the growth of populism across developed states. Globalization does not mean the end of the domestic political function, but it does alter the state's social circumstances and contributes to subtle changes in the character of domestic politics.

Globalization not only affects domestic policy but also the normative expectations of states. It facilitates longer-run changes in attitudes towards the kind of role that the state ought to play and to determinations of what it means for a state to act in an appropriate fashion. Elites, as well as the broader mass of society, have expectations about what the state should and should not do, what spheres of activity it should and should not be involved in. In many, though not all, parts of the world, states are not expected to assist failing firms, to run public services such as transportation systems or even underwrite large infrastructure projects. Globalization appears to contribute to a general trend toward ratcheting down the expectations on the state and on the sectors of domestic activity in which it is an active participant. This is not to be confused with saying that globalization is driving a relentless neoliberal shrinking of the state. Rather the expectations of what the state should be doing, and indeed what it can do effectively at home, have shrunk. Where it acts it can do so with considerable heft and the trend across the developed world is toward state expansion understood as the growth of state revenues and expenditures. The reduction, however, is one of expectation.

Finally, globalization has enhanced state powers in domestic security. The growing connections, and sophistication of the means of those connections, among the developed states have created vulnerabilities of which terrorists and others are able to take advantage (Campbell, 2002). In the wake of the brutal attacks in New York, Madrid, Bali, London and across many parts of the Middle East, many states have gathered significant powers, often with quite wide ranging remits, claiming them to be necessary measures to combat this new threat. From increased surveillance to the suspension of *habeas corpus*, states have enhanced their power precisely to protect themselves from people who take advantage of global networks to inflict damage. Quite contrary to the orthodox line of argument, in the sphere of domestic security globalization has not diminished state power but has been a clear source of a very considerable strengthening of state capacity and autonomy.

Globalization and the State: Abroad

States are inherently international creatures. Modern states are complex sets of institutions, but they are at their most coherent when they act at the international level where the singular sovereign function is most evident. In making treaties, forming alliances and generally acting as a gatekeeper to domestic society and geography, one can most clearly see the practice of sovereignty and the successful claim of exclusive authority. Is such a depiction still warranted under conditions of globalization? To what extent has globalization affected how states act in international society? When considering this one needs to pay attention to the goals states have, to the strategies they deploy to advance these goals, to the tools they use to progress the strategies and to the broader rules of the international game to which they perceive they must adhere.

Foreign policy is the central focus for state action at the international level and, more specifically, diplomacy is the most common (though not the only) tool used by states at this level. As Hill makes clear, globalization's most tangible impact in this sector has been to blur the lines between domestic and international and between foreign policy, understood in its traditional 'high politics' guise, and foreign economic relations (Hill, 2003). Foreign policy is much more intimately linked to the domestic realm, both political and economic, than before and as such has lost some of its mystery, glamour and prestige. With regard to diplomacy, globalization has led to a number of developments. First, diplomats are becoming less important. The reduction in communication costs and ease of transportation has meant that, while states will always require representation abroad, the political independence and hence significance of diplomats has noticeably diminished (Leonard, 2000; Talbott, 1997). Now that the heads of government and state can travel to all corners of the planet within 24 hours, and given the increased importance of foreign dealings to domestic political life, foreign policy is increasingly progressed by political elites as opposed to their bureaucratic representatives. Also, as summitry diminishes the political influence of diplomats and foreign service officers, it has increased the influence of advisers and staffers to the political elite. Where once treaties and alliance commitments were negotiated by ambassadors, often acting on general instruction, these deals are now cut by presidents, prime ministers and their political advisers. The task of the diplomat is to work out the fine detail and apply policy, not to negotiate agreements and make foreign policy. Evidence of this can be found in the dramatic rise of summitry in international affairs whereby high-level meetings between political elites (and not professional diplomats) drives the crucial aspects of inter-state relations (see generally, Berridge, 2005).

A second obvious change is the rise of economic matters in the priorities of diplomacy. For many of the world's less powerful states foreign policy is in effect trade and investment policy with a veneer of high politics. The business of diplomacy is still advancing the core interests of a state, but those interests are no longer understood to be geopolitical security matters, rather they are concerned with the day-to-day workings of national prosperity. Where in the past diplomats sought to preserve the balance of power, now they are more likely to be charged with achieving a balance of payments. While economic matters have not triumphed over all things geopolitical, as some in the early 1990s predicted, diplomacy, and foreign policy more generally, has a far more economic character and is consequently more complex courtesy of the changes of globalization (see generally Jonsson and Langhorne, 2004, Vol. III).

Globalization has also influenced the manner in which states seek to advance their interests at the international level. The most clear-cut way in which states have responded to the challenges of globalization is through enhanced international collaboration. States acting together in a formal fashion to try to resolve shared problems is not new. For example, the European programme of cooperation emerged in the 1950s and ASEAN was formed in 1967. However, both the level and extent of such collaboration has increased hugely in recent years. Regional collaboration is thought to be a necessary response to the vulnerabilities of the global economy and the transnational security challenges inherent in the globalization process (Hurrell and Fawcett, 1995).

Inter-state collaboration consists of three broad types: international organizations and regimes with a global remit; regional cooperation; and inter-governmental networks. The first level of cooperation is not geographically or culturally limited in its focus and involves attempts to establish properly global forms of cooperation. Examples include high profile organizations such as the WTO as well as less well-known bodies such as BIS and the World Intellectual Property Organization (WIPO). Regionally delineated inter-state cooperation was revitalized in the 1990s as states increasingly recognized the benefits of regional collaboration on the back of perceived success in Europe and elsewhere (Mansfield and Milner, 1999; Schirm, 2002). Examples include regional organizations that have sought to expand what they do, such as SADC or ASEAN, and also new forms such as the East Asia Summit or the Central America Free Trade Agreement. The third form of collaboration involves intergovernmental networks which share information to establish common standards and broadly respond to the challenge of governance while avoiding the pitfalls that have beset more rooted institutional efforts such as the WTO (see Slaughter, 2004). Collaboration ranges from technical areas, such as standardization and regulation, to monetary integration and political community building. International cooperation by states is thought by policy elites to be a necessary response to the enhanced economic, political, security and cultural linkages created by globalization. If a state's national prosperity is increasingly contingent on developments beyond its borders, it makes sense to try to act in concert with others to try to shape matters as best it can.

The intensity with which states of all kinds, both rich and poor and in all parts of the globe, are seeking to collaborate not only reflects the significance of this approach to state behaviour beyond borders it also increases the scope for non-state actors to influence proceedings. While both non-governmental organizations (NGOs) and firms have always played a role in the international system they have usually been excluded from the formal business of inter-state interaction. With the establishment of IOs, and other forms of cooperation, NGOs and firms can participate in a formal capacity beyond the lobbying and indirect activities of times past (Josselin and Wallace, 2001). Though non-state actors are still a long way from having the importance of states, institutionalized cooperation has created formal avenues for them to increase their influence in world politics.

A second shift in state strategy has been a change in attitudes about the utility of force as an effective tool of foreign policy. States are increasingly of the view that force is not an effective means to advance national interests at the international level (Bildt, 2000; Luard, 1988). Of course this is not to be confused with a belief that conflict among states has gone, rather that the linkages of globalization, along with changing political and moral sensibilities (which themselves relate to global changes), have caused most states to reduce their propensity to use force as a policy tool. Traditionally, military alliances have been a crucial strategy of states' attempts to secure themselves in an anarchic international system. This second shift relates to two trends in the politics of alliances that derive from globalization. First, there has been a decline in the popularity of military alliances. While NATO has expanded its membership, there are few other new alliance systems. States have not suddenly learned to live happily with one another, instead globalization is working to diminish that obviously antagonistic approach to organizing a state's international relations. The second has been the transformation of the purpose and function of the United States' global alliance network. Originally, its alliances in Europe and Asia were intended to thwart the perceived Soviet menace and upon the collapse of the USSR these appeared to be lacking in purpose and structure. Since that time, however, the alliance system has evolved. NATO has become an institution more focused on human security (see generally, Kaiser, 2003). For example, NATO membership is seen as a means to consolidate democratic transitions in Eastern Europe and its military operations in Europe and Afghanistan are of a distinctly humanitarian kind. Beyond Europe, the alliances in East Asia have a more traditional element in the containment of China, but they also are a means through which the allies are trying to secure themselves from the challenges of global terrorism and other less orthodox security threats (Bisley, 2006). While these developments have causes and a logic that is not all attributable to globalization, it is enhancing a sense of vulnerability and making plain that thinking about how states secure themselves and their citizens' needs has moved beyond orthodox approaches.

Elements of both diplomacy and the broader tools of foreign policy have changed, and with regard to the rules there are three central developments of particular note. First, in both the rise of humanitarian intervention and the 2003 invasion of Iraq one sees evidence of a softening of the non-interference rule. Traditionally, state interaction was governed by the principle that no state had the right to interfere in the domestic affairs of others. The growth of what could best be described as a cosmopolitan sensibility has begun to erode the foundations of this norm. Perhaps the strongest piece of evidence supporting this view is the Bush administration's swift move to use the language of moral cosmopolitanism to justify the invasion of Iraq once the claims about Iraq's security threat proved to be bogus. It is wrong to say that this has been entirely produced by globalization, but the spread of this sense – the growing awareness of human crisis and demand for action, as well as the economic interests which lie not far below the surface of such actions – relate this growth to the changes associated with the phenomenon.

The growing institutionalization of international law and its increasingly coercive character is the second discernible shift in the rules of the international game which relates to globalization. From the formation of the International Criminal Court to the growing jurisprudence of the WTO's dispute settlement mechanism, international law has a decidedly more muscular form than ever before. One should not overstate its extent, however. Legal enforcement of international relations has become distinctly more firm and this is a direct reflection of the challenges which states perceive globalization to pose. Constitutionalization of law, driven as it is by states, is a function of their recognition that some kind of certainty and coercion is needed to back up new structures of governance.

The third shift in the rules of the international game relates to the role of great powers. As recently as the late 1970s Hedley Bull determined that great powers play a distinctive role in the international system (Bull, 1977). Under globalization such claims are distinctly out of place. The lack of support for a special role for great powers in international politics comes not only from those lesser powers excluded by such a division but also by the powers themselves. This is not to say that the happy accident of P5 status is about to be renounced by the five permanent members of the UN Security Council – the US, China, Russia, France or Britain; rather that in a world of nuclear weapons, of diminishing defence expenditure, of an unwillingness to use force and the rise of a liberal economic sensibility, to say nothing of the predominance of only one power, there is serious doubt on the role of great powers as a distinctive institution of international society (see Bisley, 2007). Great powers no longer provide order to the system in the way they did in the past and certainly not in the concerted fashion envisaged in the UN Charter. The point is not that power no longer influences conduct in world politics – plainly power has a vital part to play in the structures of order – rather that the traditional understanding of the rights and duties of great powers has been undermined by globalization. Thus order in the current system is a messy compromise between the dictates of power, and most particularly of the singular power of the US, international institutions (which are subject to the whims of power), and some shared interests and other diverging values and preferences. For our concerns the interests and values which are played out in this system are increasingly more tightly woven together by globalization. This may change – it would be unwise to say that Russia, China and India will never be regional or global heavyweights with a moral and military role commensurate with such a position – but globalization, due to its transformation of the weight of economic matters and state understanding of the character of economic linkages, along with changing sensibilities has worked to diminish the once-privileged position of the great powers in the international system.

Globalization makes states more likely to cooperate than in the past and is also associated with some subtle but important changes in the rules of the game. Yet it is not clear that the underlying purpose of state action has changed. States are still primarily political entities, whose international actions have economic, cultural and military aspects, but whose conduct is at heart dominated by political preferences. The basic aims of states, to maximize their welfare and minimize their insecurity (as they conceive of it) in a world of competing political entities, remain as they were. It may be that they perceive basic aspects of human rights as increasingly a part of that welfare, or they may believe that domestic well-being is contingent on the suppression of democracy and the consolidation of one-party rule, however conceived, these aims retain their primacy. Globalization does not fundamentally alter what states try to achieve in international society but it does influence how they do it.

The State: A Powerful Idea

In many respects the idea that the state is being made redundant by global forces is not new. Marx, Angell, Cobden, Mill and Mitrany have all argued, though in quite different ways, that the state is ill-suited to cope with the challenges of modernity. Each one has been wrong, primarily because each has underestimated the power of the state and its capacity to adapt itself to changing circumstances. Globalization does not present the leviathan with an existential challenge, but it does provide further complexity for state consideration and hence it influences policy preferences and the playing out of policy decisions. The perception that states are being undermined because the disciplining power of global markets and firms cow them into submission is unfounded. From American deficits to the success of Malaysian capital controls, states of all hues have shown a capacity both for policy autonomy and for success in spite of alleged limits imposed by globalization.

As Hay has pointed out, the dominance of neoliberal ideas about the role of the state and its shrinking role does not derive from some exogenous globalization source, rather it reflects an intellectual consensus (2006). These ideas are themselves a kind of globalization, but not the singular external force of the popular imagination. Hay notes that the belief that globalization insists on neoliberal policy has become a self-fulfilling prophecy (Hay, 2006). One might go so far as to say that the appearance of a lack of policy autonomy, and the notion that policy convergence is inevitable, is not a fact of globalization but a function of a lack of imagination. The remarkable success of the Chinese economy, the growth in India and the revitalization of Brazil and Argentina emphasize not only that states can vary their policy strategies but that they can make a positive contribution to the economic welfare of their citizens. Global markets matter – the success of all of these states is due to their participation in the global economy not their attempts to protect themselves from it – but they have not pushed the state from its central role in political and economic life.

Among the voices decrying or defending the state it is often easy to overlook the fact that the state is perhaps the most successful form of globalization yet seen. The modern territorial state is the pre-eminent political entity in the world today. It has a virtual monopoly on moral authority and, with the exception of parts of Antarctica, the territory of the dry surface of the planet is entirely ruled by states. It is as an idea that the state has its most powerful incarnation. The rapid expansion of UN membership is as good an indicator as any of the popularity of the practice of statehood. The newly sovereign peoples of the former USSR or East Timor did not think the state a *passé* system of political rule, nor do the Kurds, the Taiwanese or the Palestinians.

Globalization is not destroying the state. It is not doing so because its extent is often over-stated and the capacity of the state to respond to changing circumstances – of which globalization is clearly a form –

has been a requirement from its emergence in the 17th century. The adaptibility of the state has not only been a hallmark, but central to its success. State forms have evolved, they have never been static, and the success and failure of specific instances has been directly related to their capacity to cope with the circumstances, both domestic and international, in which they find themselves. Policy-making elites in many of today's states may get globalization wrong, they may think it too powerful, they may have a fuzzy grasp of its implications, but they are not ignorant of the fact that they exist in an international system that is closely linked by movements of goods, capital, knowledge and people. For that reason, as well as those noted above, one can be confident that the state will continue to be the pre-eminent, though most certainly not the solo, actor in world politics for some time to come.

4
States, Markets and a Global Economy

The economic dimension of globalization is the site of its most fierce contestation. The high-profile backlash against globalization that led to violent protests in Seattle, Prague and Genoa was fuelled by hostility to its economic aspects. Yet for its supporters, globalization's appeal lies in its capacity to produce wealth across an ever wider population. For others, globalization's economic advantages carry substantial risk, as shown by the considerable upswing in the rate and impact of financial crises. These views are united by a belief that globalization has made market forces dominant in the international system. The critic is concerned that markets will further impoverish millions, destroy environmental standards and erode labour conditions; the supporter is enthused by the efficiency gains that will accrue from removing the distortions caused by state interference; and the third is worried that, while markets create wealth, the damage caused by volatility can more than offset these gains. Whether for good or for ill, all share the belief that markets reign supreme under conditions of globalization.

The assumption that economic forces have jumped the rails set up by states and are roaming free of the shackles of state regulation and interference has considerable currency in both the academic realm and the popular imagination. Yet the state has not surrendered in the face of globalization. The story of globalization's economic dimension is more complex than this strong market–weak state depiction. Globalization has equally important political and economic dimensions and any analysis of its broader dynamics should reflect on how these elements interact. The purpose of this chapter is thus to consider the political economy of globalization and to provide a framework to examine the way in which political systems and economic relations have interacted to produce the broader process of globalization. To that end the chapter will focus on three main issues. First, it will consider what globalization means for the core pattern and features of the world economy. Second, the chapter examines the theoretical and empirical dimensions of the current balance of power that exists between states and markets. Third, the chapter will conclude by briefly assessing the consequences of economic globalization for the wider patterns of world politics. Broadly construed, globalization can be thought of as a product of the interaction of states and markets. The current state of globalization is a function both of changes in the process of resource production and allocation and in the political and social institutions which govern these processes. Globalization is not simply capitalism run riot, rather it is the result of a complex blend of social forces in which the relationship between state and market is of vital importance not only to its broader character but also to the particular ways in which its social consequences are played out.

The World Economy in the 21st Century

During the 1990s, scholars and policy-makers increasingly began to talk about a world economy where in the past they might have referred to the international economy. This reflects a number of important developments. First, by the early 1990s, following the collapse of the USSR and Soviet communism and the progressive opening of the Chinese economy, the notion of a single world economy became a geographic and social fact. With the incorporation of all the former Soviet economies into the capitalist system the overwhelming majority of the planet's population was brought into a single economic order. The sheer number of states, and hence the number of people whose lives are shaped by global economic forces, is larger than it has ever been. Second, along with the incorporation of the former Cold War adversaries, came a widespread acceptance of a broadly liberal approach to policy-making, as well as a recognition that economic outcomes were being increasingly shaped by global forces (Woods, 2000a: 9). The idea of an international economy as something comprising distinct though connected parts seemed anachronistic as the world was increasingly unified by economic forces, in however an uneven fashion. For some this world economy was not only geographically and demographically universal, it demanded to be described as a global economy. The rise in the rate and volume of trade and investment, the growth of instantaneous communications creating new markets in media, the internet and telephony appeared to have ushered in a new and more unified phase of economic development where markets operated on a genuinely global scale. What does this ostensibly global economy look like and is it actually global?

At the heart of any economic system lies a range of fundamental issues which determine its essential character (see generally, Bornstein, 1994). These relate to the location of decision-making, the identity of the key decision-makers, the nature of resource ownership, the kind of signalling mechanisms which determine the allocation of resources and an underlying normative commitment to a set of values, whether collective or individual, tribal or class-based (for a good introduction see Cleaver, 2002: 9–31). It is common to think about economic systems from a national point of view, yet many argue that it is not too difficult to discern a global system whereby decision-makers and signalling mechanisms have a distinctly global character. The argument runs that the broad structural parameters of economic activity have a recognizably global character in which national economic activity is influenced as never before by forces from the outside world.

The world economy involves a system of production, finance and exchange for profit based on widely shared principles of private property. It consists of a vast array of markets of all kinds, some of which are strongly influenced by global forces, in the sense that geographically distant factors are key to distribution patterns, such as oil markets, and some of which are largely local, such as bread and other foodstuffs. This is overlaid by a territorially defined system of state sovereignty with which these markets have to interact. It is this interaction, its structures and variations, that drives the political economy of globalization. The workings of markets are influenced by the particular conditions established by states which can prohibit entry in certain areas, may impose tariffs or require certain standards to be adhered to if foreign firms are to act within their domain. The differing circumstances – political, geographic or resource endowment – of states and societies drives competition and the search for advantage and profit.

The contemporary world economy is, by historical measures, relatively open. International trade is conducted with very low average tariff levels on manufactured goods (OECD, 1999). Most economies are open to foreign capital movements, no longer is there widespread support for strict controls on the amount of money that can enter or leave a state. There are very few countries that try to avoid or minimize their contact with the world economy. While one can point to the many poor states of sub-Saharan Africa as examples of those excluded from the system, this exclusion is rarely self-ordained as in the case of North Korea. More generally, the contemporary world economy is distinguished by the extent of multilateral institutions that have been developed to try to influence the character of global economic relations. Given the importance of international institutions to globalization, they will be examined in detail in Chapter 5.

Trade

As discussed in Chapter 2, global trade is more important to the world economy than ever before. Sceptics often point out that trade among the European powers prior to the First World War was of a higher real value than it is today. This may be true, but trade as a proportion of global GDP is considerably greater than at any time in the modern period. The most authoritative aggregate figures note that exports as a percentage of worldwide GDP were 4.6% in 1870 and in 1998 they were 17.2% (Maddison, 2001: 363). There are a number of broad trends in global trade which are worth noting. First, the composition of trade has undergone significant changes. Manufactured goods continue to increase their share of trade and there is a marked rise in what is known as 'intra-industry' trade – cross-border trade of industry-specific goods, whether components or like goods – which accounts for around 25% of total trade (see generally Krugman and Obstfeld, 2003: 139–41). Market analysts agree that this reflects the growing integration of global economic processes (e.g. Thirlwell, 2005: 11–14). Second, services have become increasingly important to global trade and they presently account for around 19% of world trade (WTO, 2005: 3), a figure that has been relatively stable after a rapid growth phase during the 1980s and early 1990s. Where, in the past, certain sectors, such as education, retail or professional services including accounting or legal work, were thought not to be tradable, courtesy of technology as well as policies of national openness, these have become a growing part of global trade.

Trade in services, and particularly the growing diversity of services which are part of global trade, not only makes regulation more complex it also means that international agreement on common standards or practices is more difficult because they are subject to decidedly more acute political sensitivities than existed during earlier phases of liberalization. Equally, the internationalization of production which has driven the growth of manufacturing trade, and its intra-industry character, already has protectionist impulses as European and North American producers struggle to compete with the low labour costs of China and India. Unlike other key branches of the global economy, such as finance, trade has a dedicated global institution which seeks to manage the rules of the game. The WTO was established in 1995, and absorbed the post-1945 GATT regime. It has a number of purposes which together advance its ultimate aim of fostering a stable and liberal global trading system. First, it acts as an arbiter of the rules of international trade that are set out in its treaty documents. Second, it is a negotiating forum where members can further liberalize their trading commitments. Third, embodying its commitment to transparency in trade policy, it is a repository for information on international trade (Jackson, 1998).

While the WTO is generally seen as a successful institution – its rapid expansion of membership to 149 countries in 2006 is testimony to its popularity among political elites. However, the organization has some significant problems. Its sheer size has meant that negotiations have become extremely complex and, given that the majority of its members are now developing economies, its membership has quite divergent priorities. Moreover, the broad success of reducing tariffs on manufactured goods has meant that current negotiations are now on those spheres which have been politically tendentious, especially textiles and agriculture, and progress has virtually ground to a halt. The off–on–off again nature of the Doha round is indicative of this. Add to that an expansion in issue areas which are thought to be trade related (and hence subject to WTO-focused liberalization, such as investment, competition and labour standards), and many members are finding their interest in further liberalization at the WTO to be waning, although members still value its role as a rule arbiter and source of information.

Beyond these broader trends, there are two further points that are worth emphasizing. The first is the rise of emerging market economies which are subtly shifting the geography of world trade. The rapid rise of both China and India as trading powers of considerable heft is the most obvious aspect. Global trade has never been geographically global – it has long been the preserve of North America, Western Europe and Japan (see Rugman, 2005) – but this is beginning to change (see generally WTO, 2005: 9–17). Also, Russia's revival as a commodity exporter in a time of high commodity prices brings a third sizable trading economy to an increasingly crowded table. While these developments have already had considerable labour market consequences they also add a layer of complexity to the institutional issues related to global trade policy. That said, one must put the rise of emerging market economies in some perspective. Global trade is still dominated, in value terms, by the traditional Big Three (WTO, 2005) and although China is a significant force, the world economy primarily involves extensive intra-regional trade between North America, Western Europe and North East Asia. The notion of a properly integrated global trade system is some way off.

Finance and Money

The extent of economic integration through international financial and monetary markets is considerable. Integration refers to the way in which the contemporary financial and monetary regime has produced global markets which draw together the fates of firms, states and peoples from far-flung corners of the globe through their participation in increasingly global systems of finance and integrated markets for money (see generally, Cohen, 2004). The contemporary order began with the collapse of the post-1945 Bretton Woods monetary system which linked currencies in a relatively flexible manner to the value of the US dollar which was itself fixed to gold. This indirect gold standard provided monetary stability to the capitalist system during its extensive growth phase between 1945 and the mid 1960s (see generally, Eichengreen, 1996). Its major problem was the value it placed on the long-term linkage between the American currency and a static gold value. The costs of this system became unbearable to the US as its success – that is the growth of capitalist economies – raised its price to the point where the US was no longer willing to underwrite the system (Walter, 1991).

Linked to this relatively fixed currency system was a series of controls on capital movement and credit. States were able to control private flows of capital and the World Bank and IMF were tasked with controlling large-scale, long-term and small-scale short-term credit. The point of having a relatively fixed monetary system and controls over capital flow was to provide stability, predictability and international technocratic coordination of fiscal challenges. Once the monetary basis of this system fell away the logic of the financial side was no longer plausible.

As the fixed exchange basis of the system became untenable, states, in a piecemeal fashion, determined that a system of free exchange of currencies could provide a better solution to the challenges posed by international currencies than any other. This meant that the value of a currency would be determined by markets in a system of open exchange. A number of major economies moved across to this floating exchange system in the mid 1970s, and through the 1980s many smaller economies adopted the same policy (see Eichengreen, 1996: 136–50). Today almost all economies that substantially participate in the global economy have such currency arrangements. This allows market forces to help resolve balance of payment problems relatively efficiently, but at the cost of an increasingly volatile system. It is no coincidence that the number of financial crises has risen exponentially as more states float their currencies and as trade on foreign exchange markets grows (Eichengreen, 2003). The only significant exception to this trend is the Chinese currency which is still effectively set by the state. This is a source of some friction as trading partners feel that it is being deliberately undervalued to provide its exporters with an advantage. Even so, most feel that, over the longer run, China will eventually allow its currency to float. With a changing monetary order came a new financial system. States slowly removed capital controls which meant that investors could move their capital around more freely. As this occurred markets in credit began to develop as freer flows of capital provided the foundation for an international market in debt. Today a home loan that is drawn in San Francisco is as likely to be funded by capital from Tokyo as it is from New York.

The international financial system, and the monetary arrangements on which it is based, is open in that there are few constraints on the behaviour of markets. This reflects a broader consensus among the developed and developing worlds of the benefits, in spite of the risks, of a liberal system. There is a consensus that monetary and financial decisions are best determined by market forces and it is not surprising that under such conditions the currency of the dominant economy has become a significant supporting mechanism of the broader system. Not only is the US dollar used on a daily basis in many parts of the world, it also acts as a reserve currency and many commercial transactions are denominated in dollars to provide stability and confidence to cross-border deals. This dominant role is beginning to be undermined by the increasing use of the Japanese yen and the euro in international markets, but the dollar is still far from losing its primary position. This has allowed the US to run sizable current account and fiscal deficits, but it is not clear that this is sustainable in the longer run (*Economist*, 2005a).

Production

The growth of intra-industry trade and the continuing rise in manufactured goods trade are the product of the third element of the current order, the internationalization of production processes and their supply chains. There is a diverse literature on why firms invest abroad. The most influential is Dunning's theory which emphasizes an eclectic range of advantages which internationalization allows (Dunning, 1981). For example, some firms go abroad to get around tariff barriers, others do so to reduce costs through proximity to inputs and new markets, while others do it to gain the benefits of economies of scale. The advances of global financial markets and technological innovation have allowed more firms to make good these advantages through better access to finance and lower management costs.

Foreign direct investment (FDI) is the driving force behind international production. FDI refers to investment in direct productive capacity overseas (as compared with investing in foreign stock markets) such as building factories or buying a foreign company. Global FDI grew steadily in the 1980s before a rapid explosion in growth through the 1990s which peaked in 2000 and then underwent a small decline until returning to growth in 2004 and 2005 (UNCTAD, 2005). Although the rapid growth of firms investing in the less-developed part of the world has helped fuel the processes of globalization, FDI continues to be dominated by rich countries. Around 85% of FDI comes from and goes into developed economies. The major movements of investments are transatlantic with the US and the UK being the largest recipients of investment in both 2003 and 2004 (UNCTAD, 2005). In recent years, developing economies have attracted somewhat more investment than in the past, but the overwhelming bulk of this increase has gone to China. If investment is taken as an indicator, international production is still primarily a rich state affair and is of sufficient preponderance to justify questioning just how global globalization actually is.

Taking this line Rugman argues that it is misleading to talk about global production or global strategy; rather, he argues, that firm activity is more accurately described as international and the geographic character is inter-regional and not global (Rugman 2000; 2005). He makes the point that firm activities, and most particularly sales, are geographically constrained to the three developed parts of the world: North America, Western Europe and Japan. In this sense, there is no such thing as globalization understood as a properly global phenomenon. Instead, Rugman argues, we are undergoing a dramatic increase in intra-regional economic activity which links firms, states and peoples within and between these regions, but not beyond them. This perspective reinforces the views of those who argue that it is misleading to talk about a global economy. From this perspective, we should think about a world economic system in which there are dense linkages between specific regions, rather loose connections between other parts and almost no links between others.

The openness of the financial and monetary system, while dynamic, is particularly vulnerable to debilitating crises. Firms appear to have such power and capacity that many feel they are weakening states and even undermining democratic practices. The focus of FDI within the rich states is precisely the kind of uneven and exclusionary economic outcome that many feel requires rectification through systems of international governance. The structure of the global economy sits increasingly uneasily with territorially determined institutions of political authority and globalization highlights this discrepancy. This is particularly evident in the system's increasing volatility. States not only appear to have a decreasing ability to deal with such problems, but also appear unsure as to the nature of appropriate policy responses. For some a further problem derives from the way in which globalization is perceived to be exacerbating the injustice of the current order because it is increasing the gap between the rich and poor, both within and across states. This raises the vital question, how can authority be exercised over this complex system, given that the most appropriate forms of action appear to fly in the face of the institutional structure of this political authority?

States and Markets in the 21st Century

To answer these complex questions it is necessary to spend some time considering the relationship between authority and systems of resource allocation. The state has been presented with a set of complex challenges by globalization and many feel that, in the economic realm, these challenges are particularly acute. This section of the chapter is concerned with the way in which political authority (encapsulated in the notion of the state) intersects with relations of resource allocation (the shorthand 'market' is used to refer to this wide range of production, trade, investment and financial relations) under conditions of globalization. The purpose is to consider how this has been conceived theoretically and how this marries up to the empirical circumstances. The challenges that states face are not simply the result of markets trumping old-fashioned ideas and outdated institutions. Instead they warrant new approaches to the exercise of authority, alongside older forms. For students and policy-makers alike, the challenge lies in working out how best to conceive of the balance that globalization has struck between the two most dominant yet conceptually challenging social phenomena of modern times: states and markets.

The Theoretical Relationship

The issues relating to state–market relations, and their transforma-tion due to globalization, revolve around three basic theoretical questions. The first relates to the relationship's empirical status and considers how globalization may, or may not, have changed the balance that exists between economic process and institutions of political authority. The issue is essentially the practical question of how and to what extent states interfere with market processes. The second is concerned with the more normative issue of what the relationship should be, as opposed to what it is. The globalization literature is often beset by analytic problems that derive from the conflation of these two questions. The third is more analytic and considers the best way to explain how we have reached the current circumstances

There are, broadly speaking, three common ways of conceiving of how globalization has influenced state–market relations. The first sees markets as having a dominant position and that states are either unable or unsuited to play their old roles of intervention, regulation and redistribution. This view sees market-driven economic relations as creating 'natural economies' which no longer fit the delineation of authority created by states. The exercise of authority over markets, for example in the regulation of labour flows across borders, impedes these natural forces. From this perspective, the institutional config-uration of political authority vested in the modern territorial state is unsuited to the economic conditions created by globalization and it must adapt to these new realities or face extinction. This view comes both from supporters of a neoclassical approach to economic matters (e.g. Ohmae, 1995) and from those who are less enthusiastic about these developments. For example, some are concerned that MNCs dwarf the economic size and power of states and that this power discrepancy allows firms to ride roughshod over states and erode the public good (e.g. Anderson and Cavanagh, 2000), while others note that global networks of economic relations have transformed structures of power so that the distribution of resources is no longer the preserve of states (e.g. Strange, 1996).

A second group argues that globalization has not significantly altered the balance of state–market relations. This view argues that states retain a primacy in setting the rules of economic relations and that the capacity to influence questions relating to economic welfare have not been substantially altered. This view strongly contests the claim that globalization is creating transnational forces and argues that economic activity still has a primarily national character (e.g. Hirst and Thompson, 1996). From this perspective, investment decisions, pricing structure, and consumer patterns are much more strongly influenced by national rules, regulations and preferences than by global forces. Of course there is a considerable amount of international economic activity, but, this argument runs, it is largely shaped by state determinations. A related view reminds us that economic activity, of whatever kind, is always mediated through the social institutions shaped by states (Sassen, 1999). State systems of authority, rule and regulation are the interlocutors of globalization and as such continue to retain their influence over the shape of economic relations. Also, this approach reminds us that states are still substantial economic players in their own right. They employ considerable numbers, they consume resources, pay rent and buy all manner of products to undertake their many roles. At the very least the state has a heavy influence on the market as a major participant.

The third view contends that globalization has brought about a shift in the relationship which some have described as 'governed interdependence' and might be more usefully called 'complex dependence'. This view argues that both states and markets have power that derives from their differing resources and needs and that the changes of globalization have worked to subtly reconfigure the structure and dynamics of this interaction. It recognizes that states have handed over certain policy-making freedoms and that market forces require rules and systems of authority which only states can supply. For example, the integration of global financial markets, and the increased role they play in the complexities of state financing processes, means that market preferences have an important impact on state behaviour; but this system is in turn dependent on legal systems and social infrastructure provided by states. This approach emphasizes that globalization does not mean that states have no capacity to influence economic welfare, instead it means that states need to rethink the way they go about advancing these ends within the constraints imposed by international institutions and financial market discipline (e.g. Keohane and Nye, 2000; Weiss, 2003c). This group is right to point out that states continue to play an important role in economic relations. States everywhere put limits on imports, they set rules and in fiscal and monetary policy they shape the economic framework within their territory. Even when constrained by institutions and policy orthodoxy, states still matter to the basic pattern of resource allocation. In this sense it is right to agree with the sceptics that there is no global economy, at least not in the sense of a properly unified global economic system of relations which is organized around a relatively unified set of principles and practices. We have a world economy in which market forces are distributed very unevenly across the system and part of the reason for this comes from the continuing importance of state forms of authority.

Ultimately, debate about state–market relations is an argument about authority and power. Some feel that the institutionalization of political authority that is bound up in the modern state is unsuited to dealing with the specific challenges brought on by the creation of a global economy (e.g. Guéhenno, 1995; Ohmae, 1995). The ability to shape the parameters and indeed the outcomes of economic relations is thought to be increasingly diminished as global forces provide the means for markets to elude the plodding grasp of the state. In this view, market power acts to trump the way in which authority has been formalized in states. On the other hand, some argue that globalization depends on the traditional institutions of authority created by states (Sassen, 1999). Without legal systems underwritten by state power, how could modern economic relations function? As in any debate about power and authority there is often a good deal of elision between empirical arguments and normative assertions. Scholars and specialists at times slide between their observations of what they think to be the case and their belief in what it ought to be. This is particularly true of liberal supporters of markets who see in the liberalization that has facilitated globalization an inexorable move away from the pernicious effects of state intervention on economic relations. This has led some to conclude that many writers who describe markets as overwhelming states are in reality dressing up their wishes as fact (e.g. Economides and Wilson, 2001: 192–3). The empirical debate is clouded by the ideological colourings of the arguments. Some want the market to be further freed from state interference, others feel states need to do more, while yet others argue for a third way whereby markets can operate with all their efficiency but states can still act to right their many wrongs.

What are we to make of this normative argument? During the early phases of the globalization debate little was said about this aspect. Yet as the phenomenon has become more widespread and awareness of it has grown, this has become one of the most heated lines of contestation. Essentially, policy-making among the developed states and international organizations was dominated by a heavily liberal set of preferences in the mid to late 1990s and contrary voices were few. Yet by the end of the decade, this had come in for considerable criticism, both from activists and policy specialists. For critics, globalization is the means through which MNCs get rich off the backs of the poor. For policy analysts, the Asian financial crisis, among other developments, undermined much of the confidence that existed in the universal benefits of a broadly liberal approach. Moreover, the economic success of China and Brazil showed that state intervention could produce considerable benefits. As such, there is increasingly a recognition both of the limitations of markets and the role that the application of authority to economic relations has to play in generating efficient, stable and equitable social systems (see generally, Stiglitz, 2006). This is not to say that the critics and the supporters have reached an ideological compromise, rather that although considerable differences of opinion as to how the state–market relationship should be conducted still exist, the influence of the market-dominant strand is not as clear-cut as it was in the 1990s. Most agree that markets need guidance and that political authority should be exercised to help the vast bulk of humanity that has been left behind, but there is little agreement about just how this should be done.

It is clear that states have played and will continue to play, a central role in creating the conditions in which global markets operate. This is so both in an institutional and infrastructural sense as well as an ideological one. We do well to remember that markets are open because states allow them to be. Of course in some areas, such as illicit satellite broadcasting, state regulation can be flouted, but this is both unusual and a tiny proportion of the globe's economic relations. Indeed globalization, even when conceived of only in its economic dimensions, cannot be conceptualized without careful attention to the role played by states. Underlying the theoretical argument about states, markets and globalization is the gap that is thought to exist between two elements:

1. states are territorially determined institutions that embody authority;
2. courtesy of globalization, markets are increasingly delinked from territory.

Essentially, how one conceives of the state–market relationship is a function of how much this delinking process has occurred. This gap helps to make sense of the varying ways in which the relationship has been conceived, but it does not provide an analytic determination of the nature of the state–market relationship or how to reach such a judgment. One can get a better grasp on the debate, and hence on the political economy of globalization, by breaking up the broader issue into four constituent questions. The aim here is not to provide a definitive answer to each question but to establish a framework for clearer thinking on the matter. First, in any assessment of the status of state–market relations it is vital to clarify what one means by the state. States play a wide range of roles and we need to be clear which of these roles we are considering. In matters to do with the economy usually one is concerned with the extent to which markets influence state autonomy, policy efficacy, interest formation, and social goals. This is not an exhaustive list, but is indicative of the most obvious sites where globalization contributes to the market effect on states. The second issue points at the importance of territory and asks how contingent on the exclusivity of territory is the state's capacity to exercise its functions. The third asks about the extent to which markets are disconnected from territorial constraints. Markets vary tremendously, from foreign exchange markets, which are as de-territorialized as any, to agricultural products, in which territory is fundamental. The fourth question asks if there are alternative ways in which states can act to exercise authority if traditional methods are not thought to be effective.

In general terms one can determine that states and markets are mutually dependent but if one wants to go much beyond this macro-perspective then one must deploy a more nuanced analytic frame-work. The point of this question-by-question approach is that there is no clear and singular answer to the current theoretical or empirical set up of state–market relations, and it provides a way to think through the issues. It emphasizes that assessments of state–market interaction vary, and not only due to differing conceptual appara-tuses driving divergent conclusions but also because the character of institutions, the nature of economic relationships and the structure of interests varies hugely across the world, and conclusions as to the nature of this relationship are contingent on these factors. Ulti-mately, markets need states. One cannot avoid that conclusion. Left to their own devices markets often fail, they can produce warped outcomes (for example, unequal access to information can produce huge distortions), and of course they need a substantial social, political and economic infrastructure – from legal systems to social trust – to make them work. From a theoretical point of view, globalization has made clear that markets need states (or at least they need rules that derive from some kind of authority) even while it gives the appearance of making them redundant.

States and Firms

Globalization is an impersonal force. It is often hard to determine who is driving the action at any particular moment. But firms are globalization's most obvious face. MNCs are said by their critics to be exploiting workers, duping consumers and driving labour and environmental standards down around the world because of their decisive structural advantage over the rooted authority of states. Yet the relationship between firms and states is more complex than this antagonistic portrayal. Fears about the dominance of firms over states, especially those in poorer parts of the world, has been longstanding. As early as the 1970s, long before the expansions associated with the contemporary phase of globalization, there was talk that states were being denuded of their sovereignty by American firms (Vernon, 1971). Following the growth of MNCs in the 1980s analysts came to depict the state–firm relationship as a bargaining one, a relationship not necessarily between equals, but between parties which seek that which the other controls. Firms have capital, skills and knowledge; states have markets, resources and labour. The bargain struck at any particular time may favour one over the other but there was little evidence to support the view that the firm had the whiphand in all circumstances. Is this still true today?

Through the 1990s, MNCs invested abroad more than ever before. Moreover, the national origin of MNCs became more diverse as European and Asian firms played an ever greater role in the global economy. In spite of the expansion beyond American dominance there has been little movement outside the traditional North America–East Asia–Western Europe focus of firm origin and activity. Of the 500 largest MNCs only a handful come from outside the Triad and this has remained relatively constant since the 1980s (see *Fortune*, 2006). What little change there has been has involved growth within these areas, most notably the rise of Chinese and Russian firms. Perhaps the only meaningful shift has been the increase in Indian-originated MNCs, but this is still a relatively small figure. Beyond this, FDI is not a fleet-footed creature constantly fleeing from regulation or taxation (Hobson, 2003) and states have demonstrated a continuing ability to hold their own when dealing with the demands of investment capital. Few MNCs are genuinely global in operation and fewer still have an organizational culture that is different from the dominant national culture of the home state (Doremus *et al.*, 1998). Firms are rooted organizations and even the most internationalized operate, at home and abroad, within environments shaped, more than anything else, by states. Whether paying tariffs to cross borders, adhering to regulations or resorting to the courts to resolve a contractual dispute, firms operate within a state-focused environment.

So if firms are not swamping the state, what is the character of their relationship? In their influential account, Stopford and Strange argue that it involves three spheres of competition: firm–firm, state–state and state–firm (Stopford and Strange, 1991). From this perspective states compete for the attentions of firms, firms compete for the resources which states command and states and firms negotiate and bargain to maximize their respective benefits. Globalization has served not to undermine this broader characterization, it has enhanced competition within two of the spheres. Globalization has made the competition among states for inward investment more intense. This is particularly so in the emerging market economies where FDI growth rates are highest in recent years (UNCTAD, 2005) but is also true among the developed states. Second, as a consequence of globalization, firms operate in a much more competitive environment. As transport, communication and technology costs drop, more and more firms are subject to international competition. This in turn has led firms to seek the support of states to help them maintain their competitiveness in these more challenging circumstances. This has involved assistance in opening up markets, support for education, training and research (see Weiss, 2003b; 2005).

Globalization is influencing the state–firm relationship, but it is not a fundamental transformation. What was once a bargaining relationship has developed into a relationship of complex interaction. This means that the contents of the bargain and the forces shaping its outcome have changed and that their interactions have an added layer of mutual support. There is a sense that complex interaction is really a polite phrase for states acting as the handmaiden of firm interest and globalization appears to enhance its credibility. This view argues that not only is state scope for policy choice heavily constrained but it also points out that the influence of policies on firm behaviour is negligible. This rather simplifies matters. States can still choose to impose certain kinds of policy knowing acts carry a small risk cost in this regard. A commonly cited example of this argument involves Ford's 2002 closure of its assembly plant in Dagenham in the UK which is given as proof that states can do little in the face of firm power (e.g. O'Brien and Williams, 2004: 192). Yet closer inspection of the story provides a slightly different interpretation. Ford's European operation had been performing poorly and the company was under pressure to reduce costs. It determined that it needed to rationalize its production facilities and this required the closure of one of its assembly plants. When considering how to do this and which one to close a number of considerations came into play, including performance and costs. Ultimately, the Dagenham plant was selected, not only because of concerns about relative inefficiency, but also because the UK's labour laws were such that the closure costs were considerably lower than anywhere else in Europe. Thus British workers suffered not from firm dominance over the state but because the British state had established policies which made market exit less costly than elsewhere in Europe.

The lesson of the Ford closure is that state policies matter and that they shape firm behaviour. The British government doubtless felt that flexible labour market policies made it a better choice for FDI, and Britain is the single largest source of in-bound FDI in the EU. However, in this instance it suffered a reversal precisely because its policies provided it with an unexpected disadvantage, while workers in the German plant that was considered for closure benefited from state policy choice which constrained firm action. It is not telling the story quite accurately to denigrate state influence by describing modern states as simply the midwives of global capital. Neither state nor firm is free to act in any way it chooses.

Even in spite of the alleged power of firms over states, firms continue to invest where institutions of government and governance are best and they generally avoid the kinds of states to which they would more easily be able to dictate terms. A particular accolade of MNC success is to be listed on the New York Stock Exchange (NYSE). Not only does it provide corporate prestige, it also grants access to the world's largest equity market. The curious aspect of this is that the NYSE has the strictest regulations – established by state authority – of any stock market in the world (Drahos and Braithwaite, 2000: 167–8). Rather than MNCs running from regulation, in this instance firms are seeking it out. The reason is access to capital and the security that appears to come to investments that are subject to rigorous regulation. Being able to meet the onerous requirements of NYSE listing is a kind of merit badge for financial markets and investors globally. The regulatory requirements for listing, and the ongoing demands, are further testimony to the oddly contradictory character of globalization. The simplistic understanding of globalization is to see it as a force which raises the power of markets and firms at the cost of states. Yet while firms and markets do have greater influence than in the recent past, states continue to have a vital part to play. Globalization both diminishes and reinforces state and firm power at the same time.

Private Authority and the World Economy

One of the most distinctive features of the current relationship between institutional forms of authority and markets is said to be the increasing role played by private forms of authority. Traditionally, power and authority were embodied in states and occasionally, such as with the Bretton Woods system, the institutions to which they delegated that power and authority. Yet in almost all spheres of international activity one can observe private actors having an ever greater role to play. At the most obvious level, outcomes in the international economy are shaped heavily by the impersonal and almost exclusively private forces of the market. This was never more graphically displayed than in the Asian Financial crisis which was triggered by private investment firms rapidly withdrawing their short-term capital from the erstwhile Tiger economies (King, 2001). NGOs are not only more prominent today, they have an influence across a vast terrain, from human rights to security policy, that makes them important players in the international system. Criminal organizations, while not a new phenomenon, are more numerous, involved in more diverse activities – from the drug trade to money laundering, from piracy to smuggling – and more important than ever before (Williams, 2002). Private power and authority matters and its capacity to shape the international system is of growing significance.

What is meant by private authority? In essence it refers to the exercise of power to establish rules that are generally adhered to, without resort to coercion, by entities that are not states nor the delegated representatives of states, such as an international organization (Hall and Biersteker, 2002: 4). This should not be mistaken for the power to shape outcomes, where private capacity is considerably less controversial, both empirically and normatively. Rather the novel development is the enhanced role and influence played by private entities through the establishment of international economic rules and norms (see generally Hertel, 2003).

There are three distinct ways in which non-state actors influence the rules of the global economic game. The first involves the private establishment of regulations, rules and standards. Here private bodies directly set the rules in specific parts of the global economy and this is accepted as legitimate by both markets and states. The second involves markets determining norms of behaviour which are monitored by private entities. Success in markets requires certain traits, of both states and firms, and this has produced private bodies which monitor these norms and pass judgements formalizing this behaviour. The third element is slightly more nebulous, though not unimportant, whereby NGOs shape both the broader agenda of economic governance as well as the specific aspects of rule making established by states and IOs. For example, NGOs now have a formal place at the WTO table to contribute to both the broader agenda setting as well as the nitty gritty of WTO work. NGOs also influence outcomes by trying to shape market forces through changing consumer preferences. The Fair Trade movement is one of the better known examples. It seeks to get consumers to pay higher than global market prices for goods of developing country exporters through a marketing campaign in the developed world that takes a sense of justice as its primary focus.

In certain sectors private actors are very important, but in others they have little bearing on the shape of the rules. We do not have the space to explore the former in too much depth. However, key areas in which private authority is of considerable importance include internet commerce, telecommunication standards, insurance, intellectual property rights and norms, ratings agencies and commercial dispute resolution (see Cutler *et al.*, 1999; Hall and Biersteker, 2002). The establishment of standards to facilitate commerce over the internet are shaped primarily by private actors. The role played by ratings agencies such as Standard & Poor's and Moody's in establishing and monitoring modes of behaviour is considerable (see generally Sinclair, 2000). Some have argued that their capacity to validate specific norms of institutional behaviour (both of states and firms) has effectively privatized certain elements of policy-making (Sinclair, 2001), and in the realm of commercial dispute resolution there has been a marked rise in arbitration whereby private entities act as a quasi-judiciary to settle legal disputes (Sassen, 2002).

The emergence of non-state authority has a number of causes which are linked to the processes of globalization. The sheer complexity as well as the cost of certain elements of the global economy, such as internet commerce and other high technology sectors such as telecommunications, provides an opportunity and incentive for private actors to establish rules which are accepted by states (Kobrin, 2002). Second, public authorities can simply be too slow to respond to market need. In this case, markets establish their own rules as participants recognize that their absence can put investments, as well as the broader structures, at risk. Third, these changes in market conditions have been met with an ideological mindset among most developed states that is supportive of private authority. The dominance of political elites which are untroubled by, if not actively enthusiastic about, a diffusion of authority away from states and towards markets and other non-state sources has allowed private authority to flourish. The logical consequence of this, however, is that, if the normative environment shifted, the role for private authority could shrink very rapidly or even disappear.

So how important is private authority? While it is clearly of some note there is a tendency to overstate its significance and its character. Its importance varies depending on specific issue areas. Internet commerce is strongly influenced by rules that derive from non-state sources but in financial services banking regulation is firmly in the hands of states and, internationally, banking oversight is dominated by the Basel Committee of the BIS. But in the major aspects of the global economy, trade, financial and corporate regulation, authority is either state- or IO-based. That is not to say that such regulation is necessarily unproblematic or even optimal for contemporary conditions, but simply that, from an aggregate point of view, private authority is far from being the most influential source of governance.

More interesting, however, is the extent to which the exercise of private authority is contingent on state acceptance of its legitimacy and functioning. The interaction of private and public authority is a complex affair in which the public tends to hold a dominant position, even if it is only tacit. Consider the question of the rise of arbitration. Arbitration is a private version of the judicial process which, at first glance, seems to reinforce the view that the private is replacing the public. After all, arbitration is markedly on the rise in commercial dispute settlement around the world (Sassen, 2002). Moreover, if private actors can replace public ones in legal disputes then surely a Rubicon of sorts has been crossed. Yet things are not as extreme as they may appear. First, arbitration is a variation on litigation whereby parties to a dispute turn to the legal powers of the state to resolve their differences and it is no different from litigation in the sense that it is always a matter of private choice and not a matter of state compulsion. Second, private arbitration is backed by laws and linked to state-delegated authority. It is not a completely private process free from the state, rather its appeal lies precisely because it is backed by established legal process and ultimately state coercive power. If arbitration is just the state at one remove, why is it popular? One reason is practical, it tends to be quicker and cheaper than litigation. Second, by being private, disputes can be resolved behind closed doors and out of the public scrutiny inherent in most systems of law. Arbitration thus represents neither the victory of the private over the public nor simply a delegation of the public frame, but a blend of the two which is increasingly popular due to its distinctive appeal.

Arbitration, like any of these forms of private authority, is contingent on the acceptance and support of states and is a reflection of state recognition that contemporary economic circumstances require some delegation of authority. This delegation is temporary and liable to be reversed if circumstances were to change. Moreover, it is always exercised somewhere, that is in a legal and institutional context, and presently that context is established and dominated by states. In short, private authority plays a small role in the global economy. It is accepted by states and indeed requires this legitimacy to be effective but it remains contingent upon the normative conditions which gave it life to allow it to continue.

Under conditions of globalization states and markets exist in a relationship that can be described as complex dependence. The world economy is structured so that traditional state approaches to the exercise of their power over domestic and international economic matters are no longer especially effective. States have been crucial to the establishment of conditions under which they have less capacity and influence than in the past. In simple terms, states have essentially traded off certain policy choices for what are perceived to be economic gains accruing from a more liberal approach to market relations at home and abroad. While the exercise of authority over the world economy is beyond the control of any one power the most important institutional actor shaping the conditions of economic relations under conditions of globalization is still the state. One way in which states are dealing with these challenges is to cooperate in economic governance and this will be discussed in more detail in the next chapter. The political economy of globalization shows that zero-sum conceptions of state–market relations are not particularly helpful when thinking about authority and capacity in the global economy. Cooperation in the exercise of political authority varies tremendously due to differing circumstances, preferences and power discrepancies, but it is simply wrong to see the binding of tariffs via the WTO as something which simply comes off the ledger of the state and gets added to the ledger of globalization. States continue to underpin the basic structures of the global economy. The way they do this may be more sophisticated than in the past, but that basic fact cannot be ignored.

New Global Economy, Old World Politics?

While many think of globalization as a largely economic phenom-enon, one cannot help but conclude that, at least in the economic sphere, globalization is not properly global. While firms and states perceive themselves, at least in their rhetoric, to be part of a global economy, the realities of patterns of investment, trade, production and distribution are not at all global, rather they are decidedly regional. Equally, it is clear that states have not been conquered by markets. Their fates, and those of the societies they rule, are of course heavily affected by economic decisions at some remove from themselves. But the nature of these decisions and the flows of capital, goods and services that they trigger are inter-regional. There are some changes around the margins, and these may yet change further – Brazil and Argentina may provide scope for expansion of invest-ment and trade in South America, while India and China are rapidly making their presence felt – but while globalization has added a dynamism and energy to the world economy it appears to have reinforced the dominant distributions of wealth and networks of trade and investment. Thus far globalization has not yet made a properly global economy, rather it has fostered a world system of more tightly linked regional clusters. It is perhaps prudent, therefore, to avoid the term global economy, which implies a more unified global economic system, and retain the idea of a world economy, for there clearly is a world economy – in a macro sense all the inhabitants of the planet are, to some degree, affected by the system – but it is far from unified and certainly not at all global in any geographic or distributive sense.

For the broader concerns of the book this chapter has a number of conclusions. First, for all its power and pervasiveness, globalization has not broken the links between states and institutions of economic authority. These systems may not be as effective as they were and are dominated by a mindset which sees the openness of globalization as necessarily a good thing, but the underlying dynamics of power and authority are still heavily tilted in the favour of state forms. Second, the impact of globalization on the state–market relationship is a function not only of the power of markets but of the relative capacities and capabilities of states (see also Woods, 2000a). Third, while the notion of the global economy is perhaps not warranted, globalization has created a world economy which is universal in the sense that its impact is experienced by all, but the character of this experience is particularly uneven. Fourth, it implies that states need to operate collectively in some areas to achieve influence over aspects of the system. This is of particular importance both to the broader concerns of this book and to the growing place of institutions in world politics and is the focus of the next chapter.

All of the above underlines the fact that globalization has not removed the centrality of political institutions and interests from the structures of the world economy. Orderly international economic relations, and the social systems to which they relate, are not simply created by establishing the right technical settings, they are the product of compromise and conflict among political interests. Globalization has not changed this, indeed it has underlined the extent to which this is so.

Finally, we tend to forget that central to the success of the post-war order of the global economy was the Cold War context in which it operated (Hufbauer, 2003). The East–West conflict not only provided a kind of military Keynesianism to economic relations it also acted to discipline the Western bloc. Moreover, the patterns of success and failure in the global economy were closely linked to developments in geopolitics. Stagflation in the US, while linked to the Oil Shocks, was also related to the disastrous Vietnam War. The development and broader conditions of the contemporary world economy are equally shaped by the security environment and their future development will be bound up with developments in international security. The general absence of great power rivalry and conflict has been vital to the expansion of globalization and to the economic openness and cooperation among states which has facilitated it. We must recognize that these conditions are the result of the geopolitical preferences and policies of states and are thus contingent on the security environment providing them with sufficient oxygen to thrive. Without a security setting that does not impinge heavily on state willingness to open markets to investment and trade and to cooperate on broader matters of regulation and policy coordination then the foundations of the world economy, and of globalization, will be extremely weak.

5

International Institutions, Governance and Globalization

There appears to be a growing gap between the political structures of the international system and the processes of the global economy. An important means through which states have sought to close this gap is multilateralism and international institutions. While multilateralism has been around for some time, in recent years it has become central to contemporary diplomacy and international relations (Ruggie, 1993). Multilateralism's significance derives not only from a belief that multiple mechanisms are more effective at resolving the sorts of transnational diplomatic problems that currently predominate but it is also thought to be necessary for the legitimacy of so much that goes on in the international system. The US-led intervention in Iraq was criticized for a raft of reasons but it was thought by many to be a problem simply because it was not multilateral enough. While there was a thin multinational coalition it was nothing like the number of countries that had supported the US-led response to Iraq's invasion of Kuwait. If UN approval could have been achieved then America's position would have been greatly strengthened.

A function of the rise of multilateralism has been the massive growth in number, remit and scope of international institutions and organizations. So extensive has this been that it has become impossible to discuss the broader workings of international politics without careful assessment of the place of the UN, the international financial institutions and regional bodies in the structure of the system. Not only do IOs serve to enforce rules, they embody norms, articulate values and have become international actors in their own right. While some of the more obdurate realists may quibble about their efficacy and their ability to stabilize the system, it makes little sense to try to come to terms with modern international relations without recognizing the distinct place of international institutions.

International institutions feature prominently not only on the vista of the international system, they are important components in the processes of globalization. The globalization of the world economy has encouraged the trend to institutionalize international relations and particularly to use IOs to exercise authority. It is not by chance that anti-globalization protesters have focused their attentions on the buildings and summits of international organizations and groupings around the world. Protesters are concerned that globalization is enhancing the power and influence of organizations such as the WTO, the IMF and the EU to the detriment of people the world over. Whether one agrees with this or not, it has become a commonsense position that globalization is increasing the reach, power and authority of international institutions and organizations. Yet while this has an intuitive appeal – globalization tests the efficacy and limits of territorially focused institutions and its scale appears to be beyond the reach of even the most powerful of states – the reality is that international institutions are not thriving in the current environment. Indeed many of the IOs that are cited as examples of this trend are facing varying degrees of crisis. The WTO, the EU, NATO, APEC and ASEAN, to say nothing of the problems of the World Bank and the IMF, are just some of the groups that are finding the forces of globalization to be rather more challenging than straight-line logic might lead one to expect.

The purpose of this chapter is to examine the relationship between globalization and international institutions. It does so firstly by looking at the ways in which institutions are thought to shape the broader parameters of world politics. Secondly, it examines the extent to which globalization has changed the role that international institutions play in world politics. The experience of institutions set up by states to cope with multi- and trans-national issues under conditions of globalization is contradictory. While IOs have had their structural position enhanced by global forces, their ability to capitalize on this appears to be limited. Organizations are not becoming the new centres of power in world politics, indeed in some cases globalization is showing institutions to be decidedly ill-equipped for contemporary circumstances.

International Institutions in the International System

What Purpose do Institutions Serve?

This chapter is concerned only with international institutions and organizations that are inter-governmental in nature. Although there is a wide range of non-governmental institutions that influence the broader workings of the international economic and political system – the significance of NGOs, such as Amnesty International and Greenpeace, as well as their less liberal confreres, such as the Muslim Brotherhood or Hezbollah, is undeniable – these are not considered here. They have been omitted because they play a distinctly different role from that of intergovernmental organizations precisely because of their detachment from the formal institutions of statehood. The chapter does not discuss private international institutions, such as those bodies which have a regulatory function accepted by states, such as IATA or the *codex alimentarius* (which has more corporate representation than state). The focus here is on the particular role of organizations formed by states, whose membership is composed of states or their representatives and whose policies are implemented by states.

Scholarly interest in the role of international institutions came to the fore in IR during the 1980s and early 1990s when theoretical debate was dominated by arguments between realists and liberals about their role and relative importance (e.g. Baldwin, 1993; Kegley, 1995). As the debate progressed the more interesting and pertinent issue has come to be the determination of how and to what extent institutions influence events in world politics (Martin and Simmons, 1998). This debate identified a range of functional purposes that international organizations serve. Even if institutions outgrow their initial purpose, in the way NATO has after the Cold War, their creation has always been the result of a desire to achieve some end.

The international system is famously described as anarchic and international institutions are said to mitigate the consequences of anarchy (e.g. Keohane, 1989). There are generally two ways in which they are said to do this. First, institutions can constrain the behaviour of the powerful (Ikenberry, 2001) and can help build trust and promote reciprocity among states. The anarchic nature of the system means that states have an interest in distrusting others and being confident only in themselves. Institutions act to limit this effect and shift the incentive structure so as to promote trust. Second, institutions are thought to be able to resolve collective action problems at the international level (cf. Sandler, 2004). Social systems, under all conditions, are prone to problems which can only be resolved through cooperative action yet resolution fails to be achieved as the incentives for cooperation do not exist or are insufficient to prompt necessary action. For example, international collective problems such as pollution are especially difficult to deal with. Not only are there insufficient incentives for states to act together to limit it, some see pollution controls as a means for the rich to prevent the poor from developing further. As Martin and Simmons explain 'individually rational action by states would impede mutually beneficial cooperation. Institutions would be effective to the degree that they allowed states to avoid short-term temptations to renege, thus realizing available mutual benefits' (1998: 744). International institutions are thought to be an effective means to remedy this situation.

International institutions also help to align interests and help coordinate policies among states (Cooper, 1989). For example, states fail to cooperate not because they are inherently selfish, but because they have insufficient information about other states' actions and intentions and thus act in ways that can be mutually detrimental. Institutions can promote cooperation by improving the flow of information which can lead to mutually beneficial action. There are also thought to be several broad-ranging purposes to international institutions (see Abbott and Snidal, 1998). At a basic level they promote norms of behaviour, the most prominent of which is the international rule of law. This should not be confused with a naïve view that institutions provide a rule of law – they manifestly do not – rather they promote the adherence to certain rules and force states to pay some price, even if it is only symbolic, if they breach those rules. Changes in domestic policy do not happen in a vacuum and the consequences of reform can be importantly shaped by the international environment. Thus institutions provide an international means to help states pursue domestic reform and to lock it in so that subsequent governments cannot undo the changes. Institutions also provide international or global public goods (e.g. Kaul *et al.*, 1999). For example, just as in the domestic setting the state acts when markets fail, such as in the provision of funding for the performing arts, at the international level institutions can act to coordinate responses to global market failures.

The array of purposes mentioned here provides some sense of the scholarly debate, as well as the sorts of functions which institutions are thought to provide. These functions tell us why institutions exist in the sense that they highlight that they are all ultimately efforts to resolve problems that stem from the sovereign-state basis of the international system. Institutions exist as a response to the particular limitations of an international system that is structured on the principles of sovereignty, legal equality and non-interference. For some, taming anarchy is known as governance. Indeed in much of the policy and academic realm, the language of governance has become almost hegemonic. But what does it mean?

The idea of governance came to prominence in the 1990s as a term that was applied to a very wide range of policy matters, at both the domestic and international level (e.g. Rhodes, 1996; Rosenau and Czempiel, 1992; Young, 1994). The term was enthusiastically taken up by scholars and policy-makers and its capacity to detach the practice of authority from the institution of government was of particular appeal to those grappling with the growing power of markets and the authority of private actors. The popularity of the term has led it to be used so widely as to undermine its utility. 'Governance' describes everything from the coordination of industry standards to codes of behaviour in corporate boardrooms. In IR, governance has been used as a synonym for international order. It can refer to the practices of authority, the projection of power and describe the normative ends which some rules try to advance. Indeed governance can refer to almost anything that influences rule making and the practice of authority in any environment, whether public or private.

The concern here is with governance understood as an attempt to provide some order in a realm without clear lines of authority. Without the dominance that the state has in its domestic sphere, and even the most liberal of states still has final authority over private actors within its domain, attempting to influence or control what goes on in global markets or in response to transnational environmental problems is problematic. Perhaps the best definition of governance notes that it refers to 'the structures and processes that enable governmental and nongovernmental actors to coordinate their interdependent needs and interests through the making and implementation of policies in the absence of a unifying political authority' (Krahmann, 2003). It is precisely this coordination of action at the international level that IOs try to achieve.

Institutions and Governance in World Politics

There are four ways in which this broader process of governance is played out in world politics. First, institutions embody and enforce norms and rules. The institutionalization of codes of conduct acts in several ways to shape the nature of international politics. Codification sets standards of conduct, deviation from which must be justified in some way. It does not equate to law-like powers, rather it involves the establishment of a system of costs to constrain behaviour, for example, the UN's rules on the use of force or the WTO's embodiment of a liberal norm on trade. Second, institutions influence the preferences and decisions of their members. The international actions of states are the product of a wide range of factors, from domestic political pressures to geopolitical considerations, and institutions play a role in this process in a number of ways. The most obvious example of this involves committing oneself to specific policies or rules of behaviour through treaty agreements, such as giving up the use of landmines under the Ottawa Convention. Rationalists see this process in a slightly different light. Institutions act to change the payoffs of a given decision at the international level and thus shift state preferences by altering the logic of preference formation. From this perspective institutions promote, for example, economic policy coordination because it provides payoffs to members to do so which otherwise would not exist. Equally, decision-making can be influenced when states see a value in supporting or promoting an institution for its own sake, even if it does not necessarily entail a prohibition on a specific policy. For example, while many in the Asia–Pacific are sceptical of APEC as a means to advance economic integration, most see it as a body that has some potential worth in other areas and thus they behave in ways which support its continued existence.

Third, international institutions influence the strategies that states use to advance their interests. When states consider how to achieve their goals the potential of international institutions is seen by many to be considerable. The appeal varies from sector to sector, in military security one sees greater scepticism than in trade. But the possibilities for states to seek their aims through the creation of or participation in international institutions is vast and is widely supported among policy elites around the world. Finally, institutions play an important role in world politics as actors on the stage in their own right (Barnett and Finnemore, 1999). While some may describe institutions as little more than the sum of their member states' interests, this depiction is increasingly out of kilter with the autonomous status of many organizations. In the office of the UN secretary general and the Commission of the European Union one sees only the most striking examples of the kind of personality and influence institutions can have. The functional purpose intended in their creation has provided in many cases the basis on which institutions can pursue a specific agenda or aim (Barnett and Finnemore, 2004).

In security and economic matters, as well as the environment and the field of rights and values, one can discern the distinctive role of international institutions illustrative of the points described here. At the broadest level, institutions exist to coordinate collective responses to security challenges. This involves a range of roles from formal alliances to confidence building bodies, from dialogue and informa- tion sharing to enforcement of the rules of international security. The UN is the most obvious example of this but regional bodies such as the ASEAN Regional Forum, the African Union and the Southern African Development Community's Organ on Politics, Security and Defence, as well as ECOWAS and the Arab League, all have institutionalized aspects of international security cooperation. This diversity is reflected not only in institutional form but in efficacy as well. Some institutions have a limited scope and are thus more able to meet their ambitions, such as the ASEAN Regional Forum (ARF), while others have more ambitious goals which they often fail to achieve.

Security matters are the subject of a large number of institutions and organizations and while often derided for having little influence – conflict and insecurity abound in spite of the alphabet soup of security institutions – are of considerable importance to the structure of the international security environment. First, the UN has established the rules determining the legitimate use of force in international affairs. Force may only be used in self defence or with Security Council approval, and while there is considerable debate as to what self defence means, as well as a wide range of purposes that the Security Council sees fit to authorize, as a codification of a practice it is reasonably successful (Roberts, 1996). Beyond the global body one can see effort at the regional level to shape norms of behaviour that relate to war and peace. For example, ASEAN not only seeks to encourage adherence to the UN approach but also sets out codes of conduct for its membership which have a resonance in the Asia–Pacific more generally (Emmers, 2003). These include a formal renunciation of the use of force, commitment to non-nuclear principles and treaties on security cooperation and neutrality. Third, institutions provide a setting whereby conflicts can be resolved. This can involve conflict resolution short of the use of force, mediation to conclude protracted conflicts as well as diplomatic resources to head off crises before they become conflicts (Jentleson, 1999). In the 'good offices' of the UN secretary general, third-party mediation by regional organizations or more broad-ranging preventive diplomacy efforts of ASEAN and the Southern African Development Community (SADC), international institutions tangibly shape the terrain of security in world politics.

International institutions also establish and advance specific conceptions of rights and values and set standards against which states can be measured. They also provide key support for the advancement of particular rights regimes (Risse *et al.*, 1999). These are most commonly associated with the UN's Universal Declaration of Human Rights, and the commission established under the UN's Economic and Social Council, but it occurs at the regional level as well. The European Convention on Human Rights and the African Charter on Human and People's Rights are two distinct variations on this theme. The latter, known as the Banjul Charter, while incorporating ideas of fundamental human rights, emphasizes the culturally specific content of those rights as opposed to the universal application more common in the Western ideas embodied in the European and UN charters. Institutions formalize ideas about appropriate human behaviour and through this shape the material conduct of world politics as well as the development of ideas and values.

Traditionally international relations was a strictly statist affair: only states had any legal personality in international law and individuals mattered only in so far as they were members of a state. The institutionalization of rights, understood in a non-state fashion (whether as an individual or a community), has brought a new moral dimension to world politics. It is testimony to the success of this process that *raison d'état* is no longer seen as a sufficient justification for state action and that the moral language of rights has a political power, even if associated with dubious acts, that was previously unthinkable. The institutionalization of rights and values also makes explicit the relationship between sovereignty and political values. While sovereignty has always had a moral content, as a function of the success of the rights regime, sovereignty is no longer seen as giving *carte blanche* for states to act in any way that they please.

The structure of world politics means that the pursuit of environmental protection requires multi-state action and institutions have been perceived as a means to achieve this. Their purpose is to try to align interests among states so that all are made aware of the collective benefit from actions that may damage any one state. The intention is to get states to see worth in, for example, limiting greenhouse gas emissions that offset the economic harm that may accrue to any individual state. Institutional attempts to establish global environmental rules are also an example of a response to market failure. Whether understood in the economic sense of an externality – that is a product of a market relationship that falls outside market purview – or simply as a realm to which market logic has yet to be properly applied, environmental policy beyond state borders requires coordination to underwrite a global public good.

The range of activities, agreements and regimes that collectively make up institutional responses to the environment can be grouped into three broad sectors of activity. The first involves institutional efforts to coordinate and achieve a specific environmental outcome such as the Kyoto Protocol to the UN Framework Convention on Climate Change which seeks to reduce world-wide carbon emissions through the establishment of a targeted reduction regime. A second kind establishes rules and regulations to manage the global commons, such as the UN Conventions on the Law of the Sea. The third kind involves the adoption of specific environmental policies and broader policy prescriptions of functional international organizations and regional organizations. This refers to, for example, institutions such as the World Bank and the WTO adopting environmental goals in their functional activities (e.g. Weinstein and Charnovitz, 2001). It also includes the extensive environmental programmes of the EU and other, less deeply rooted, efforts in regional organizations such as NAFTA and ASEAN (e.g. Elliott, 2003; Stevis and Mumme, 2000).

Finally, in the economic sphere institutions play their most significant role. International economic institutions try to mitigate the consequences of market and policy coordination failure which inheres in a global market system that is overlaid by a series of legally equal sovereign states. They also provide stability to markets which, if unfettered, can produce dangerously volatile outcomes. Third, they help advance particular social goals in the world economy, most notably the reduction of poverty, the improvement of living standards and the inclusion of ever more states and societies into the world economy. On the one hand institutions provide what might best be described as a technical management function for the global economy and on the other they try to drive particular normative goals.

What are the key institutions of economic governance? The IMF has monetary matters as its focus and its primary (though not sole) purpose is to advance international monetary cooperation and particularly exchange rate stability. It is best known for its coordination of short-term injections of capital to states that suffer from balance of payment crises. The World Bank is concerned more with the organization of longer-term capital distribution with the aim of advancing economic development among the poorest states. The WTO is concerned with ensuring a functioning liberal trading system through the establishment and enforcement of rules and support for the provision of an international environment conducive to liberalization. A less well known institution, the Bank of International Settlements (BIS) is concerned with financial and monetary cooperation. Often referred to as the central bankers' central bank, it monitors international finance, provides advice to its members and more generally coordinates the activities of its members' central banks. The G7 lacks a secretariat and a permanent home but it is a regular forum for the seven richest states, plus Russia, to meet to discuss the coordination of economic policy matters. The OECD acts to assist the coordination of economic policy among its members through advice and reports rather than through rules and regulation. It acts as a kind of cheerleader for fiscally prudent and generally liberal macro-economic policies. While trade, finance and money all have relatively successful regimes and institutions, nothing of note exists for investment or production. There have been a number of efforts to create broader agreements, such as the Multilateral Agreement on Investment (MAI) and the Code of Conduct on TNCs (transnational corporations), but agreement of the kind which brought about the WTO has never been possible.

Overall, institutions matter to the structure and pattern of behaviour and outcomes in world politics. International organizations embody and advance normative shifts, they reconfigure preferences and provide states with a wider range of policy mechanisms through which they advance their interests. Of course, institutional efforts are extremely uneven in their capacity to achieve the goals their supporters have for them. The UN's inability to cope with a wide range of problems in recent years, from the Iraq debacle to the immobility on the humanitarian disaster in Darfur, is typical of shortcomings on the security front. The failure to incorporate the world's largest producers of carbon emissions into the Kyoto regime and the ongoing stagnation of the Doha trade negotiation round are only some of the more obvious problems faced by environmental and economic groupings.

International Institutions and the Challenge of Globalization

International organizations reflect the interests and values of those who construct them and are the product of the broader circumstances in which states and peoples find themselves. In that sense it is not unreasonable to expect that institutions will adapt to changes in their environment or, if they fail to do so, will eventually disappear from the scene. The reduction of the costs of distance on social transactions has drawn the fates of peoples and states ever closer, and as such, ought to provide an environment well suited to international organizations. As one of the leading scholars of international institutions has pointed out, globalization increases social friction because self-interested actions affect the well-being of others and globalization significantly enhances the transnational effects of social action (Keohane, 2002: 246). This means that action must be taken to mitigate these effects and institutions are the only realistic means to do so. From this perspective, it is in everyone's interest to increase the influence and efficacy of institutions. There has been considerable expectation that globalization was going to usher in a new era of institutionalized multilateral global governance. The incentives of the global structures of production, finance and trade would drive states to recognize their own limits and focus organizational efforts at the supra-national level. Others pointed to the widespread and unexpected chaos unleashed by the East Asian financial crisis and its contagion crises in Russia and Brazil as evidence that the brutal realities of the financial 'global herd' would drive states to more advanced levels of cooperation in matters of financial governance. Has this come to pass?

Growing Influence?

Contemporary circumstances have improved the systemic position of international organizations. The increasing number and remit of such organizations, to say nothing of the clamour to join groupings by states, rich and poor, is testimony to their appeal (Shanks *et al.*, 1996). Equally, it is fair to apportion much of the motivation to participate in these organizations, particularly those associated with the global economy, to globalization. On the one hand, decision-makers feel that it is an unavoidable part of the globalization process. They perceive that globalization is an inexorable force to which one must react to optimize one's chances and as such one must sign up to the institutions or risk missing out altogether. Given the challenging circumstances of so many states this view – that globalization insists one must join the WTO or establish regional organizations – is understandable. State decision-makers also feel that institutions provide an important means through which they can advance their interests given the complexities of an increasingly globalized economy. For example, ASEAN states, traditionally reluctant to take their institution too far toward functional policy commitments, are seeking a range of economic agreements, relating to trade, investment and financial services, as a direct response to globalization. They feel that if they fail to make some sort of effort along these lines they will lose out to competitors in North East and South Asia (ASEAN, 2005).

A further source of the growth in support for institutionalized international collaboration comes from the way in which globalization changes the balance of domestic interests in many states. Globalization makes domestic actors increasingly susceptible to changes in their external conditions and thus have an interest in encouraging state elites to adopt institutional solutions. A state may feel particularly threatened by ozone depletion or global warming, as many in the South Pacific are, and thus their interest in institutional responses is heightened. Also, the dynamic but fragile nature of the global financial system and its penetration of so many societies and states means that bankers in New York, wine makers in France and car manufacturers in Japan, have an interest in financial stability and probity in Thailand and Malaysia. The point is not that domestic interests will inevitably lead to effective global institutional responses, rather that the balance of interest in the domestic environment is shaped by globalization to create circumstances in which the chances that a policy issue will get pushed up to the international institutional level are greater than in the past. But domestic pressure may push for international cooperation that undermines existing institutions, as some argue that the rush for preferential trade agreements (PTAs) does. A further example is the recently established Asia-Pacific Partnership on Clean Development and Climate which brings together some of the world's leading carbon emitters (and non-signatories to Kyoto) – Australia, China, India, Japan, the US and the Republic of Korea – to work on an alternative cooperative framework that better suits their preferences. Domestic incentives exist for international cooperation but these do not align with existing institutions or frameworks, thus the six established their own, less onerous, regime. Critics feel it undermines Kyoto and is not an adequate response to the problem of climate change, and it illustrates how globalization does not drive an inexorable move to embrace existing institutions and organizations.

For some, the enhanced structural role of institutions is necessary to globalization itself. When leading scholars write that 'globalization depends on governance' (Keohane, 2002: 267) and that governance is best provided by institutions, they do not simply mean that globalization is being fostered by international institutions. Rather, they mean that the continued existence of globalization requires the support of international organizations and institutions to provide the necessary infrastructure. In this sense globalization needs institutions to supply the rules, coordination and reciprocity necessary for its functioning. The sovereign state structure of world politics prevents the necessary exercise of authoritative rule making, norm creation and enforcement central to the globalization process.

This structural-strengthening argument should not be confused with a straight-line conclusion that institutions have a greater impact on the system than previously. Instead, it points toward a more measured interpretation, that globalization has increased the situational importance of organizations but does not guarantee increased power, influence or effectiveness. Nor does it imply that existing institutions will necessarily be well equipped to respond to the challenges. The demand for and expectation of international organizations has, on the whole, grown due to the transformations of globalization, and an opportunity has been created for institutions to increase their influence. Whether they are capable of so doing is a separate issue altogether.

Globalization and the Institutions of the World Economy

Recent developments do not support the view that globalization is producing a more effective institutional framework for the governance of the world economy. A number of institutions are coming under stress as increased membership and the expansion of their role, as well as the more traditional problems of states protecting their entrenched interests, are hindering institutional function. Also, although there are a range of efforts to try to establish a new 'financial architecture' so as to reduce the volatility of global financial markets, they are not making much headway. As such, states are increasingly turning to regional, as opposed to global, efforts to cope with the consequences of globalization when they perceive that existing institutions are either failing or are inappropriate to their circumstances. One area in which there has been some important movement is the efforts to expand the number of states which are able to influence key structures as a means to enhance the legitimacy, and through this the effectiveness, of global economic governance. Globalization is straining old systems of governance and producing new strategies as states attempt to come to terms with its shifting demands.

The WTO-centred trading system is coming under increasing strain and is becoming less able to advance its core business of trade liberalization. This is not to say that its members no longer think that it is useful; its growing membership shows that states continue to feel it is a club in which they wish to participate and all agree that its dispute resolution mechanism is vital. But, its success has created significant technical and political problems which show little sign of abating. There are three core problems. First, the size of the membership has made decision-making extraordinarily difficult as the members have wildly diverging interests and requirements. Moreover the institutional structures cannot adapt themselves to effective decision-making under such conditions. After the debacle at Cancun, Pascal Lamy, Director General of the WTO described its procedures as 'medieval'. Serious reform of organizational decision-making and its relationship to members' priorities is required if the WTO is to overcome its current stasis (see Ostry, 2003). Second, the current round of negotiations is in abeyance. This derives from the first problem but also from the expansion of the agenda to include not only the higher-profile matters of development but also new trade-related issues, such as government procurement, the environment and competition policy. These are seen to be far more intrusive than the traditional focus of tariffs and hence subject to much greater member-state sensitivity. The success of the system in the longer run has derived from its capacity to deliver results and this is growing harder and harder to achieve. Third, trade is more politically sensitive than ever before and elites have a greater incentive to protect some aspects while at the same time trying to open up other markets. This is leading many in the developed world to focus on other means to advance their trade aims because the WTO is seen as unable to deliver the goods or might be the source of less-desired outcomes. The most obvious consequence of this has been the rapid growth in regional PTAs which have become the focus for many developed and developing states' trade liberalization agencies. Rather than seeing globalization driving a global opening of markets via the WTO, globalization is increasingly encouraging a rise of preferential trade and seizing up the multilateral system. As Thirlwell points out, the GATT/WTO system, which was born in 1947, successfully completed eight rounds of negotiations in 57 years, yet since 1979 only one successful round has been concluded (2005: 47). This is hardly evidence of a globalization-fuelled cosmopolitan sensibility overcoming the entrenched power of vested national interests.

The financial crises that rocked the globe in the 1990s caused many to demand a new 'financial architecture' for the international system. Precisely what this meant, however, was less than clear. Some argued that the global financial system needed the level of confidence that a lender of last resort plays in domestic economies, and that the IMF could be transformed to play this sort of role (Fisher, 2000). Others felt that coordinated regional responses might be more effective with Japan proposing an Asian monetary fund. Yet others argued that the Tobin Tax – a mechanism to damp down market volatility through a taxation system – should be introduced into global financial markets. Yet while proposals have been many, concrete action has been sparse. To date, the only meaningful developments relate to the surveillance of market and state actions and involve little intrusion into the workings of global financial markets. These developments include the monitoring of private sector investment moves, particularly firm exposure to potentially dangerous circumstances, surveillance of financial markets, especially offshore centres, and improved coordination between the IMF, the World Bank, the OECD and the BIS. This is being done by new committees and revamped groupings within existing organizations such as the establishment of the Financial Stability Forum (FSF) in the BIS and the Capital Markets Consultative Group in the IMF. The aim is to reduce the chances of crises emerging by increasing market awareness of risk and encouraging less risky behaviour by states and firms.

One of the more concrete developments in this sphere is the Chiang Mai Initiative established by ASEAN and China, Japan and Korea in 2000 (Henning, 2002: 11–31). The initiative was intended to help avoid future crises and to provide states with policy assistance if a crisis were to eventuate. The participants agreed to monitor capital flows, improve surveillance of financial markets and establish a set of currency swap agreements. The aim is to provide states with low cost external support in the case of currency crisis. While most feel that the initiative is not sufficient to protect states in the event of a substantial crisis, it is indicative of the kind of regional response to crises and of a region-focused 'financial architecture' that signify the partial character of supposedly global economic governance.

While states recognize the inherent risks in the present structure of the international financial system they prefer the wealth opportunities it allows over a more secure but less energetic system. Whether this preference is a function of the bullying power of markets, the cravenness of political elites or a considered judgement is unclear. The reality of the current system is that global financial markets are not governed in any proper sense of the word. The developments that have emerged do little more than codify contemporary market expectation of good behaviour. There appears to be little abiding interest in advancing any serious alternative to the current structure of the global financial system.

But the news is not entirely gloomy. There have been a range of efforts to expand the number of states which can influence institutional governance, as well as attempts to increase the transparency of these institutions. This attempt to be more inclusive and more open is a direct result of globalization. Much of the criticism levelled at the institutions of global economic governance by the anti-globalization movement has focused on both the secretive nature of much of the decision-making in these organizations and the fact that most of the decisions are made by a handful of states who, unsurprisingly, tend to nudge developments in a direction commensurate with their interests. Also, states have come to recognize that the effectiveness of governance rests not only on the technical efficiency of supervisory and collaborative mechanisms but also on the political support that such systems receive.

The two elements most central to this are the creation of the G20 and the FSF. The G20 is a group of nineteen of the largest and most dynamic developed and developing economies, as well as the EU, which meets regularly at finance minister level to enhance global economic stability through coordination of policy, dialogue and the further development of the institutional setting of international finance and monetary matters. It includes the largest markets in the world and, most crucially, the most dynamic economies. On top of the G7 it brings the large and dynamic economies of Russia, China, India and Brazil alongside a broader geographic range of states such as Saudi Arabia, Turkey, Australia and Mexico. It is both technically and politically a much more compelling place to have cooperative economic action than the G7. Moreover, its present agenda, which includes reform of the Bretton Woods institutions, managing the challenges of demographic change and macro-economic policy coordination, stands a much greater chance of success due to the nature of those represented around the table and their respective stakes in successful cooperation programmes. The FSF brings together representatives of central banks and financial authorities, international institutions and international regulatory bodies. The FSF is intended to improve stability through better policy coordination, enhanced monitoring of vulnerabilities to the system and the provision of a central point to supervise action to remedy weaknesses. Both the G20 and the FSF represent the first genuine efforts to broaden the geographic scope of states involved in financial and monetary governance. The FSF includes not only national authorities but also involves non-state representation from regulatory agencies as well as the European Central Bank, the OECD and the World Bank. It brings together a broad cross-section of those who influence the structure of the global financial system, including state and institutional perspectives. Of course, this is no UN General Assembly, but that is not necessarily a bad thing. Effective governance requires striking the right balance between inclusiveness and legitimacy, on the one hand, and the requisites of functional efficacy on the other. In the G20 and the FSF we see reasonably judicious examples of such a balance. The IMF, World Bank and WTO, through attempts to become more transparent and more inclusive in their decision-making, are trying to improve their public image. At the WTO, NGOs now have a formal place at the table, the World Bank is slowly beginning to provide input from advocacy groups and the IMF has begun to reconfigure its approach to conditionality, as well as responding to demands about broader matters such as human rights and the environment and changing the representation in the key decision-making bodies.

Globalization and its attendant pressures have begun to make states recognize that changes are required in the institutional infrastructure of the global economy. Particularly there is a recognition that governance is not only a matter of getting the technicalities of information dissemination, financial regulation and fiscal policy coordination right, it is also increasingly recognized that governance is inherently political and its efficacy is closely linked to legitimacy and inclusion (Germain, 2001). Although such moves are slow and fairly circumscribed they do mark a decisive break with past conduct of global economic governance.

There are also examples of more geographically constrained attempts to establish some institutional economic governance. Some of the more notable include the EU, APEC, ASEAN, MERCOSUR, and the GCC. These are examples of states getting together on a geographically limited basis to collaborate on economic and other matters: the establishment of rules and procedures and the advancement of common economic aims. Regional efforts tend to be dominated by economic concerns with a particular preference for trade liberalization and trade facilitation, although in some cases they involve considerably more extensive economic cooperation and governance. For example, ASEAN has adopted a range of measures designed to harmonize standards across its membership to promote trade. The ADB seeks to enhance economic development in the Asia-Pacific and the EU has a strong commitment to redistribution of wealth across its members, most notably through the Regional Development Fund.

Although the EU is distinct in both the scale of its governance structures and the success of its economic integration, there are other examples of ambitious attempts to move beyond the more limited cooperative efforts embodied in trade agreements. Specifically, there are attempts by states in Southern Africa and Southeast Asia to try to construct single markets and common currencies. These may be overambitious given their circumstances but they reflect the concerns of many states about the conditions of globalization and how best to respond to them. ASEAN states are increasingly in favour of more extensive cooperation because of concerns about competitive pressures emanating from China and India. In some parts of the world regional cooperation is of much greater importance than global efforts.

Not all regional efforts are an unmitigated success. APEC, which burst onto the international scene in the late 1980s and sought to become the focus for trade liberalization in the Asia-Pacific region, has stagnated in recent years (Ravenhill, 2000). Equally, the South Asian Association for Regional Cooperation (SAARC) has never moved much beyond a broad statement of intent and several small-range and limited policy agreements. SAARC and APEC show that, even as globalization provides pressures and incentives for states to cooperate and integrate their economic policies, these efforts may not all work. Regional cooperation may be an effective strategy for some states to cope with economic aspects of globalization but it is still subject to a wide range of national political and economic pressures. Globalization may change the economic calculus for policy-makers, but it does not always trump political circumstances. To take the APEC example, by the late 1990s the organization was lacking leadership as many, such as the US, Japan and Australia, were no longer interested in devoting political capital to the institution as their domestic political preferences lay elsewhere. In addition, there was a growing perception that the organization lacked sufficient benefits to make it worthwhile. The story of regionalism as a strategy for responding to the challenges of globalization is not, therefore, one of simple market victory over state power nor of states seeing the benefits of cooperation as inevitably compelling.

Finally, the question of institutional governance has tended to be treated as primarily technical, and only latterly as somewhat political. Yet there is a third determinant of its success which is only tangentially related to globalization. Institutional efforts and their success are shaped by geopolitical circumstances. Whether in South Asia, the Middle East or Northeast Asia, geopolitical and security concerns are preventing the kind of institutional governance that some have come to expect as a natural consequence of globalization. While global markets can be profoundly powerful actors, both as distributors of resources as well as shapers of policy, they can be severely hit by conflict. The kind of communication, trust and general goodwill that are necessary to facilitate institutional efforts to govern the global economy require changes in the existing geopolitical framework. Globalization has increased the currency of economic matters but it is a long way from making them trump geopolitical and security concerns. Without the requisite levels of stability and security, globalization could easily become very badly unstuck.

Mixed Experiences and Their Sources

While the appeal of international organizations is broad-ranging, there is considerable variation in demand as well as expectation among states, and in issue areas. The stark differences between regional approaches to economic institutionalization noted above are clear evidence of this. What about issue areas? In the security sphere – a sector that is just as bound up by globalization processes (see Chapter 6) – one sees a much more ambivalent attitude to organizations. The UN is beset by political disagreement over even the most basic issues, typical of which is the ongoing wrangle over a definition of terrorism. The Security Council is still heavily influenced by old-fashioned geopolitical concerns and the preferences of the major powers and is increasingly ill-equipped to face the complex realities of the security challenges thrown up by globalization (Malone, 2004). Elsewhere there is a good degree of enthusiasm to create new institutions or adapt existing ones for dialogue, confidence-building and information-sharing (albeit of a limited kind) to cope with challenges such as transnational crime and terrorism, infectious diseases and human security crises. These can be seen, for example, in the ASEAN Regional Forum, the SADC Organ on Defence and Security, NATO's Partnerships for Peace programme and even the APEC Secure Trade in the Asia-Pacific Region Initiative. These are all moves that involve either strict limits on cooperation or commitment-free dialogue rather than substantive cooperative action. In the security realm there is reasonable demand for institutional action but the expectation of what can be achieved through these means is significantly lower than in the economic sphere.

This mixed experience is a function of traditional concerns. While states may realize that collective action to resolve transnational security challenges is more pressing due to globalization, they are still largely of the opinion that the costs of cooperation outweigh the benefits. In some sectors states feel it is better, even in what they may realize are sub-optimal conditions, not to take the risk that they may be even worse off under new circumstances. Traditional thinking in many parts of the world still predominates, a lack of trust and the dominance of traditional security approaches to military and defence policy militate against the kind of cooperation which many realize is vital. But this is only part of the explanation. Institutions and organizations have always had a limited capacity to deliver the results that their founders had intended. For every EU-style success, one can point to a raft of under-performing organizations such as the OAU or SAARC. The problem is not only related to the broad-ranging challenges of international institutional efficacy but to the particular impact that globalization has on the ability of institutions to achieve their ends. In short, many institutions are finding that their capacity to deliver intended results is constrained, and in some instances severely hampered, by globalization (Milner, 2005). The most obvious examples are the IMF, the World Bank and the G7, although one could argue that this is also the case in many other organizations such as the WTO and APEC.

There are a number of reasons why globalization is not enhancing organizational strength and instead undermining institutional efficacy. At the most simple level, globalization is increasing the workload put on organizations, yet they are not receiving the necessary increase in resources to cope with the rising demand. Globalization is increasing the role of trade in the global economy and a wider range of states and societies are affected by the world economy. Yet institutional capacity, whether in terms of available funds for the IMF to assist in times of crisis or credit for the World Bank to assign, or of bureaucratic resources to assist the WTO's trade function, has not come close to keeping pace (Milner, 2005).

A second reason is that globalization is creating circumstances to which existing institutions are not, in their current guise, especially well-suited. A typical example of this is the Asian financial crisis of 1997–98. The crisis did not fit the usual model. Yet the IMF insisted that Indonesia, Thailand and Korea all undertake a range of measures that were designed to remedy an entirely different situation – the traditional current account–loose fiscal policy-driven currency crisis (Blustein, 2003). The IMF's approach not only failed to curb the crisis it made conditions considerably worse (see generally Noble and Ravenhill, 2000).

Institutions of all kinds are notoriously slow to change to meet new circumstances, and international institutions are especially tardy because of the sovereign character of their membership. While most agree that adapting existing institutions is much easier than creating new ones from scratch, the speed of globalization, its apparent dependence on institutions and its ever wider consequences are all making life extremely challenging for these organizations, even though many thought that their fit with the needs of globalized world politics would put them in a dominant position. At a broader level, globalization is revealing the structural limits of organizations which are based on sovereign states. States turn to organizations to resolve common problems or to advance common aims. Yet these institutions are, with few exceptions, not only susceptible to the whims of their members (Woods, 2000b), they are prone to conceiving solutions and implementing policies in statist terms. This should not be read as approval of the standard realist critique of institutions which sees them as little more than the sum of their states' parts (e.g. Mearsheimer, 1994), rather it emphasizes that their very nature as inter-state creatures makes conceptualizing and operationalizing other ways of acting – that is *not* via states – almost impossible. They are products of the statist conceptualization of modern politics and their capacity to cope with globalization will, therefore, always be tested. Institutions can adapt to new situations and are not instantly rendered obsolete by new circumstances, but they are beset by the problems of their nature, that is by the interests of states and the limits of statist solutions to problems thrown up by globalization.

The final reason for institutional difficulty with globalization derives from a more basic fact. With the exception of a number of regional organizations, most of the key institutions in world politics were created in the aftermath of the Second World War. As such it is unsurprising that even with reform and restructuring they are not especially well suited to the contemporary era. The collaborative problems of the early 21st century are markedly different from those of the post-war period, and the institutional structure of these organizations is similarly out of line with the interests, powers and priorities of the current era. Why should Britain, France, Russia, China and the US have a veto power on the Security Council when other nuclear powers do not? Why are Africa, South America and South Asia not represented in this group? Why are some of the largest and most dynamic economies not included in the steering committees of the global economy, such as the G7? Globalization is challenging not only the technical capacities of the post-1945 multi-lateral institutional order, it is asking pressing questions of its political foundations.

Institutional Transformation

The circumstances of globalization have not been plain sailing for the international institutions, but we should recognize that some have tried to respond to the new challenges. Most obviously, the UN and its agencies have begun to take globalization seriously as an issue that requires a decisive and thought-through institutional reaction. In a famous and widely cited remark UN Secretary-General Annan made this imperative clear: 'The central challenge that we face is to ensure that globalization becomes a positive force for all the world's people, instead of leaving billions of them behind in squalor' (Annan, 2000: 6). While other institutions have made changes that may not have been self-conscious reactions to globalization, they are clearly motivated by the transformations it is bringing.

The UN system is a notoriously sprawling set of institutions and its hallmark has been a 'silo' mentality. Its various parts plan, think and act almost as if they were separate entities. One leading scholar (and erstwhile participant in the system) argues that, in contrast to this history, globalization has prompted the UN to adopt a more integrated approach (Ruggie, 2003). This closer working relationship among the functional agencies, the councils and the secretariat consists of a number of elements. The first involves a conceptual convergence among groups on the nature and character of globalization's challenges as well as on the appropriate policy response. This means a cross-institutional acceptance of a broadly liberal approach to economic management and a particular emphasis on the need for 'good governance'. The second is an increasing unification of institutional priorities, at least as far as the developmental aspects of globalization are concerned. This is best embodied in the Millennium Development Goals, which set clear aims to reduce poverty and enhance human development. Such initiatives can focus the minds of key players, but, more particularly, they provide a unified vision for cross-UN work. Yet even here the aims and work of the institution are being stymied by the membership which famously failed to support concrete action in support of the Goals at the 2005 World Summit.

Beyond development matters, adaptation of the UN system is much more limited. This is most obviously the case in the security sector with the Security Council showing a particular recalcitrance (Malone, 2004). State interests predominate, the permanent members constrain action when it suits them, coordination is limited and the capacity to respond to the multidimensional security threats posed by globalization is severely hampered by the continued constraining effect that state interests build into the structures of the system. Moreover, there is a continued unwillingness to make any significant or substantive changes to these structures. The UN as an institution has made considerable efforts to respond to globalization. The success of these efforts, however, is constrained by the interests of the members and, at times, positively hampered by the system's structural flaws. There is no willingness to change the system and the considerable increase in workload that globalization has presaged has not produced a commensurate increase in capacity.

The UN's recognition of the need for institutional efforts to advance development goals is typical of a broader trend among IOs, especially those have not traditionally taken development as a focus of their activities. This is most notable at the WTO. In part this is a product of the interests of the members. Since the formation of the WTO in 1995 its membership has increased by just over 30%. Of these new members the overwhelming majority are developing states whose primary interest is to gain the economic benefits of the liberal trading system. Around two-thirds of the WTO membership now comes from developing economies and this reflects a consensus that trade is a central mechanism through which states can achieve their development ambitions. In fact, the latest round of trade negotiations has been dubbed the Development Round because of the centrality of development-related issues. The ministerial statement which sets the framework for discussion makes this plain (WTO, 2001).

It is not only in the current Round's focus on development that one can discern WTO adaptation to globalization. First, the whole range of issues which are on the table reflect the way in which globalization is changing trade: services, intellectual property, investment, e-commerce and competition policy are central parts of the 'work programme' which is the broadening WTO remit. Second, the WTO recognizes that its success requires more than the achievement of enhanced liberalization among members, it is also contingent on significantly improving its legitimacy. Globalization has made clear to many that what goes on at the WTO matters to them. Just as globalization has increased the range of issues whereby the social consequences of economic decisions are more widely felt, it also makes clear the need to manage the system in an accountable and legitimate fashion. The WTO may not be doing this particularly effectively but globalization is pressing institutional change. Yet, just as the Doha Round appears set to fail, any meaningful reform of the structures of the organization is hard to envisage. As with the UN, the WTO's work is being severely impaired by the continuing presence of state interests and by the members' unwillingness to give it the necessary autonomy to play the kind of role that it sees for itself and that so many feel is necessary to the success of globalization.

There is a broader sense that institutions, and particularly the international financial institutions (IFIs), have failed to respond adequately to the new circumstances. Few would dispute that the processes of globalization have notably increased the opportunities for wealth creation around the world. Yet, as many argue, the existing international institutions have not acted to help direct these opportunities to assist the poorest and most deprived. In essence, the IFIs are charged with having mismanaged globalization for the least developed countries (e.g. Stiglitz, 2002). These institutions have a range of tasks, but central to these is assisting poorer countries to join the global economy. As globalization has transformed the nature of the economy the institutions appear increasingly unable to meet this task (e.g. Easterly, 2001; Vreeland, 2003). Many reasons are given for this: institutions are thought to have inappropriate policies; they are captured by the vested interests of the developed world, both state and private; their efforts are undermined by domestic problems in less developed countries (LDCs); their work is attributed to dysfunctional institutions which lack accountability and transparency (e.g. Bueno de Mesquita and Root, 2000; Thacker, 1999; Vaubel, 1996).

In response, the IMF and the World Bank have begun to implement small-scale change in structure and policy prescriptions, and have tried to improve their transparency. These organizations, along with the UN and the WTO, have become more overtly committed to bridging the gap between rich and poor that globalization appears to have exacerbated. Yet the barriers to significant transformation within these organizations are considerable (e.g. Mallaby, 2005). Not only do the vested interests of those within the organizations constrain significant structural shifts, but states are not willing to provide the autonomy of action that many argue is necessary. Equally, it is still far from clear how, technically speaking, development can be pursued more effectively by institutions. There is nothing like a consensus among scholars and policy-makers about how one might construct better policies or more effective aid programmes. In short, globalization does not do enough to override the vested interests and institutional limits that prevent significant transformation.

At the regional level one can discern a range of interesting developments related to globalization. In the most widespread response, regional institutions have reacted to globalization by attempting to enhance levels and degrees of economic integration. This is most obvious in the explosion of preferential trade agreements among not only bilateral partners but regional groupings. ASEAN is pressing on with a range of economic cooperation activities the centrepiece of which is its own free trade agreement and two extra-ASEAN agreements, one with China and the existing agreement between Australia and New Zealand. This trend is evident also in Latin America with the Central America-Dominican Republic agreement concluded in 2004 and the integration efforts of MERCOSUR. While the rise of leftist politicians in Venezuela and Bolivia may stymie the Andean Pact, and possibly the continent-wide Free Trade Agreement of the Americas, they are committed to alternative regional trade promotion activities. In Africa, as well, one sees regional trading agreements seeking to lock in benefits of existing groupings. This was led by ECOWAS in the early 1990s and has been followed by SADC's and WAEMU's trade agreements at the turn of the millennium.

The Social Limits of International Institutions

Overall, while globalization has increased the hand of institutions it is not inexorably leading states toward a global multilateral future where global trade is open and overseen by the WTO, development is achieved by the World Bank and global security is carefully advanced by a unified and representative United Nations. The experience is considerably more mixed. The expectation of many that globalization would create an irresistible case for global multilateral solutions to transnational challenges has not been forthcoming. Even though states recognize that institutions provide a particular opportunity to advance their collective interests and make a better fist of globalization, they are still reluctant to hand over power and authority to organizations or even to improve cooperation. Although globalization reveals the limits of existing approaches to governance and authority there is no reason to think that these shortcomings will necessarily lead to the sensible construction of better alternatives.

There can be little doubt that the wide-ranging changes brought about by globalization – increasing dependence on foreign markets for economic well-being and the enhanced vulnerability of states and peoples to threats from terrorism – present existing institutions, both domestic and international, with a decisive challenge. Much of what is central to the smooth functioning of economic systems – the probity of leading institutions, the required capital base of finance houses – is beyond the reach of many states. The gap between the requirements of the global economy and the capacity and reach of national institutions is considerable. This is even more clear-cut in regard to questions of environmental preservation and the transmission of infectious diseases. But even if an organization is not well-suited to its environment, it does not follow that it will collapse or somehow automatically adapt to these circumstances in a rational and optimal way. Just because the circumstances in which organizations find themselves provide them with an excellent opportunity to enhance their power and promote better policies, it does not mean that they will.

There are a number of reasons why the existing institutions are unable to achieve the sort of technocratic efficacy that their supporters might have hoped. These include the ongoing political constraint that states put on institutional behaviour and the broader fit of the post-1945 institutions to a 21st century world (see also Woods, 2000b). But a further challenge to institutional efficacy derives from its ability to satisfy not only technical exigencies but normative and social ones as well.

It can be easy to forget that international organizations are social institutions and like any such creature require a normative anchor in their social constituency if they are to succeed. Modern states have been particularly successful institutions because of their capacity to legitimate themselves through ideas of nationalism and to effectively construct a social foundation for their power through mechanisms which allow them to penetrate society and govern without the need for coercion at every turn. This capacity has been described as the 'infrastructural' power of states (Mann, 1993). International institutions need to create some autonomous infrastructural power, and globalization has made this especially evident. To do this, and thus to make good on their potential, they need to do three things. First, and most obviously they must improve their legitimacy. Second, they need to improve the efficacy of implementation at the local level. It is evidently not enough to rely on states to carry out action. Third, they need to construct networks of relations that make the societies they influence feel as if they have some stake in their activities. In the anti-globalization movement one sees these shortcomings in their starkest form. The violent demonstrations that accompanied a raft of institutional meetings in the late 1990s and early 2000s chastened many institutions. The protests also remind us that the actions of the institutions have real social consequences and that organizations need to work to ensure that they are more effectively embedded in the societies they influence (Halliday, 2000). This is not to say that all institutions must act to advance specific normative ends, such as gender equality or economic redistribution, rather that they need to negotiate the complex terrain whereby they can become more effectively rooted in their constituent societies.

Some feel that one way to do this is to embrace norms of accountability, transparency, equity and social justice (e.g. Karns and Mingst, 2004: 514–20). Given the importance of these ideas to political life in many societies, this may provide some means of achieving a more compelling social basis than that which currently exists. The problem is that the mix of state and institutional predilections appears to make this unlikely. Without a more effective social basis international institutions are unlikely to significantly enhance the role that they play in world politics. More importantly, globalization has a very real chance of fostering a backlash against its effects. Vital to preventing the kind of reaction that brought the previous era of globalization to a devastating end is a concerted effort to link the structures which govern globalization to the norms and values of the vastly differing societies which live through it. Institutions need to be able to take seriously social concerns about globalization. They need to do so both to minimize the chance of a revolutionary rejection of globalization and to function more effectively in determining the appropriate technical settings to manage global processes. Until they do this there will be little chance for meaningful shifts in the role, function and success of institutional efforts to govern globalization.

International organizations play a greater role in the international system due to the changes associated with globalization. They are an immediately available means of solving the collective action problems and coordination difficulties that beset the world economy. But they are limited by their circumstances. The statist institutional limits of international organizations, their organizational pathologies and their social failings present them with manifest problems. While at first glance globalization might be seen as a fuel to drive such groups to new heights, perhaps to become the moral equivalent of states in the coming century, there is little evidence to suggest that this might come to pass. If anything, the trend is moving in the opposite direction. International organizations are fundamentally political institutions. As such they are constrained by the interests of their state membership, as well as being more hemmed in by the continued hegemony of a nationalist and statist conception of modern politics. Globalization, some thought, would dislodge this dominance by demonstrating its instrumental shortcomings and provide institutions with a means not only to enhance their power but to make the world a better place. Yet while globalization clearly matters, it has so far failed to provide the necessary radical transformation to push the dominant structural system of politics from its hegemonic position.

6

Globalization and the Changing Face of War

In the opening years of the 21st century which followed the bloodiest yet in human history, war casts a curious shadow. Out of the carnage and brutality of total war a series of finance, production and trade networks has emerged that has intertwined the economic interests of so many states and societies that many have begun to think that war is on the wane, at least among those that have the good fortune to be part of these networks. For those excluded from these links intra-state ethnic and tribal wars, as well as organized anti-systemic violence, is carrying on as before. In some cases the situation has even worsened as these networks have become more interlinked.

The character of warfare has always been a good index of the conditions of human existence. Wars reflect the technological and economic levels of development of their eras; their aims and manner of conduct provide an excellent means to assess the political, economic and social priorities of the societies which fight. Even the most committed 'neoclassical realist' (Gray, 1999), one who argues that in essence war has not changed over the millennia, recognizes that the manner in which wars are fought – on horseback or in tanks, by stealth bomber or infantry charge – and the political ends which they advance say much about the social conditions out of which wars have emerged. The wars of the mid 20th century were different both in conduct and motive from the wars of the 1990s. These differences reflect technological developments, as well as shifts in political priorities, forms of social organization and changes in perceptions of moral worth.

Analysis of the character of war is necessary beyond the insight that it provides into the nature of contemporary social conditions.

There is a pervading sense that war itself is undergoing a significant transformation, and in part this is thought to result from globalization. War is subject to globalization as well as being a force which contributes to its ongoing dynamic. Given the scale of issues related to warfare and globalization, and the space constraints of the chapter, it is necessary to focus on the core issues. To that end, the chapter will firstly consider the extent to which globalization increases the vulnerability of states and societies to threats, as well as the way in which globalization can also limit how and to what ends the organized use of force is deployed. The second section examines the conduct of war and assesses how globalization has changed the way wars are fought. The final section examines the purpose of wars and sets the growing sense that the use of force in the international system is illegitimate alongside the continuing incidence of low-intensity war and a growing interest in humanitarian, or what one leading scholar has called 'humane', war (Coker, 2001).

War and Conflict

Prior to delving into these issues it is necessary to clarify how the concept of war is being used here. From the very earliest traces of human civilization war has been central to social experience. One need only look at the centrality of war to human cultural expression and valorized symbols to grasp its ubiquity. From the defining myths of nations – Kosovo for Serbs, Gallipoli for both Turks and Australians – to the memorials and monuments to fallen warriors, such as Des Invalides in Paris or Yasukuni in Tokyo, war is a central component of our modern sense of identity. Yet while it is intuitive to speak of war in such a fashion, in the context of the study and practice of war it means something relatively specific. Some argue that war is ultimately best understood and analyzed as a specific variation of the much broader category of conflict (e.g. Burton, 1990). This view sees human conflict as a form of violent behaviour and thus war, in all its guises, is an extension of violence at the individual level. From this perspective, war has its roots in the sorts of disputes over basic human needs which are the source of individual manifestations of conflict and violence such as domestic assault or mugging. Of course war is more complex and sophisticated in motive, organization and operation, but at base it shares sufficient social traits to warrant such a classification. To put it plainly, war is different in scale but not in substance from domestic violence.

In drawing attention to the brute force which lies at the heart of war, such a view has something to recommend it. Yet, there are some important aspects which are lost when associating it with such a broad category. The most crucial aspect of war which the war-as-conflict approach overlooks is its political character. The essence of modern war was best articulated by Clausewitz, who recognized that war is a social phenomenon that is geared toward political ends (Clausewitz, 1976). War is violent, unpredictable and complex, but it is set apart from other forms of violence and conflict by the political purpose to which it is put. War is the organized use of force advanced to achieve political ends.

There are a number of reasons why some contemporary critics argue that this understanding is outdated (e.g. Gray, 1997; Van Creveld, 1991). For one thing, argue critics, Clausewitz's views are specific to the social and technological conditions of his time. Just as the cavalry charge is of little use against Sherman tanks, so they claim, this understanding of war has little to tell us about war in the 21st century. This criticism sees the aims, methods and conduct of war today to be so different that insights from the Napoleonic era have little relevance. That the conduct of war has changed is clearly true, yet there is little convincing evidence that much of the organized violence in the international system is not directed toward decidedly political ends. Whether one looks at FARC guerrillas in Colombia, RUF fighters in Sierra Leone or KLA irregulars in Kosovo, to say nothing of the ambitions of US forces in Iraq, NATO forces in Afghanistan or Russian forces in the Caucasus, it is hard to see a motive that is not demonstrably political. Of course, there is a considerable degree of organized force which has economic or religious ends, but these are not, analytically speaking, wars. More precisely, while such forms are of importance, the deployment of force for purely economic and religious purposes is limited in scope and application in the contemporary system.

A second line of criticism argues that the forms of modern military force make their deployment for political purposes virtually impossible. As Van Creveld writes, 'military power is simply irrelevant as an instrument for extending or defending political interests over most of the globe' (1991: 27). The problem, as he sees it, is that modern war's ability to bring about effective political change is undermined by its all-encompassing destructive power and thus its utility as a tool of statecraft is compromised (Van Creveld, 1999). For traditionalists, the political ambitions of Clausewitz's understanding is limited to war as a policy option of states in their dealings with other states. Critics maintain that he is of little help in an era of nuclear weapons, total war, and the predominance of low-intensity conflict driven by non-state forces.

To a certain extent the critics have a point. Total war and nuclear weapons do change the calculus of war and its effectiveness to advance political ends. Yet, tying the political purposes of war to the specific policy ambitions of states takes a far too restrictive understanding of the political ends which organized violence can advance. There is a clear distinction between force used to advance political ambitions – that is those related to the structure, distribution and institutions of social power – from economic or criminal aims. These political aims may relate to states using force to achieve policy aims (such as US forces in Afghanistan), to groups seeking to advance their state ambitions (such as the PKK in Turkey) or even among groups seeking to dominate a specific territory but not to advance claims to statehood (such as the FARC in Colombia). But it is a mistake to argue that the political character of war must only mean physical contests between states or conflicts to achieve strictly state-defined aims. War is about political ambition; how that ambition is played out is a secondary consideration. From this perspective one is able to talk of a huge range of tactical variations and a wide variety of political ends. Indeed it is in this variety, of method, conduct and purpose that the experience of globalization plays itself out.

Globalization and the Opportunities of War

Globalization is a contradictory process. Just as the consumer in Strasbourg benefits from cheaper goods produced by lower wage workers in Shenzen, the workers in Alsatian factories suffer job losses as their firms lose their competitiveness. In the economic realm we are more familiar with such developments, but in the realm of warfare, such contradictory moves are less well understood. For some, globalization reduces the incidence of war as complex networks link states' interests in such a way as to make war literally unthinkable (Mandelbaum, 1998). For others, globalization and its loosening of state power in many spheres heralds a new era of barbarism, violence and warfare (Kaplan, 2000). The rich may be safe behind their walls, but beyond this realm a vicious anarchy awaits. Such an either–or view, however, is misplaced. The linkages of trade, finance and culture work at once to provide both constraints on the war-fighting instincts as well as motives for violence and opportunities to use force to achieve political goals in novel ways.

Constraining Force

One of the most common claims made about globalization is that its economic dimension makes states reluctant to use force to achieve their policy objectives. Economic linkages tie state interests to the extent that the costs of using force make it rationally unthinkable. The fact of economic interdependence is thought to be a reason why policy-makers and scholars should be reasonably sanguine about the possibility of great power war. For example, some feel that while the dispute over Taiwan is one of the most likely sources of this kind of war, the huge inward investment by Taiwanese in the People's Republic of China (PRC) and the cheap consumer goods imported by Taiwan will ensure that this does not eventuate.

This is not the first time that we have heard people arguing that economic interests are capable of trumping diverging political priorities. In the 19th century, liberals such as Cobden and Mill argued that international trade and investment would reduce the chance of conflict between states. One of the most systematic elaborations of this thesis came from the liberal thinker, Norman Angell, who attempted to show how the politics of statist nationalism of his era were wildly out of step with state economic interests (Angell, 1933). The current international system appears to closely resemble that which Angell described:

> the interdependence here indicated, cutting athwart frontiers, is largely the work of the last 40 or 50 years; and it has, during that time, so developed as to have set up a financial interdependence of the capitals of the world, so complex that disturbance in New York involves financial and commercial disturbance in London. (1933: 147)

Angell tried, unsuccessfully, to show that the costs of war in an era of complex economic interdependence were unspeakably high. The tragedy of the Second World War, and its recasting of the international system's political and economic balance, were confirmation of Angell's basic point. Perhaps the most significant difference between the contemporary period and Angell's is that statesmen and women are aware of the character of their societies' economic interests and that these perceptions constrain the tendency to use force to achieve policy goals.

The argument that economic integration reduces the likelihood of war has a number of elements. First, wars were traditionally fought to make strategic and economic gains from the losses of others. If one needed, or desired, gold, oil or diamonds that were not on one's territory then conquest was required. Of course, trade could be used to acquire limited quantities, but if sufficient strategic weight was placed on the good, such as oil, then one would be loathe to leave oneself open to the vulnerabilities which trade dependence bred. Thus imperial Japan sought to make up for its lack of geographic endowment through the seizure of oil, rubber and other commodities in East and Southeast Asia. Today, it is recognized that trade is not zero-sum and that it is cheaper and easier to buy goods rather than conquer their sources. More importantly, there is widespread support for the view among elites that the vulnerabilities of trade are not as severe as once thought and, with sufficient care, can be ameliorated or at least offset. The strength of these perceptions lies not only in the economic argument but in the fact that sufficient numbers of state elites think this way. Rosecrance takes a slight variation on this position. He argues that changes in the nature of economic production are creating conditions in which conflict over territory makes less and less sense (Rosecrance, 1999). Essentially he argues that the key factors of production have moved from being land and resources (over which one can fight) to being knowledge and capital (over which one cannot). Thus economic transformation has removed the central source of conflict among wealthy states. Of course in those parts of the world where land and resources continue to be key, war will continue, but elsewhere, the logic of globalization is, he argues, reducing the likelihood of war.

The second aspect of the economic constraint argument is more basic. States have become so dependent on international economic activity for their own domestic prosperity that they realize that international conflict, especially of the large-scale variety, is a considerable risk to domestic success. This derives from a belief that policy-makers are acutely aware of the character of their domestic economic structures and their actions are disciplined by international markets in such a way that they would not put these at risk. Alongside the domestic concerns of statesmen and women, prudence is counselled by corporate actors whose self-interest in their enterprise promotes a cautious hand in defence and foreign policy.

Some argue that in contemporary China one sees a good example of this process. The Communist Party has staked its domestic political fortune on economic prosperity which is in turn dependent upon international markets and foreign investment. Thus there are clear international and domestic pressures not to act in a militaristic fashion, whether in disputes with Japan, over Taiwan or in the South China Sea. An even more clear-cut example is the EU. The economic integration of European markets has meant that the principal catalyst of European warfare for the past two centuries – differences between France and Germany – is now implausible. There are many reasons for this, but the marrying of economic interests by the forces of globalization plays no small part. In tying states' interests into a complex web in which no state can feel itself insulated against global forces, globalization is said to reduce the propensity for states to use force for political ends.

Globalization, Vulnerability and Grievance

While globalization may constrain the urge to use force among the well off, the linkages which bring states and economies together also increase the vulnerability of those societies. Many are beginning to kick against the forces of globalization. They are reacting against both the spread of Western values and culture around the world, as well as the extremely uneven way in which its economic benefits are distributed around the globe. The World Bank notes that in the last quarter of the 20th century GDP per capita in rich states nearly doubled, but remained almost static for around two-thirds of the planet's population (UNDP, 1999). It is unsurprising that such discrepancies fuel a distinct sense of grievance. Not only does globalization provide something against which to rage, its networks of trade and finance, and the technologies which facilitate the rapid movement of people and ideas, provide both targets and the means through which force can be projected. The most obvious example of this is terrorism, which is thought to involve a substantial reaction against globalization just as its mode of delivery is made possible by the same networks (Campbell, 2002). One could not get a better display of globalization than the horrific tableau of September 11 2001. A group of well-educated middle class men from Saudi Arabia and Egypt hijacked airliners and used them as weapons to attack symbols of American power in New York and Washington, DC. The attack was planned in Afghanistan, Germany and the US, it was financed through international networks and broadcast across the globe as a live action drama. The blow that was struck, while not of great economic or strategic significance, presaged a wholesale shift in the foreign policy of the world's most important military power and, whether due to shock or jubilation, has deeply embedded itself in the psyche of all those who watched.

Terrorism and globalization are particularly well-suited bedfellows: acts of violence are motivated by global injustices exacerbated by globalization; and terrorists are able to thrive in the complex networks that transnational space has created. As one leading analyst points out, globalization appears to increase the lethality of terrorist attacks, it allows the geographic activity or 'global reach' of terrorists to be greatly enhanced, and it has increased the opportunity for terrorists to enhance their financial resources (Cronin, 2002: 46–8). More generally, the permeability of borders has created what can be described as an environment of opportunity for transnational terrorists.

Globalization has increased the options available to those who use force for political ends, it has expanded their menu of targets, and enhanced their ability to orchestrate strikes against a state or society from a great distance. The means of transportation that the processes of globalization rely upon – airliners, crude oil and LNG tankers – can be both lethal weapons and targets. As the bombings in London and Madrid made painfully clear, highly urbanized societies have an extraordinary vulnerability to indiscriminate attack. The computerized systems which run banking systems, manage traffic lights and the logistics of food transportation are all easy targets with potentially high payoffs to an interested party. A state that aims to undermine the military capabilities of an enemy would do as well to attack information systems as it would to bomb traditional military targets. In sum, globalization makes the distribution of relative capabilities in an anarchic system frighteningly complex (Cha, 2000; 399–400).

Beyond increasing the vulnerability of states and societies, and the opportunities for those who wish to exploit them, globalization is a source for war in three other ways. First, globalization provides further means for financing wars and, as will be discussed below, can provide a motive force for conflict (Berdal and Malone, 2000). Second, rather than producing a homogenized one-world culture and society, globalization appears to exacerbate the sense of social differences experienced by many. This has facilitated a growth in identity politics and has provided political momentum to some of the more vicious wars of the latter part of the 20th century. While Huntington may have over-stated his case, he is right nonetheless to draw attention to the way in which globalization has fuelled conflict through driving a sense of dislocation which has allowed elites to drive exclusivist agendas (Huntington, 1996). The world may not be on the cusp of a 'clash of civilizations', but perceived differences and ethnic politics have fuelled conflicts on the fertile ground that globalization has prepared. The remarkable degree of support for the brutish acts of al-Qa'eda is evidence of this phenomenon.

Already one consequence of the more brutal reactions to globalization has been the closure of some of the networks of global transactions. In this respect, globalization is contributing to its own closure, if not its own demise. From the increased regulation of the movement of money around the world, especially cash remittances, to the heightened costs that business have to bear through rising insurance premiums and other cost hikes that derive from terrorism and other realized threats, it is clear that globalization is not necessarily commensurate with unfettered openness. As much as many may have thought that the opening of markets was a one-way street, recent experience has shown that, under certain circumstances, markets can be closed off and transactions altered so that political priorities and not market efficiencies determine outcomes. But for some, the threats that have emerged are simply part of the package of a process which rewards some and impoverishes others (Hoffman, 2002). If we want to resolve these problems there seems little option but to wind back the openness and integration of globalization. Such pessimism is to a certain extent misplaced. Although globalization clearly enhances vulnerabilities to terrorism and other unorthodox forms of violence, and can magnify the capacity and effect of attacking groups, as a number have argued, globalization can also act to reduce threats to states and societies.

The view that globalization can work to reduce vulnerabilities has two dimensions. From the first point of view, globalization can be a means through which some of the more atavistic tendencies in human society can be ameliorated. It can enhance the wealth of the poor and reduce significant sources of tension and conflict in the world. Many have argued that the main source of international terrorism is the sense of hopeless exclusion felt by so many in the poorer parts of the planet. In a direct counter to those that argue that globalization makes societies more unsafe by provoking a sense of exclusion, the argument runs, through opening up economies, and participating in global trade, production and finance networks, the life opportunities of the poor will be enhanced and their grievances diminished. In this sense, terrorism can be overcome if globalization improves the lot of the entire planet. The second view is more technical. As noted above, one of the more typical responses to the challenges of terrorism is to close down avenues of international interaction; for example, increasing the regulation of international monetary movements, or limiting the ways that hazardous material is produced or traded across borders. Yet, for some, the best way to cope with challenges of this kind is to open borders and increase collaboration among states and firms. As Hoyt and Brooks show, state action to reduce international collaboration among firms that work with biological agents erodes the capacity to develop appropriate responses to the threat of WMD. They argue that the opportunities for cross-border and inter-firm collaboration made possible by globalization can be a potent means to combat some of the more pressing challenges posed by terrorism and other forces which have their opportunities to use force enabled by the globalization (Hoyt and Brooks, 2004).

Globalization has been attributed with being able both to reduce the likelihood of war as well as being a source of conflict and grievance. It binds states' interests and constrains the use of force. Yet it also increases the opportunity to use force for political ends in unorthodox ways, and that it enables terrorists, both in terms of increasing targets and the capacity to damage those targets from great distance. In the early years of the 21st century these actions have provoked the world's mightiest military power to undertake wars in Iraq and Afghanistan to secure its interests in what it perceives to be a world made more dangerous by globalization.

Globalization and the Conduct of War

Although we are increasingly sensitive to the insecurities which globalization brings with it, due primarily to terrorism's dominance of the popular imagination, perhaps the most important aspect of globalization's relationship with war is in its conduct.

Mercenary but not Mercenaries

Wars are still primarily fought by states (IISS, 2006). The professional armed forces of the wealthy developed states are the most effective, although some of the world's largest defence forces, such as those of the PRC or India, still rely on the strategically inferior basis of conscription to provide the bulk of the force. In raw numbers and capabilities, the panorama of modern war appears much as it has in the recent past. Military force is dominated by states. Even though high technology has allowed those bombing targets in Kandahar to do so from bases in Western Europe and even the Mid-West in the US, the concentration of military power lies with states. That said, an interesting phenomenon has emerged at the fringes of modern warfare: the growing number and influence of private military actors (PMAs).

PMAs are military and security actors who operate independently from states and undertake activities ranging from the provision of security to MNCs undertaking work in Iraq or the Caucasus, to the training of regular state-based military forces. Typical of this trend was the relatively high-profile, botched coup in Equatorial Guinea in 2004 involving PMAs from South Africa and Zimbabwe (see Roberts, 2006) and the extensive role they play in post-invasion Iraq (see Pelton, 2006). PMAs usually operate as firms and, as Singer points out, they follow the same basic aims as traditional firms, that is they seek profit and are disciplined in their behaviour by competitive pressures from the market. Importantly, as they operate on an ongoing basis, their behaviour is shaped by obligations such as corporation law and corporate regulatory frameworks (Singer, 2002: 192). In this sense these groups are not rogue gun-for-hire mercenaries, rather they are firms who provide a service for which there is a particular demand in the contemporary era. While PMAs are commonly associated with shady activities in poor and undeveloped parts of the world, with a particular affinity for Sub-Saharan Africa (e.g. Lock, 1998; Musah and Fayemi, 2000), they operate in all continents and undertake work with and within large and small states, with the rich as well as the poor (Avant, 2005). PMAs operate out of headquarters in Australia, the UK, South Africa, the US and many other countries. They have undertaken work in Sierra Leone, Ethiopia, Brazil, Russia, Iraq, Afghanistan, the Malacca Straits, Papua New Guinea, Colombia, the US, the UK, as well as many other locations around the world. This is not simply a phenomenon confined to the poorly governed and war-prone parts of the world.

Part of the reason for the geographic diversity of PMA activity lies in the wide range of services that they supply. Once again the image of the mercenary is at odds with the reality of the private provision of security service. Singer identifies three distinct types of activities that PMAs undertake (Singer, 2002: 200–2). The first, and best known, is the provision of military forces in the operational environment. The PMA can act as a private army that will fight your battle for you, or assist your forces in the operational theatre. The second is the provision of military consulting services. This service involves advice and training to military forces (whether they be state- or non-state-based) and covers a wide range of activity from infrastructure services, such as military reform and reorganization, to more hands-on operational and tactical training of regular forces. The third is to provide logistical support to military activities such as supply chain management, technical support and other supplementary services. If PMAs were only involved in the first kind of service provision then their use and geographic reach would be considerably smaller. But the huge range of services that they provide allows them to serve a much wider market and to influence the important, though often under-appreciated, areas of international security that are not at the coal face of international conflict.

For some, PMAs mark the return of mercenary to international affairs and, as harbingers of a new medievalism, are a depressing sign of a retreat of state capability in the face of globalization. For others, the emergence of PMAs is a positive development allowing the possibility of stability in parts of the world where states lack capacity and where the interests of the major powers are insufficient for them to take a stabilizing role. Many who write about PMAs also point out that they represent a significant break with the traditional Weberian understanding of states and sovereignty (e.g. Avant, 2005; Mandel,

2002; Singer, 2002). They argue that, given that the state is defined by its monopoly of the legitimate use of force, the introduction of legitimate private actors deploying force somehow undermines the state and transforms sovereignty. These concerns are misplaced. In part this is because the Weberian interpretation of the state is a rather narrow understanding of the practice of modern statehood. What states are, how they function and the kinds of role they play are defined by a great deal more than the monopoly of the legitimate use of force (see Bisley, 2004, Ch. 2). Moreover, PMAs are not replacing state power, rather they are supplementing it and are subject, ultimately, to state dictates and controls. PMAs pose more interesting questions about the ethics of the use of force. Whether one is concerned about human rights, just conduct in war, civilian control of the military or constitutional limitations on the use of force, PMAs present a series of considerable challenges to existing norms of behaviour. While the market may provide some incentives to follow the laws of war, profitability may drive action in another direction. Although the penetration of pecuniary interest into the business of war is as old as war itself, the evolution of the conduct of war in the 20th century did much to change bad habits. Some of these developments, to do with respect for human rights, the status of combatants and constitutional limits on the use of force, can be undermined by the role of private interests and actors, who are independent of the moral sanction and political control of state forces, in international security.

Why have PMAs emerged on the international stage at this point? In the past twenty years there has been a substantial change in the environment of international security (see Singer, 2003). This is, in part, to do with the end of the Cold War, but there are other reasons which relate to other forces in the international system. On the supply side, the end of the Cold War brought about a considerable downsizing of military forces the world over. From the wealthy powers, who cut their defence spending throughout the 1990s, to the client states, whose militaries had been propped up by Soviet and American support, shrinking militaries was the order of the day. Large numbers of skilled military operators were available to fill a niche which had suddenly emerged because many states had been left without the capability to cope with a rapidly changing security setting. The lingering wars in Angola, Somalia and on Russia's southern periphery are typical of these problems. But, beyond the fact that the major powers were less willing or able to provide discipline outside their core areas of interest, the number of parties interested in or requiring security services has grown significantly. One of the consequences of post-Cold War instability in much of the undeveloped world was that firms which did business in that part of the world – such as mining enterprises – began to provide demand for security service provision. It was not only instability that prompted this but also the expansion of western firms into parts of the world that had hitherto been off-limits due to Cold War politics, such as the resource-rich territories of Russia, Angola and the Central Asian republics. As Mandel notes, globalization supports what he refers to as 'the privatization of violence' because it enhances efficiency, promotes the tendency for firms, and others, to take on risk, while at the same time acting to reduce state capacity (Mandel, 2002: 36–8).

Equally, general instability prompted NGOs and IOs, as well as some insecure countries, to turn to the market for security provision. For poor countries, PMAs supply expertise and capacity they could never hope to provide for themselves and at a relatively affordable level. For NGOs and IOs, PMAs provide a flexibility of service and a political neutrality which can be useful in their line of work. The other factor which facilitated the emergence of PMAs was the rise of privatization as a public policy of choice across the developed, and in some areas of the developing, world. Pioneered by Pinochet and Thatcher, by the 1990s, almost nothing was thought to be exempt from the benefits of market provision. Spheres of public policy which had hitherto been considered the core business of the state became ripe for private provision: public transport, elements of law enforcement and the running of prisons are only three of the more notable. In such an environment, it is hardly surprising that the tendering out of security services to private contractors came to be seen as an appropriate strategy. Singer also argues that the character of modern warfare, the high-technology approach preferred by the wealthy states requires a much closer operational link between public and private spheres (2002: 195–6).

In some respects the linkages between globalization and PMAs is relatively clear but it is worth spelling out some of the salient and less evident issues. The emergence of capable and well supplied PMAs has been a response to the integration of markets around the world but it also facilitates this action as well. Where once firms might have been loathe to become involved because the risks were too high, security insurance, in the form of PMAs, is now available. While globalization may enhance some aspects of international instability, the market for private security can assuage some of the concerns that firms may have. Not only has globalization been assisted by PMAs, global financial markets make service provision more straightforward, both for clients and PMAs. The international financial system allows capital to be raised more easily so that PMAs can enhance their operations, merge with other firms and generally take advantage of the same commercial opportunities as other international firms. On the other hand, the complexity of the system can allow those who want their involvement with these organizations to be less than clear – whether this be criminal groups who wish to raise their technical capacities or states who want to keep the involvement of PMAs from public view – to act with relative anonymity. The rise of private military service providers makes access to military power cheaper than ever before and more widely available to both state and non-state actors. Where previously the costs of maintaining a high technology weapon system or a well trained special forces unit was beyond the reach of all but a few very rich states, now firms, poor states, rebel movements and criminal organizations can tap into cutting edge weapon systems and military units to advance their own ends.

Overall, therefore, PMAs make the international security environment more complex and more morally adaptable. While it may be opportune for firms to take advantage of these services, for states and their military forces, rules of engagement with PMAs are less than clear, as are lines of responsibility and accountability. The small but growing role of PMAs in the international system is indicative of a subtle but important shift in the balance between public and private power and authority. Hitherto dominant public authority is being slowly moved by the capacities and ideals of the private sector (Muthien and Taylor, 2002). PMAs have not fundamentally revolutionized warfare and international security, but the environment of modern warfare has a new element which reflects some of the more salient features of globalization.

Barbarism and 'New' Civil Wars

Along with the return of military force in the service of profit, it is argued that many wars in the contemporary era share a number of characteristics which indicate a break with the classical Clausewitzian understanding of war (for examples of this literature see: Collier, 2000; Gray, 1997; Holsti, 1996; Kaldor, 1999; Keen, 1998). First, they are said to involve a high degree of barbarism and gratuitous violence. Force has ceased to be a means to a political end, instead it is gratuitous and its brutality goes far beyond that driven by the instrumental logic which is at the heart of traditional wars. Second, it is argued that these wars are driven by emotional and identity-based motives and not political state-based ambitions. Third, wars are said to be funded in novel ways and produce distinctive means through which they can generate wealth for their protagonists. Rather than relying on state financing through taxation and other means, conflict is funded through access to global markets where loot from the conflict is traded for ready cash, through financial networks and from diaspora communities. These networks provide a distinctive means not only to finance conflict, but also to line the pockets of the elites. In some cases the raising of revenue is said to have become the purpose of war. For example, Charles Taylor, the former rebel leader and President of Liberia, is reported to have made around USD 400 million per year from the Liberian civil war of the early 1990s (e.g. Duffield, 2000: 82). As a result of these traits, these conflicts are extremely hard to resolve and their very nature inhibits reconciliation and rehabilitation.

From this view, new wars are not fought for political purposes, nor are they informed by a state oriented ideology. Instead, war has become a criminal endeavour characterized by brutality and an emotive character. For these writers, war has become 'economics by other means'. Yet, many of these claims have been contested in recent years. In spite of the ethnic colouring to conflict in the former Yugoslavia and elsewhere, scholars have shown that these identity based conflicts had a significant political dimension (e.g. de Graaff, 2005; Sambanis, 2001). Moreover, the barbarism of wars in Sierra Leone, Chechnya, Kosovo and Angola may horrify but it is hardly a new phenomenon of war. As Kalyvas shows, to argue that needless violence in Africa is new overlooks the gratuitous and unjustifiable violence of so many old wars. From the Somme to Dresden, the bombing of Tokyo to North Vietnam, excessive force of a barbaric kind was the hallmark of many of the classical wars of the 20th century (Kalyvas, 2001).

While these authors are right to point out the novel ways in which global markets provide opportunities to fund conflicts and to profit from them, they go too far to argue that it is greed and not grievance that drives conflict. While it may make for interesting rhetoric, the wars spluttering along in Sri Lanka, Colombia, Angola and elsewhere are manifestly not, as Lévy claims, wars without meaning (Lévy, 2004). Their meaning derives from old-fashioned political ends. These political ends may be more local in origin than once they were, to do with class or tribal cleavages, but again there is nothing new in this (Kalyvas, 2001). Civil wars have always been complex networks of competing loyalties, shifting and often uneasy alliances. To emphasize this as something new is to forget the old and badly underplays the perennial political character of contemporary conflict (see Berdal, 2005).

That said, we should not utterly ignore studies of new wars for they draw our attention to a number of pertinent issues, the most obvious of which is the shifting character of war. While it may be that war has certain basic features, it has a huge variety of modalities and in the contemporary international system the predominant form of war is low intensity civil conflict. Moreover, claims about new wars underline the ways in which globalization provides opportunities for war. Global networks enhance funding opportunities, they provide increased scope to access material and the expertise to fight a war.

Revolutions in War

Among the wealthy, where one finds the most militarily significant, the element of strategic life that has been of greatest interest since the mid 1990s has been the introduction of technologically sophisticated war fighting systems that, in the eyes of some, have ushered in a 'revolution in military affairs' (see generally Freedman, 1998). Revolutions in military affairs (RMAs) are regular, if infrequent, occurrences. The use of longbows at Agincourt, revolutionary France's *levée en masse* and the emergence of ballistic missiles and long range nuclear weapons are thought to be archetypal (Knox and Murray, 2001). RMAs are associated with radical changes in the technology of war fighting, but, as Gray points out, they do not necessarily produce enhanced strategic effectiveness in the sense that they do not always help force to achieve political ends more effectively than the old ways (2002).

Following the perceived success of the 1991 Persian Gulf War, the sense that an RMA was emerging derived from the rapid application of stealth technology, widespread electronic surveilance and target acquisition equipment, and the acquisition of precision munitions and sophisticated networked communications by all parts of the armed forces. While aspects of the RMA are experienced in many states across the world, it is primarily associated with the transformation of the American military. These technologies provide a decisive advantage to the holder and they were used to assuage the political concerns of the populations of wealthy states who had become particularly casualty shy (Freedman, 1998; O'Hanlon, 2000).

The evidence thus far supports a more cautious assessment of the 1990s RMA. As recent experience in Iraq and Afghanistan has made all too obvious, the US has found it much harder to turn this RMA advantage into strategic effectiveness than expected. That is to say, the policy ends which the US seeks to achieve through its use of force have not been achieved. In part, this is a problem with the American military (see Gray, 2005), but it is also due to a recognition by opponents that the advantages of technologically sophisticated American military power can be negated through the adoption of effective tactics. Indeed, as a recent survey of military matters notes, the strategic environment which western military planners now face is a long way from the one they had expected in the late 1990s (IISS, 2005: 411).

While the RMA has not provided the US and its allies with the kind of decisive strategic advantage that some of its more enthusiastic proponents had envisaged, the US is continuing to pursue a policy of technologically advanced conventional predominance. This dominance is the most important element of global strategy at present and has prompted several key reactions. For allies of the US, American predominance has led to a general tightening of alliance relationships and there appears to be little interest or appetite for any conventional attempt to balance American military power. Although European politicians may mouth platitudes about defence capability their unwillingness to spend enough even to maintain alliance commitments, let alone establish some kind of replacement for American power, is typical. In the Asia-Pacific, allies are snuggling ever closer to the US, with the notable exception of South Korea, and while the PRC may not be pleased with the situation it realizes that, in the short term, its interests are best served through the current strategic setting. There is not, and nor is there likely to be, a conventional strategic competitor in the short to medium term. The only possible source of anything resembling a challenge appears to come from the PRC but that is many years away and even then not especially likely.

Of greater significance has been the response of America's self-styled adversaries both state- and non-state-based. The terrorist forces of al-Qa'eda, insurgents in Iraq, the Taliban, as well as Iran and North Korea, have all undertaken strategies to mitigate or negate American conventional strength. They have undertaken what are known as 'asymmetric approaches', that is, they adopt tactics that make conventional strength either ineffective or redundant. For example, they undertake combat in unforgiving terrain where US force is much less effective or they pursue nuclear weapon acquisition which provides insurance against conventional force superiority (IISS, 2005: 412–15).

Globalization is clearly shaping the arena of conflict, it provides opportunities for a vast array of actors, and particularly those with unconventional tactics, to make decisive strategic actions in world politics. Globalization has changed the character of strategic threats and the means through which force is organized, and also provides opportunities to respond to threats through enhanced global communications and organization. Yet while strategic effectiveness is still shaped by the predominance of politics over force – something which globalization has not changed – the modalities of conflict and the tactics to advance political ends are undergoing transformation. As Guéhenno notes, 'global leaders of today have probably more power and less control than their predecessors' (1998: 19).

Why Fight? Globalization and the Purposes of War

The motive and purpose of wars is central to any assessment of the character and indeed nature of warfare. Determining when to fight and for what ends has important strategic, tactical and operational consequences. From determination of large-scale spending priorities to the basic training of enlisted soldiers, the purpose of war is a fundamental concern. As a cursory glance at any of the multitudinous volumes on the causes of war will show, wars are fought for many reasons (e.g. Howard, 1983; Waltz, 1959). While there has yet to be any definitive scholarly consensus on the causes of war, the motives for fighting wars are nonetheless evident and speak to dominant interests and values in the societies which fight. The idea of honour, as well as fear and power, have all played a fundamental part in motivating wars across the centuries. In the oft quoted words of Thucydides: 'what made war inevitable was the growth of Athenian power and the fear which this caused in Sparta' (1972: Book 1, 23). War has been fought for instrumental reasons, to expand territory and to acquire wealth and treasure, and to resolve international disputes. In the 20th century ideology and revolution were central components of many of the more devastating conflicts (Halliday, 1999; Walt, 1996). Freedom from foreign control has been a further motivation for war and a relatively recent development has been wars fought in the name of humanity and human rights (Coker, 2001).

One of the most notable developments in the history of warfare has been the radical change in attitudes to war that emerged during the 20th century. It is not widely recognized, but the system of international law centred around the UN has been remarkably successful at changing the moral attitude toward and conduct of war. The use of force has become far more narrowly proscribed – under the current system it can only be used legitimately for self-defence or when approved for specific purposes by the UN Security Council – and, most crucially, this proscription has been accepted by the vast majority of the UN member states. This does not mean that war has been outlawed, but the past century has witnessed a radical transformation in attitudes toward the use of force: its role in dispute resolution, in advancing economic interests and, more generally, as a legitimate tool in the foreign policy kit has been severely curtailed (Finnemore, 2003). The final section of the chapter explores the relationship between globalization and the changing attitude to war. Specifically, it looks at the claims made about the obsolescence of major power war and the rise of humanitarian wars.

The Death of Major War?

There are a number of empirical propositions which have established a correlation between the absence of conflict between states and specific socio-economic conditions within them. The most prominent of these is Michael Doyle's observation that, thus far, no mature properly democratic states have fought wars against one another (Doyle, 1983). The key to this empirical claim lies in the definition of democracy, but with a relatively robust conception (involving full franchise, a stable electoral system where governments come and go along constitutional lines and a relatively open system of governance) the empirical observation appears valid. Another, less sophisticated, view is that countries which have a McDonald's hamburger chain do not fight wars against each other (Friedman, 1999). This was true until the NATO bombing campaign of Yugoslavia in 1999 when the presence of the recently-opened McDonald's in Belgrade put paid to that claim. But the logic underpinning the view has some purchase. There seems to be some empirical basis to the fundamental view that once states achieve a certain level of economic development they no longer fight each another.

These trends have led a number of scholars to argue that major war among the large, wealthy and militarily most capable is becoming obsolete (Mandelbaum, 1998; Mueller, 1989). These scholars argue not that war among major powers is an impossibility, rather that large-scale conflict among wealthy, militarily capable and strategically significant states is extremely unlikely. And globalization's linkage of interests, as well as a recognition of this state of affairs, reinforces this trend.

There are a number of reasons why this is thought to be the case. One strand of thinking sees the obsolescence of major war as part of a longer-run historical tendency (e.g. Mueller, 1989). The recognition that war fails to achieve viable political results and a broader moral rejection of war is thought to be making its practice obsolete. Although war appears to be something we must simply endure – thought to be normal, necessary even – this line of thinking argues that war is a product of normative preferences and, as such, is subject to change. Slavery, duelling and gold as currency were all thought to be indelibly part of the human condition, yet they disappeared. In such a fashion, major war is being made a thing of the past. Of course, just as slavery persists in parts of the world, war continues, but rather than the norm it will be as exceptional as slavery is today.

A second line of thinking makes a more instrumental argument. This approach puts the increasing cost and the diminishing benefits of war at the heart of its obsolescence. The costs of large-scale war – understood in financial, political and human terms – are thought to be simply too high for any wealthy state to bear (Mandelbaum, 1998). When these costs are put alongside the perception that there are few benefits to be gained from war that cannot be acquired more cheaply and effectively through less violent political means, then major power war is thought to have little future. A third view is that the highly destructive nature of nuclear weapons, and modern warfare more generally, has nullified war's political effectiveness (Van Creveld, 1999). How can war achieve any meaningful political goal when fighting one produces such utter devastation?

Is globalization supporting this trend? At first glance, it appears to reinforce the historical trend against major power war. Not only do the networks of production, investment and trade produce the constraints against war noted earlier in the chapter, it is the global recognition by policy-makers that economic benefits are positive-sum and not zero-sum that has changed the minds of statesmen and women. Moreover, the flow of information through global media networks has also served to reinforce the growing sensitivity to casualties among the wealthy states. Given that all of the OECD economies are democracies this appears to have an added heft. Conflict may be thought to have some electoral cachet, but large-scale casualties, of the kind experienced by America in Vietnam or Korea, are politically unthinkable.

But on closer inspection, the analysis is not entirely compelling and realists see this kind of thinking as naïve at best and downright dangerous at worst. While few can dispute the recent empirical basis of the obsolescence thesis (the Iran–Iraq war was the last major state–state conflict fought among relatively well-off powers) the reasoning underpinning the argument, some claim, is wrong. There are two strands of response. On the one hand, some argue that war among major powers is an inevitable product of the structure of the international state system (e.g. Mearsheimer, 2001; Waltz, 1993). While the circumstances of the 1990s and early 2000s have been relatively peaceful, to say it marks the end of great power war based on this experience is akin to saying that gravity has been banished by the invention of aircraft. No amount of economic or cultural inter-connection will remove the underlying conflictual character of the system. The other argument draws on a more basic understanding of human character. Human beings have always fought. There is no evidence that the basic elements of human character have changed in recent years and that, for as long as people have competing political ends, then war will be part of the human condition (Gray, 1999).

How can we reconcile these two views? It is clear that globalization is making states perceive that their interests, and particularly those related to their economies, are more reliant on developments beyond their borders and are thus more likely to avoid war as a means to advance them. Moreover, most of the wealthy major powers are to be found in strategically stable parts of the world and are still heavily influenced by the Cold War perceptions of friends and enemies. So while globalization contributes to the trend of the declining chance of great power war it is not its prime cause. However, while globalization has changed the configuration and conception of interests we must recognize that interests and politics are not coterminous. That is, interests are only one aspect of the political ends to which the use of force is put. Nationalism can be highly valued and have a political premium even though it may not serve any clear-cut economic or rational instrumental purpose. The important point that scholars such as Gray reinforce is that states conceive of their political ends in broader terms than many liberals believe. Equally, the politics of alliances and credibility can contribute in vital ways to the escalation of conflict, as we saw with Kosovo. As such, unless globalization significantly reconfigures state conceptions of political ends, major power war cannot be said to be off the menu of world politics.

Globalization contributes to the forces which have reduced the likelihood of major power war. But it is not some kind of irreversible process by which war among nations has been banished. That said, there is little evidence to support the view that there has been a shift away from a purposive and rational understanding of modern war. Of course globalization has changed the context and the mechanisms, but there is little evidence that it has changed its nature.

Humanitarian War

Among the wealthy and more globalized states and societies it is clear that large-scale war is something that few are interested in or prepared to undertake. That is not to say that war has gone altogether, rather that economic interests and political structures, alongside the massive predominance of American military power, make large-scale war an unlikely proposition. But it is a mistake to conclude that this is indicative of a moral rejection of the use of force. War and warriors have not succumbed to some kind of law of diminishing returns for valorization. The population of wealthy states may have a distaste for the violence of war, but their appetite for memorials to the fallen and praise of the warrior continues unabated. The wealthy continue to value the idea of war even if they are uneasy with the reality of conflict. The growing sense that the use of force as a tool of foreign policy is illegitimate is also tempered by a considerable enthusiasm for humanitarian wars and the deployment of force to deal with complex emergencies. Indeed not only is the use of force to advance humanitarian ends and to protect human rights seen to be the kind which wealthy states support, there is an emergence, though not a consensus, that there is a moral imperative to undertake these kinds of actions.

Some argue that 'humanitarian war' is an oxymoron and they may be right. Any examination of the wars fought in the name of humanitarian intent in the 1990s shows little longer-run humanitarian benefit. Whether in Kosovo or Somalia, East Timor or Rwanda, humanitarian forces arrived too late, exacerbated the violence and left too soon to achieve the kind of outcomes envisaged (see e.g. Welsh, 2004). Yet in spite of this and a broader moral move away from war, there is definite support for the deployment of force to deal with humanitarian crises.

If the rich do not fight one another, yet they retain considerable military budgets, to what ends do they put their military force? With the exception of the US, whose military dwarfs all others in terms of size, geographic scope, role and function, wealthy developed states are willing to use force only under very specific circumstances. They will fight in the name of international law (1991 Persian Gulf War), they will fight to defend themselves if attacked (Britain in the Falkland Islands) and they will fight to achieve humanitarian objectives (the NATO campaign for Kosovo or the British deployment to Sierra Leone). The deployment of force is strictly limited to these circumstances (and preferably, though not exclusively, with the blessing of the UN Security Council) and it is very hard to envisage circumstances in which most wealthy states would undertake military action of any other kind.

The first and third of these circumstances have been particularly influenced by the growing authority of cosmopolitan rules, norms and institutions. The growth of a sense that shared values and obligations warrant particular kinds of action has been fuelled to a certain extent by globalization (see generally, Brown, 2002, Ch. 8). The increasing awareness of distant events that is the product of global media networks and a much greater sensitivity to global events which stems from economic interdependence reinforces the notions of common belonging and common obligation. That said, the use of force is rarely undertaken simply for the sake of ideals, interests of a political and strategic kind are still necessary to mobilize and justify deployment. Yet, it is telling that, in the build-up to the US-led intervention in Iraq in 2003, the *casus belli* was portrayed in traditional security terms: Iraq posed a clear and present threat to international security of such an acute kind and had contravened UN Security Council demands so many times that action was required. Yet once the intervention had revealed that such claims were largely hollow, the justification for war very rapidly turned to the language of human rights, democracy and humanitarianism. Suddenly Iraq had become a large-scale response to chronic human rights abuse. Military action in this case could be defended on humanitarian grounds – an exercise in cynicism equal to the novelty that the circumstances reflected. Globalization is not the sole cause for the heightened political purchase that humanitarian ideals have in many parts of the world. Rather, it is the linkages which it fosters – through the mass media as well as through trade and investment flows – that reinforce the ability of these ideas to resonate and thus contribute to action being taken.

Globalization, War and the International System

The kinds of wars societies fight and the way they fight them reflect their technological capabilities as well as political and moral priorities. The industrial revolution turned warfare, always a brutal business, into mass slaughter and paved the way for the blurring of distinctions between civilian and soldier, and total war which was so characteristic of war in the 20th century. In so doing not only did it change the technical practice of war-fighting, it changed the way war related to politics. It did not transform the nature of war, but the way war was fought and the ends to which it was put were different from what had come before. While globalization, so far, has not matched the radical social transformations of the industrial revolution, it has already contributed to some important, though subtle, shifts to the face of modern war.

Most significantly, globalization has helped to change the strategic and security environment of international politics. Globalization facilitates a widening of threats against which states and societies need to secure themselves. Terrorism is the best known and most widely appreciated example, but the volume and speed of airline travel has hugely increased the chances of infectious diseases travelling rapidly around the world. The most disastrous social event to befall the Asia-Pacific in recent years was the 1997–98 financial crisis, an event that demonstrates the dual opportunities and challenges presented by global financial systems. Second, globalization insists that traditional responses to threats need to change. Moreover, as groups such as al-Qa'eda have shown, globalization provides strategic opportunities both for attack and for defence and states which seek to deflect these threats need to show an equivalent nimbleness. Traditional approaches such as deterrence, at least as conventionally practised, are often simply inappropriate in this new environment. Third, globalization has increased the number and character of actors in the international strategic environment, it has improved their access to sophisticated weapons and has advanced their capacity to have strategic effect. Whether through PMAs, or attacks on the vulnerabilities opened up by globalization, a much wider range of groups is able to apply lethal force across considerable distance to remarkable effect. This kind of organized lethal force was once the preserve of powerful states. Now not only has there been a huge explosion in the number of states, the vast majority can access sufficient force to make trouble, to say nothing of the expanded range and reach of terrorist and criminal organizations. As such, globalization has decisively enhanced the power and influence of private actors in the international system.

Although the obsolescence thesis has some empirical validity, and globalization acts to increase the linkage of interests among states, it does not mean that war among states has disappeared altogether. Equally, violent political conflict is presently manifested most prominently in civil wars and low-intensity conflict. The power and capacity of the wealthy states to fight large wars is matched by their inappropriateness for the majority of conflicts in the world today. As the US intervention in Iraq demonstrates so clearly, it is virtually impossible to defend against America's overwhelming conventional military power – a force that is geared for large-scale high-intensity warfare. If the US wanted, it could probably successfully invade and defeat, in conventional military terms, almost all of the members of the UN. But as Iraq has equally shown, success in the military conquest of a state is only one part of the process through which political aims can be achieved. In part, US difficulties in Iraq reflect the structure and training of the US military. But it is also a function of a disjuncture between policy goals and the military means to achieve them. The lack of fit between most of the military forces in the world and the strategic challenges thrown up by globalization should be cause for serious policy reflection. It is not that major war is never going to happen again, but the military challenges faced by Britain, France or South Africa are of a kind that are unsuited to a conventional military trained to fight large-scale wars. War is still, as the Prussian general observed, politics by other means. Globalization has made the 'other means' more complex and the aims and ambitions of the political actors, and the structures they seek to change, have likewise been subtly changed.

7

Identity, Nationalism and Globalization

Many argue that globalization is not only transforming how we live, and the institutions which govern us, it is changing who we are. Globalization is destabilizing the traditional cultural systems that forge individual and collective identity and is creating new mechanisms through which individuals find meaning and a sense of belonging in an increasingly complex world. From novel cultural forms to the global spread of McDonald's, the force of globalization is said to be transforming the means with which we make sense of ourselves and the larger world. The view that globalization is driving a reconstruction of many facets of identity and culture is articulated most directly by those who feel that it is a process of cultural homogenization (e.g. Latouche, 1996). The forces which unify markets and drive political and moral authority away from states are also serving to homogenize culture and identity and draining national and local forms of their meaning and capacity to mobilize popular sentiment. For some, this involves not a new melange or hybrid creation but an overt Americanization of other cultures (see Holton, 1998: 166–72). In the ubiquity of Starbucks, Hollywood movies and the transformation of dietary habits and patterns one sees the forces of a cultural imperialism made more disturbing by the eagerness with which it is embraced. For others, globalization threatens societies by projecting new ideas and practices across borders, destabilizing existing cultural values and institutions. Globalization is thus thought not to be a source of unification or homogenization but of division and social discord (see e.g. Barber, 1995). Perhaps the most clear-cut example of this is Huntington's controversial argument that the increasing interaction of globalization increases the sense of difference among peoples and exacerbates conflictual tendencies which derive from a growing sense of otherness and cultural threat (1996). Violent clashes will flare up where different cultural and identity-based groupings bump up against one another, what he refers to as the 'fault lines of civilization'. From this perspective globalization will transform the source of conflict, where in the 20th century it was produced by diverging ideologies and interests, in the 21st it will derive from the value systems that underpin different cultures and civilizations.

From the often reproduced pictures of Masai tribesmen in Southern Africa talking on their mobile phones to the celebration of an American Sumo wrestling champion's promotion to the highest rank, globalization appears more real in culture than in almost any other sphere. In that sense one cannot consider the contemporary character of globalization without spending some time on this dimension. Moreover, while few accept the Huntington thesis in its entirety, many sense that the consequences of changes in identity and culture for social, economic and political structures may well be considerable. Equally, there is a growing recognition that questions of culture and identity are increasingly important to the patterns of world politics (see e.g. Jacquin-Berdal *et al.*, 1998; Lapid and Kratochwil, 1996). The focus of this book, therefore, requires consideration of how matters of culture and identity are being influenced by globalization. The sprawling terrain of such a field, from music to religion, class to popular art forms, means that one cannot do justice to all the ways in which this occurs in the confines of a single chapter. The focus here will be restricted to the ways in which globalization and processes of collective identity intersect, with a particular focus on the dynamics of modern nationalism.

The 20th century was, in many respects, the century of nationalism. In the contest of political ideals it vanquished virtually all foes. It lay at the core of the fascist challenge to socialism and liberal capitalism, it was central to the collapse of Soviet communism and it sits at times uneasily with the political structures of modern democracy. Its genius lies in its capacity to forge a profound link between two extremely powerful forces: human desire to belong to a group and the modern state. Nationalism acts as a kind of sociological glue which binds the abstract principles of sovereignty and statehood to the populations over which they hold sway. In short, nationalism serves to make states real. Yet if globalization is changing the material structures of states, and society is being influenced by both these changes and shifts in the economic realm, it is not unreasonable to conclude that something must be afoot in the politics of identity and its relationship with nationalism given that it acts as the bridge between these two spheres.

This chapter will analyze the ways in which globalization is influencing dominant forms of collective identity and will consider the contradictory ways in which identity formation is intersecting with globalization. The chapter first looks at the notion of identity and provides an overview of the dominant way in which this is manifested in world politics. Second, the chapter considers the challenges of globalization to culture and identity and considers how these influence the politics of collective identity in world politics and concludes with an assessment of their consequences for the international system.

Identity, Nationalism and International Relations

There is a growing realization of the importance of questions of identity in IR (e.g. *Millennium*, 1999). This is evident in the growing recognition of the importance of nationalism to world politics. From students of war and strategy to international economics few would deny the power and pervasiveness of nationalism for the conduct of the modern international system. The revival of a more bloodthirsty variety in the 1990s in Europe, Africa and beyond has further reinforced the view that one cannot talk meaningfully about the structure of modern international society without discussing nationalism. Nationalism is a protean social phenomenon and its highly variable manifestations, both progressive and retrograde, has thus generated an extensive debate in the scholarly literature (e.g. Day and Thompson, 2004). As a central point linking processes of identity formation and consolidation with world politics and globalization it is necessary to provide a brief sketch of the basic notion of identity and how it relates to the various meanings attributed to nationalism.

Varieties of Collective Identity and Nationalism

In general, notions of identity relate to the ways in which a sense of being and belonging is created and sustained and is generally thought of as the means through which individuals make sense of themselves. In this sense identity formation is the means through which cultural processes intersect with both individual cognitive mechanisms and broader political and economic forces to foster a specific notion of being and belonging. The individual's cognitive faculties absorb cultural, political and economic forces on a constant basis and the process of identity formation involves the interaction of these in such a way that it forges a sense of self in relation to these external and internalized forces. Material, cultural and ideational factors all shape an individual's sense of themselves and the way in which they relate to others. Identity is thus a particular configuration of ideas about self-definition and about the links individuals forge with others. It refers to the way individuals make sense of themselves in the world but it also presents them with a place in the world. Identity is not only individualistic, in the sense that it provides an internal mechanism for being and belonging, it locates the individual within broader human society. Identity is not only about who you are but it is also fundamentally bound up in the groups to which you belong. The nature of the relationships the individual has, both with others and with other groups, is fundamentally influenced by the shape of one's identity. It provides not only a basic feature of human existence, it lies at the heart of many questions relating to rules, laws, duties, distribution of resources, and politics more generally.

Collective identity refers to the way in which the emphasis in the individual's sense of self is shaped by a set of collective relationships. The term denotes the means through which people construct their sense of self by group affiliation. Collective identity does not necessarily mean that the individual is less important than the group, rather it refers to the way in which modes of identity place greater emphasis on collective being and belonging than on an individualistic version. Collective identity can derive from a shared religious affiliation. For example, the Islamic notion of the *ummah* conveys the idea that all followers belong to a larger group of faith. It is constructed through the production of ideas, images and symbols which are said to describe and denote group distinctiveness. The processes of identity formation, both collective and individual, are primarily conducted through cultural means. The writing of history, the building of museums, the telling of stories are all cultural mechanisms through which it can be fostered. In the 20th century, nationalism has become the dominant form of collective identity. Of course individuals have many collective identities and they do not demand exclusivity: one can be British, Catholic, a member of a trade union and a season ticket holder at Arsenal Football Club. But, the most widespread, most politically powerful, and for the concerns of world politics, the most significant form of collective identity is nationalism.

It is tempting to say that there are as many definitions of nationalism as there are nations. The origins of this lie, in part, in attempts to craft a final theory of nationalism which covers all its varieties, one that explains its revitalization in recent years and its mobilization capacity, as well as its association with some of the more horrific political programmes of modern times. Even when one moves beyond attempts to craft master theories of nationalism one can see widely diverging assessments of its nature and character which relate to different versions of how it constitutes collective identity. Perhaps the most basic distinction is between those versions of nationalism which argue that it is a political phenomenon and those which argue that it is fundamentally cultural. For some, nationalism is, at its heart, a political ideal that is most closely associated with the achievement and defence of statehood. The nation is a function of the political institution of the modern state and collective identity is a product of centralized political institutions and conjugated through political and legal mechanisms such as citizenship (e.g. Motyl, 1999). The nation is a means to organize society, to bind it to the central bodies of authority and power and to provide it with the social coherence required to meet the demands of modern life.

In contrast, some argue that understanding nationalism as a functional political process cannot adequately explain its capacity to resonate in people's minds. The power of this form of collective identity – its ability to unite highly disparate and sizeable populations – comes not from the cold legalism of political institutions but from culture. Nationalism, from this perspective, is about the advancement and preservation of distinctive cultural communities, whether they embody the institutions of statehood or not (Connor, 1994). This view does not deny the political dimensions of nationalism, instead it emphasizes that politics is not necessarily central to the phenomenon and it stresses that the political manifestations of nationalism are not only limited to questions of statehood. A third view sees nationalism as a programme which fuses politics and culture. From this perspective, nationalism is an overt social programme creating and reinforcing a particular form of collective identity which is inherently both political and cultural. In the words of one of the leading authors of this position, it involves the '"culturalization" of politics and the "politicization" of culture' (Özkirimli, 2005: 21–2).

Nationalism's harnessing of individuals' identity-needs has a purpose (to achieve statehood or to maintain a cultural identity), and argument about that purpose leads on to debate about the means through which these ends are achieved. If one feels that nationalism is about forging collective identity to create political community, how does it go about this process? There are two major approaches which distinguish between the different ways in which group sentiment is created and, implicitly, suggest differences in degrees of openness, malleability and rootedness of forms of nationalism. Ethnic nationalism is perhaps the best known form. It takes the view that nations are a product of ethnic markers such as race, religion, language and culture (see generally Connor, 1994). Ethnic understandings of nationalism are premised on the view that cultural communities are homogeneous, that they are fixed by these markers and that creation and defence of the nation derives from the valorization of these properties. In this sense, it is said to be overtly exclusionary and, in many cases, highly deterministic. You cannot choose to join a nation; it is chosen for you. You may move territory but you never leave your nation behind. It is often associated with nationalism's more vicious manifestations, such as the bloody attempts to create ethnically 'pure' territories out of the former Yugoslav Republic. Yet in both Japan and Germany one sees less vicious but equally fixed views of the nation whereby laws of citizenship and notions of national identity are linked to birth and blood and not loyalty oaths or shared values.

As distinct from this, civic nationalism sees common identity as deriving from a shared set of values. Membership of the nation is not contingent on the capacity to speak a language, profess a faith or demonstrate bloodlines but from a consensual acceptance of the rights and obligations of the political community (e.g. Ignatieff, 1994). Civic nationalism is generally associated with the idea of the nation as a community of equals where sovereignty lies with 'the people' but it can equally have an illiberal character. Collective identity can be based on a shared commitment to the principles and institutions of fascism just as it is based on liberalism. It emphasizes that the creation of the nation through forging a powerful sense of collective identity does not derive from fixed ethnic markers but from civic and political principles and institutions. Perhaps the best contemporary example of this is modern American nationalism (Lieven, 2004). Civic nationalism is thought to be more open: membership of the community derives not from determination but choice and it is open to all who subscribe. For ethnic understandings the opposite is thought to be true. Indeed for many it is precisely its closed and fixed nature which makes it so appealing. Yet most citizens of the supposedly civic nations acquire their citizenship from birth not choice. Equally, while civic nationalism is more open than a nationalism built on blood or ethnicity, the opportunity to join and participate in a political community in practice is never as straightforward as the adherence to a creed.

Nationalism's dominance of the politics of collective identity, both in domestic and international terms, is a product of its remarkable capacity to fire the minds of people to such an extent that they are willing to lay down their lives for the idea. Precisely how it has this effect is unclear. For some the answer lies in its origins. Nations derive their power over people from the basic human desire to belong to groups. Thus the cultural basis of modern political communities is much the same as it has ever been – it derives from humanity's innate desire to be part of a group. In contrast, some argue that the national version of collective identity is decisively modern; it is not only the language of nations and nationalism that emerged in the 18th and 19th century, but the idea of nations, exclusive political and cultural communities that belong to a particular territory, and which command absolute loyalty from the population is thought to be a distinctly modern creation. For some, the idea was self-consciously created by elites to advance their interests and aims (e.g. Kedourie, 1966). For others it was the product of the needs of industrial capitalism which required the construction of a uniform national culture (Gellner, 1983). Others argue that industrial production technologies allowed people to imagine that they belonged to an exclusive community in a way and form that was hitherto impossible (Anderson, 1983). The Marxist understanding of nationalism is emblematic of these views: nationalism is a product of a stage of human development that will pass away when those economic conditions which gave rise to them also pass on (e.g. Hobsbawm, 1990).

Yet these modernist-functional explanations do not satisfactorily answer the core question. Why should we feel impassioned by what is little more than a cultural by-product of the industrial revolution? Why do we feel that it is right to fight and die for the nation if it is but a concept created by elites? In response, Smith argues that, although nations are modern, their capacity to resonate derives from their ability to link contemporary sense of identity with a past and an imagined future. He argues that its power is derived from the authenticity of the link that collective identity has with the past: the linkage of modern institutions with premodern symbols, images, myths and memories creates the national affiliation (Smith, 1998; 2001). The quasi-spiritual power of the national idea derives from its invocation of premodern social forms and their ability to strike a chord with modern society and to bind individuals to a group with a past, present and a future.

Where one stands on questions related to the purpose, mechanism and origins of nations and nationalism is likely to shape one's assessment of its interaction with globalization and the central question is the relationship of nationalism with the state. The state is able to achieve three related though distinct ends through nationalism. First, it provides a compelling and efficient means to achieve social cohesion within its territory. Second, nationalism provides the state with legitimacy and facilitates state institutions, particularly novel formations, in their efforts to embed themselves in society. Upon coming to power in Iran, Khomeini and his supporters used a strongly internationalist rhetoric, yet when faced with internal instability and external threat from Iraq, the language, imagery and policies of the Iranian state took a distinctly nationalist turn (Abrahamian, 1993). Third, nationalism provides a means through which social transformation can be achieved. This refers both to the brutal attempts to create racially or ethnically 'pure' societies, but also to the efforts undertaken by many states to transform the economic basis of their society. Economic nationalism, a vital part of the international economic order, is often neglected in studies of nationalism yet viewed either from the international or from the state point of view it is an important part of the picture (but see Mayall, 1990).

This chapter is interested in nationalism understood as a programmatic political principle that fuses states with the societies that they rule through the assertion that a specific population belongs

Table 7.1   Summary of theories of national collective identity

---

Essential dynamic of collective identity
- *Political* – identity is determined in relation to political institutions
- *Cultural* – identity is a function of cultural community
- *Fusion* – identity is a fusion of political and cultural processes

Mechanism of inclusion
- *Ethnic* – membership of collective is a function of ethnic markers such as blood lines and language
- *Civic* – membership of collective is a function of participation in civic community

Origins
- *Perennial* – national collective identity is a result of inherent human desire to belong to groups
- *Modern* – national collective identity is a function of modern social conditions such as capitalism and industrialization
- *Ethno-symbolist* – national collective identity gains its power from real historical ethnic origins

State use
- *Social cohesion*
- *Legitimacy*
- *Instrument for change*

---

exclusively to a particular state. It places a moral and political priority on the national form of collective identity. It does not insist that all other forms of identity are extinguished, but it does make clear that when forced to choose among differing forms, the national prevails. It can be played out in ethnic, civic, economic and cultural ways, but its primary function is to provide social cohesion to a population that is governed by a state. It can be used to mobilize action to create new states and societies from existing states or to claim territory or populations not presently recognized as their own.

In choosing to limit our focus of collective identity on nationalism in this way does not deny the reality of nationalisms which are less concerned with statehood or which see cultural homogeneity as an end in itself, nor does it deny that there are other forms of collective identity at work in world politics. Rather our interest is with the dominant form of collective identity and with the way in which it interacts with states and the international system. Nationalism is the central social mechanism which links individuals with states and the international system. In this sense we must accept that many nationalist symbols and images are arbitrary and invented. However, it does not mean that they are any less powerful for so being. Quite the contrary, one of the abiding lessons of the 20th century was the capacity of invented traditions, symbols and communities to fire the minds in astonishing ways. In Germany in the 1930s, in Israel in the 1940s and South Africa in the 1990s one witnessed recently created symbols crafted to reinforce newly restructured political entities work with astonishing effect.

Nationalism and the International System

It is only relatively recently that nationalism has come to be perceived as an important dimension of the international system. Most theoretical accounts have tended to give it short shrift. It does not warrant an index entry in Bull's *Anarchical Society*, it is under the radar in Waltz's *Theory of International Politics* and both Marxist and Liberal traditions tend to pay it little attention. Although theory in its more recent variations has neglected nationalism, historians of international relations have given it some systematic shape such as Hayes (1948), Carr (1945) and Hinsley (1973). There is also little systematic consideration of the impact of nationalism on the workings of the broader international system. At one level, the principle of nationalism supports the foundations of the contemporary system. It is predicated on the notion that the territory and populations of the planet are divided, however unevenly, among a set of equal political entities each of which has final and absolute authority over its territory and people. Nationalism, in essence, is the idea that people belong to states and that they have a right to exist independently of others. This provides a moral underwriting of and legitimation for the principles of sovereignty and non-interference which underpin the system. Yet the idea also challenges it due to its ambivalence about which people belong to what state. Thus a segment of a state's population that wants to be part of another state or have a state to call their own have a principle which says that they have a right to do so. The challenge of secession (or irredentism for that matter) puts the idea of nationalism squarely at odds with a stable system of states. Thus the parallel evolutions of the modern international system and the ideas of nationalism have made it fundamental to, yet always slightly in tension with, the practices of the system. This is illustrated in the legal status of statehood as compared with the always unclear status of nations. For a state to exist in a formal sense it needs to satisfy basic criteria such as an effective rule-making capacity and a functioning economy, but most importantly, it must be recognized by other states as being one of them. Without that, as people in Taiwan know only too well, one does not have a state and thus no formal standing in international society. For the nation something as basic as this does not yet exist, rather it is subsumed in the state recognition process.

Mayall argues that nationalism and international society have had a relationship of challenge and accommodation. Nationalism has challenged the content of certain principles, such as the domestic basis of sovereignty and international legitimacy, but has not fundamentally recast the system: 'the primacy of the national idea amongst contemporary political principles has modified the traditional conception of an international society, but has not replaced it' (Mayall, 1990: 145). Nationalism has caused a modification of the practice of international society through the transformation of the social basis of sovereignty and subtle shifts in the principles which determine legitimate conduct. But nationalism also makes its presence felt in the strategies through which states advance their interests: by recasting the content of national interests it introduces new domestic political constraints on the exercise of foreign policy.

The international system of states is governed by principles, the most important of which include sovereignty, legal equality, and non-interference. As it has developed the system has shown a capacity to respond to changing circumstances either through the transformation of norms or through the adoption of new strategies. For example, sovereignty understood as final authority was thought to provide little more than a formal statement of the realities of absolute state power. Yet as political norms have changed and democracy grown in sophistication, sovereignty has come to refer not only to final authority but also to the location of that authority in 'the people' or even 'the nation'. Where once sovereignty was an end in itself nationalism has become a legitimizing principle of the system of states (hence the tendency to misname inter-state relations as being inter-national). Sovereignty is the means through which nations find legitimacy and the state system is therefore the means through which groups derive not only their distinctiveness but their membership of a broader community of similar unique entities.

Beyond this nationalism influences the contemporary system through the principle of national self-determination. Although not formally part of the UN Charter it has come to have quasi-legal status. In so doing it provides a reinforcing sense of legitimacy to the existing state order but it also poses a serious challenge to any state in which groupings feel aggrieved. Iranian and Turkish attitudes to Kurdish demands, Chinese fury about Taiwan and Russian responses to the Chechens are only the most obvious examples of how the threatened react to the challenges this principle poses. The international system is a system of states and those states are not freely floating above their societies but are linked to them through the principle of nationalism. A politically powerful mode of collective identity is embedded in the basis of the international system as the national idea has become the organizational basis of statehood. Through the 20th century, and particularly since 1945, it was the social underpinning of international politics but it is also a source of considerable instability and conflict.

The Challenge of Globalization

From statistics which indicate the global dominance of the media by a handful of Western firms to images of young women dressed in hijab eating McDonald's hamburgers in Jakarta, the cultural impact of globalization is visible in our everyday lives. Moreover, the images and artefacts of cultural exchange are often conflictual due to the fusion of old and new, of the local and the global. It is not surprising that there is a growing sense that the destabilization of existing orders, images and symbols is contributing to a shift in forms of identity. Some feel that it is revolutionizing modes of human identity while others argue it is simply reinforcing existing systems, and particularly the dominance of the national form. For yet others, the destabilization of identity systems is not merely of sociological interest, it is positively dangerous. In recent years it has become common wisdom to assert that globalization is fostering a 'maelstrom of conflicts' (Kaldor, 2004; Smith, 1995). In India, the Caucasus, the Balkans and the Horn of Africa, as well as many other places, globalization is thought to be exacerbating the conditions fuelling nationalist sources of inter-state and secessionist war, the root causes of which are ascribed to ethnic and identity politics. It is not only in the underdeveloped part of the world that globalization is thought to be dislodging existing modes of collective identity. In the rich and highly globalized world, nationalism is thriving in a peculiar way. Not only is it reinforcing the electoral success of nationalist politicians, whether extreme or more moderate, it is contributing to the growth of collective identity formations below the national level, that is the nationalist sentiment of nations that lack a state to call their own (Guibernau, 1999).

In the first flush of the globalization debate, some felt that old forms of identity, such as nationalism, would be dissolved by the forces of global integration. As economies and fates become intertwined, as images and symbols and the identities they create became increasingly detached from their old moorings, nationalism's power as a focal point of identity, and hence its capacity to provide political mobilization, would be irreparably diminished. It was not only Marxists who felt that nationalism would become outmoded, many liberals thought national forms of identity were rapidly becoming irrelevant. Events have not been kind to such propositions. The national form of collective identity retains a dominance even while alternative forms have emerged. Opinion is divided as to how to interpret the interaction and one can identify four strands of argument about the relationship between globalization and nationalism.

The first strand argues that globalization is not transforming the character of nationalism nor undermining its central role in cultural and political life. While globalization may be exposing people to a wider array of symbols, images and ideas with which to make sense of themselves and the world, this position argues that there is nothing in the emergent global culture which would supplant nationalism's power. For example, Smith argues that nationalism retains its dominance as a mechanism for collective identity because of the authentic link between past, present and future which it embodies. In an era of globalization, with cultural dislocation caused by the rapid transnational flow of ideas, images and values, the sense of location provided by nationalism becomes of ever higher value. As he writes, 'a global culture seems unable to offer the qualities of collective faith, dignity and hope that only a "religion surrogate", with its promise of a territorial culture-community across the generations, can provide' (Smith, 1995: 160).

Others simply argue that globalization is not revolutionizing people's sense of place. While one cannot doubt the increasing cultural connections among disparate communities, nor the growing awareness of this among populations, they argue that 'attachments to the nation remain strong throughout the world' (Day and Thompson, 2004: 189). For those taking this position the fact that a jungle hut in Vietnam has a poster of David Beckham adorning its walls or that a German student in a British university is learning *capoeira* (the Brazilian dancing martial art) does not indicate a profound transformation of identity. Rather it is indicative of the ways in which people have always been able to adopt external cultural forms without compromising dominant systems.

Finally, this line of argument recognizes that in many of the technologies that make globalization possible the state has a new array of mechanisms through which it can 'manage' national collective identity. While some see in the information economy the means to subvert nationalism others see mechanisms through which states can enhance their position and hence reinforce the role of nationalism. In global events such as the Olympics, the football World Cup or the opportunities provided through electronic mass media, states have a greatly increased capacity to create and disseminate a homogeneous culture (Guibernau, 2001). From this view globalization can be said to be slightly enhancing nationalism's capacity to mobilize political action.

A second view argues that globalization is fostering nationalism. Nationalism's hegemonic position is not merely being reinforced by globalization, it is producing new manifestations and novel formations. At the most basic level the resurgence of nationalism is thought to be a reaction against globalization and its attendant insecurities. As production processes relocate to lower cost centres they put people out of work, as traditional social roles break down and women join the workforce, the capacity of nationalism to provide some unifying response to social dislocation appears to increase. In Europe the electoral success of xenophobic nationalist parties in Holland, Italy, France and Denmark is thought to be evidence that it is not only in the economically developing world that nationalism finds fertile ground. Beyond the basic notion that globalization provides nationalism with new fuel, there is a further view that nationalism can be invoked as a form of resistance. As some argue the 'age of globalization is the age of nationalist resurgence expressed in the form of reaction to the established nation-states' (Delanty and O'Mahony, 2002: 157). From this view, globalization does not re-create nationalism as such, rather it provides opportunities for it to be manifested as anti-systemic movements.

A variation of this argument portrays globalization as responsible for the evolution of a new form of nationalist identity. For some, the return of atavistic nationalism in places like Armenia, Serbia and India is not a product of the revival of timeless hatreds, or the melting of Cold War constraints, but is due to globalization creating new forms of national collective identity. Changes in the structure of economic relations, particularly the rise of the 'information economy', the shift beyond the limits of print technology to electronic communications, such as the internet, satellite television and mobile telephones, and in the character of war, are said to be crafting a new form of nationalism (Kaldor, 2004). For these writers this nationalism is new because it is the product of a moral as well as a functional transformation, it makes use of novel means to reinforce the national idea and can have a semi-religious character or deploy religious ideals and imagery in a distinctive way (e.g. MacDonald, 2002). Nationalism, from this perspective, is resolutely a function of the structural conditions of its social existence. As these change, and from this view globalization represents such a shift, then nationalism is bound to be transformed. This view does not see structural change as driving nationalism out of business, rather it is helping it to evolve into something new. Moreover, as Kaldor acknowledges, these 'new nationalisms' coexist presently with older nationalisms and their interaction is explosive.

The third strand sees globalization as the source of a cultural process of hybridization that is diluting the power of nationalism to dominate the politics of collective identity. The fusion of cultural forms that comes from globalization is thought to diminish nationalism's ability to act as an effective focus of identity. Cultural markers, such as dress, music or literature, are influenced by global forces that are said to render the state's capacity to make political utility of fixed notions of culture increasingly ineffective. The cultural flows of globalization, the lack of constraint that geography places on the creation of a sense of political community and the increased range of opportunities to advance, fund and defend competing forms of identity has brought this about. As one commentator observes, 'the central paradox of ethnic politics in today's world is that primordial loyalties have themselves become globalized' (Özkirimli, 2005: 134).

At a basic level globalization allows what some refer to as long distance nationalism or 'portable nationality' to destabilize established and fixed forms of identity and political affiliation (Anderson, 1998). This refers to the capacity of diasporic communities to imagine affiliations with their homelands such that they fund liberation movements and lobby for political recognition all while they maintain their lives in other states (see generally Østergaard-Nielsen, 2001). But this affinity for Tamil independence from Sri Lankan émigrés in Toronto or Melbourne is only one part of the kind of duality that globalization is thought to foster. At a deeper level globalization is creating new cultural forms by facilitating the rapid fusion of cultural elements from around the world (Hannerz, 1996). Culture and identity are said no longer to be fixed in exclusively national forms, rather the cultural linkages which bring Australian rules football to Japan or which create Irish bars in Nigeria are crafting hybrid cultures that diminish the power of national forms (e.g. Nederveen Pieterse, 2004).

Although there is a tendency to focus on the more parochial and atavistic tendencies of identity based reactions to globalization, it is also increasing the scope, number and appeal of cosmopolitan attachments and for some blurring the distinctions between nations (see generally, Scholte, 2005: 239–52). The notion of national distinctiveness, whether ethnic, religious or civic, is said to be increasingly untenable due to the enhanced cultural awareness that globalization fosters. The growth of cosmopolitan theories about obligations and duties to humanity as a whole is thought to be indicative of the shift in perceptions that is being fostered by global forces (e.g. see Held, 2003; Linklater, 1998; Pogge, 2002). One sees also the dramatic growth and influence in activist and civil society groups which seek to advance global and human causes that clearly identify interests and basic questions of being with the human community, and indeed with the planet, as opposed to the narrow conception of the national. There is no doubt that cosmopolitan senses of identity are growing and their reaction to globalization stands in contrast to the localizing tendencies in some parts of the world.

Globalization is creating new loyalties and increasing awareness of the fluidity of old forms of identity. This process is also said to be eroding the nation state's capacity to monopolize loyalty (Appadurai, 2000). The view from this perspective is not that nationalism is simply dissolving in a sea of globalization, rather that the overlapping loyalties and cultural connections are making distinctly national understandings of culture less and less effective. This leads to a reduced meaning of national identity which translates into a diminution of the political power of nationalism. This view sees globalization as loosening the political link between state and society and the hybridity which is at the core of this vision of nationalism is eroding its capacity to provide the social basis for the modern international system.

The final strand of the transformation literature takes the hybridization argument slightly further and sees globalization as an opportunity to create post-national forms of political community. This represents a more overt attempt by some to drive the changes prompted by globalization in a specifically non-nationalist direction. Rather than seeing globalization as a means by which nations without states can achieve statehood, this view sees in globalization an opportunity to create utterly new forms of community and belonging that do not take the idea of the nation as a reference point (e.g. Özkirimli, 2005; Appadurai, 1996). In the breaking down of territorial constraints comes the possibility to forge new non-national public spaces. The range of groupings which can provide social resonance in the fluid and fragmented world of globalization not only loosens the binds of national systems, it enhances the possibilities of non-national political and ethical claims. Globalization provides a real opportunity, for some, to challenge the functional and moral dominance of the national idea by exposing the constructed and arbitrary character of so many of the supposedly sacred and unarguable claims of nationalism.

As this short survey (summarized in Table 7.2) shows, from those who argue that globalization reinforces nationalism to those who see

Table 7.2   Four views on globalization and identity

1. Globalization reinforces the dominant mode of national identity construction
2. Globalization enhances nationalist forms of identity
3. Globalization dilutes national forms of collective identity
4. Globalization helps to create post-national forces of identity and political community

global integration forcing its demise, the terrain of debate on globalization and collective identity is vast. While many of the observations of this process are valid, a number of common mistakes have been made. The first is to see a direct fit between cultural forms of collective identity and political nationalism. Nationalism refers to an extremely wide variety of social processes. Thus, while it is correct to note that globalization is creating new cultural symbols and practices which fuse geographically and politically disparate cultures, it is wrong to then assume this undermines nationalism as a means to link state and society through national visions of collective identity. Nationalism's continued electoral success, its social power and importance in most democracies as well as in many non-democracies, shows that one must analytically keep cultural and political mani-festations separate.

A second common error is to assume that the reduction in state authority that many associate with globalization undermines the efficacy of nationalism. It may be true that states have agreed to bind their hands and that they have reduced their authority over more policy spheres, it does not necessarily follow that nationalism will logically become less effective. This linkage, which sees people's affinities to a national idea reduced as the capacity of the state is reduced, seems to imply far too much rationality on the part of nationalism. For one thing, collective identity is constructed on more than just functional grounds. Linked to this is the assumption that globalization is changing nationalism in a fundamental way, that nationalism is the dominant form of identity at the personal level all of the time. If it were then the kinds of changes identified probably would be as radical as claimed. Yet national identity is only one element which constitutes an individual's sense of self. It is significant and its resonant power considerable, but it is not dominant at all times. Moreover, the fluidity of both intensity of experience and the nature and form of its existence provide a flexibility, and hence a resilience, that many overlook.

While writers such as Guibernau are right to emphasize the links between state, society and nationalism, they are wrong to assert that a change in the aims and means through which states advance their interests, necessarily requires a change in the character and func-tional role of nationalism. If a state decides to open up previously protected parts of the economy as part of an attempt to foster an economic restructuring required to cope with globalization it will have to face all sorts of social challenges. Unemployment, social dislocation and the like are very real possibilities, yet it does not follow that the functional role of nationalism will change. Experience thus far supports the view that social dislocation that derives from economic strategies intended to cope with globalization can produce demagogic nationalist political actors or can shift the way in which nationalism is played out, but it does not appear to change the basic nature of the national ideal and the powerful bonds it fosters between individuals and the idea of the state.

So what are we to make of nationalism's encounter with the changes of globalization? At the most basic level there is little empirical evidence that nationalism is becoming less politically effective under conditions of globalization, nor that this dominant mode of collective identity is being swept away. One indicator is the EU's Eurobarometer polls which consistently indicate a clear preponderance of national identity over European sentiment (European Commission, 2000b). There has been little electoral success in democratic political systems for those who deviate from variations on the national script. Although it might be somewhat unfair to expect globalization to instantly cast existing practices of politics into the darkness, the continuing political salience of nationalism is clear.

It is also clear that globalization is changing the context in which nationalism mediates the political relationship between state and society. While there is little to support the extreme claims, the process by which states and societies are not only increasingly interlinked but increasingly conscious of the economic, cultural and political connections which bind their fates is of significance to forms of collective identity. If one thinks that nationalism has an international and domestic dimension – one to do with mediating social existence in a system of like political entities and the other to do with cohesion within the community – then globalization most obviously influences the international dimension. In providing an international context which is destabilizing and the source of greater potential threats, both new and old, real and imagined, states have a more fertile ground to use nationalism to advance their aims. For example, nationalism in the PRC is used to legitimate one-party rule and globalization has provided a means through which this can find more effective purchase amongst society (Hughes, 1997). In China the idea of nationalism – whereby the idea of cultural distinctiveness is transformed into political power – is particularly influential. But this process is not limited only to one-party states looking to justify communist party rule. In the US nationalism of an astonishingly powerful variety was elicited by the trauma of the September 11 attacks (Lieven, 2004), which, as discussed earlier, were quintessential expressions of globalization.

The position taken here sounds similar to that associated with Smith's defence of nationalism's power. In some respects it is. Globalization has not presented a fundamental challenge to the efficacy of nationalism. The reason for this, however, is where we part company with the ethno-symbolist. The inability of globalization and emerging hybrid-global cultural forms to displace national ideals is due not to nationalism's capacity to link the contemporary with some authentic past, but because it does not present a threat so profound that the social process, whereby identity and political power is mediated by nationalism, cannot cope. In this sense the argument here sees nationalism as the cultural and social means through which the political system of states is produced and reproduced and there is little evidence to support the argument that this important role will be meaningfully transformed. This view does not imply that the practices of nationalism will carry on unaffected. On the contrary, although the fertility of the soil has been increased by globalization, states will need to adopt new strategies to be able to make use of these opportunities. The creation and advancement of symbols, values and cultural markers that effectively bind a society together and to the institutions of authority is a particular challenge under globalization.

To take one example, since the fall of European imperialism many states in East Asia have put statist economic policies at the centre of their nationalist programmes. The national idea in Singapore, South Korea and Taiwan was fostered both by the functional advances achieved through subtle (and not so subtle) forms of economic nationalism as well as overt cultural and education policies intended to construct a robust sense of political community. Economic statism in many respects created the idea of the nation. Yet globalization makes statist approaches to economic policy-making very hard and thus economic success as a means of nation-building becomes considerably more complex. If the national idea is founded on economic success and that success fails to be maintained or the policies which have created it are no longer effective then there are some very serious problems lying in store. Instability in Indonesia after the 1997–98 financial crisis was very much a function of the breakdown of policies which had hitherto fostered social cohesion. In this sense, globalization presents a significant challenge to nationalism as an explicit political programme. States that had used economic nationalism need to adopt more sophisticated means of achieving their economic ends and need to link this to the national idea in a new way. Yet the point that must be emphasized is that economic nationalism has not yet undermined the more basic functional role of nationalism. The form of national policies is clearly at some risk but the fundamental function of nationalism as a politically powerful form of collective identity is not threatened. Globalization provides new and challenging circumstances for nationalism but these do not yet mean that states or other political entities are being driven by new political principles.

The capacity of nationalism to survive, indeed to flourish, given globalization's emergence should not be thought of as a reflection of the eternal genius of nationalism. Rather nationalism's persistence is a function of two things: the limits of globalization and the capacity of political institutions to adapt to changing circumstances. At base the national idea maintains its grip in the face of global forces because of the lack of fundamental challenge these forces present to the basis of existing institutions, values and cultural associations. This is not to say that things will stay forever as they are, but the changes advanced by globalization do not as yet provide sufficient challenges to the social basis of nationalism's power. To a certain extent, writers like Guibernau are correct to emphasize that changes in the state and the nation will necessitate a transformation in the practice of nationalism, but such changes have yet to be presented by globalization. The radical changes in social organization which presaged the rise of nationalism – the linkage of secular and territorial principles, industrialization, urbanization and imperialism – involved significant ruptures in existing social and cultural practices. Globalization has, thus far, not involved ruptures of this kind and has not created significantly new social structures – it has accelerated moves toward industrial and post-industrial forms, but not anything substantively new – and thus it is unsurprising that nationalism retains its power.

As a programmatic political principle, nationalism is able to call on a vast array of images, values and ideals to achieve its ends. Any principle that can be deployed to advance the interests of the Chinese

Communist Party, or the American government and to inspire soldiers in Eritrea clearly has an elastic capacity that should not be underestimated. When considering the impact of globalization on forms of identity it is vital to recognize that the nationalist version has a decisive advantage due to its inherent fungibility. It is capable of adapting to changing circumstances and should not be thought of as something forever tied to a narrow set of social circumstances. For example, a state may have crafted a nationalism which is built out of a history of mass migration, yet it can still effectively deploy a deeply anti-immigrant nationalism to great effect generations later. Under the relatively limited cultural and ideological transformations thus far brought about by globalization nationalism has been able to adapt with ease. Equally it is not a principle that requires cadres to reinforce its dominance at all times and all places. Reinforcement through dominant values, education systems and a hegemonic consent allows of much greater malleability than systems of outright coercion.

The International System, Globalization and National Identity

For traditional scholars of the international system, especially those from the classical realist tradition, the politics of identity and culture are a nuisance; they get in the way of prudent statecraft and the rational management of power politics. If the aristocratic approach to diplomacy and statecraft could be revived, such arguments go, if the emotiveness of nationalism could be kept in check or avoided altogether, then the system of sovereign states could function in a more efficient fashion. Some might have hoped that globalization would weaken the grip of nationalism and help return world politics to an ostensibly more civilized age. Such aristocratic yearnings are, of course, in vain. The nationalist genie has been let out of the bottle and neither globalization nor rational pragmatism will get it back in. It is as hard to imagine an international system overlaid with globalization without nationalism as it is to imagine a return to 19th century European diplomacy.

What does the foregoing discussion have to tell us about the international system? At the very least it underlines the importance of culture and identity to the workings of the international system. Too often we tend to associate world politics with the dry matter of trade, investment, alliances and balances of power and can overlook the rich social and cultural systems which underpin the structure of international politics. Without nationalism as the social glue which binds people and their dreams to the abstract matter of sovereignty and statehood then world politics would look very different. What then of the continued importance of the national idea in a world where globalization is of clear influence? At the most basic level the answer is straightforward, globalization's failure to erode nationalism's dominance reinforces the conclusion that globalization does not translate into a political or normative restructuring of the international system. However, to say that nationalism still matters to international relations is not to say that the currents of globalization are irrelevant for the nationalist circumstances of the international system.

While globalization has not removed nationalism from the map of world politics it has changed some of the ways in which this form of collective identity influences the pattern of relations. New national strategies and indeed new nationalisms will propel novel developments in the international system. This is no more evident than in the economic sphere. Economic nationalism, while continuing to be important, is presently being pursued in a new form. Nationalism deriving from economic success can no longer be feasibly pursued through old techniques of protectionism or demand management. Globalization has forced states to adopt new approaches to economic policy-making and to the economic dimensions of nationalism such as strategic alignment via trade agreements or a structural binding of hands via the WTO.

One important feature of the contemporary international system is regionalism. Geographically limited inter-state cooperation is an important facet of world politics. From the deeply rooted integration of the EU to regional trade pacts such as the Central American Free Trade Agreement, regionalism is an important tool in state foreign policy. One of the chief motivations for the creation of the EU was to try to reduce the political impact of destructive nationalism and to that end it has been remarkably successful. But nowhere else is regionalism promoted as a means of containing nationalism, indeed in many parts of the world regionalism is a response to globalization and used as a means to advance statist goals in more challenging conditions. In East Asia, this has been particularly striking (see He, 2004). Its prominence in international affairs is precisely an example of states advancing new strategies without undermining the national ideal.

Nationalism's position as the moral and sociological basis of the current international system has been reinforced by globalization even while it continues to exist in an uneasy tension with these flows. What Özkirimli calls minority nationalisms (2005: 134), such as those of the Basques, Catalans and Scots, are given succour by globalization. Yet the proposition they embody is not a radical rejection of existing modes of identity and their link to political institutions. There is tension in the sense that the established map of nations and states does not sit easily with a process which encourages sub-state sensibilities but the system of sovereign states has in nationalism an ideal which resonates with populations, that is adaptable to changing conditions and which provides a moral legitimacy in tune with the times. Nationalism is at once in tension with and yet strongly supportive of the international system. This contradictory existence is also evident in nationalism's relationship with globalization. Not only does globalization provide sustenance for this powerful phenomenon, nationalism is a political idea which may shut globalization down more effectively than anything else. If a severe economic crisis were to emerge it is all too easy to imagine a return to the closure of times past and a nationalist defeat of the openness of globalization. In the anti-immigration policies of many democracies one sees some of the least edifying responses to globalization and the seeds of possible future backlash. In less speculative terms, nationalism is still the source of significant instability and potential conflict in the system. Whether in the Caucasus, East Asia or the Middle East, political instability has a nationalist face. This derives from nationalism's central political role as a mediating process between international system, state and society. Through this, nationalism provides elites with opportunities to reinforce their domestic position. Typical examples of this can be seen in Putin's Russia and the CCP's policies in the PRC. Yet, as the example of China shows all to readily, stoking nationalist flames, whether over Taiwan or Japanese history textbooks, can have very dangerous consequences (Zhao, 2000). The CCP has established a nationalist programme on which its own success rests, but which risks war over Taiwan and significant geopolitical competition with Japan. These are outcomes the CCP does not particularly desire but which may be hard to avoid given the central part that nationalism plays in its political programme.

While the UN and most of its members are not enthused about many more new states taking their place at the international table, it is hard to see how the system can prevent the continued redrawing of maps while the national idea has such resonance. Taiwan cannot continue to live in limbo, it will gain formal independence or be absorbed by the PRC. The West Papuans, the Kurds, the Palestinians, the Tamils and the Chechens all show a fierce determination to achieve independence and globalization provides them with opportunities to advance their claims in novel ways. Nationalism will continue to be a source of both conflict and inspiration for the foreseeable future and its moral weight will continue to create an uneasy balance between order and instability. Huntington was correct to emphasize that globalization will help drive identity-based sources of conflict in the coming years but wrong to see in the religious mumbo-jumbo of 'civilizations' the source of that conflict. Indeed the source will be much as it has been for many years – the desire for political communities, however constructed, to be able to determine their fate as others are able to do. Globalization has not changed that basic proposition, and thus nationalism still provides the social embedding of the system of sovereign states. The problem is that the social forces which ground the abstract principles of international politics do not necessarily sit easily with the existing geopolitical map and in globalization one has an array of transnational forces which can be deployed to advance nationalist causes and to re-write the cartography of world politics in dangerous ways.

Nationalism is part of the international system just as globalization is and it brings the politics of identity to the centre of the workings of the current order. Yet its capacity to prompt instability, especially when propelled by the social dislocation caused by globalization, is considerable. Whether the political and social consequences of globalization will ultimately undermine traditional social forms and hence foster a new cosmopolitanism or craft new non-national forms of collective identity and political community at this stage seems unlikely. At present it is safe to conclude that globalization most certainly does not herald the end of nationalism nor the conclusion of the admission of new nations to the status of sovereign statehood.

8

Still an Anarchical Society?

Although much of this book has sought to damp down the enthusiasm of many of the early globalization boosters the argument presented here should not be confused with that of the arch sceptic. Globalization is an important feature of the current international system. From the challenges of terrorism to the dynamism of global financial markets, the influence of globalization can be discerned in almost all fields that shape the character of contemporary world politics. The norms and rules of international politics, as well as the strategies of states, cannot be analyzed without considering the impact of this complex and multifaceted phenomenon. Yet due to precisely this diffuse character, it is extremely difficult to pin down just how its impact is being felt. Globalization matters, on that it is hard to disagree. How much it matters, where and to what extent is a much more complex affair. When one is dealing with something as conceptually slippery as the structure of world politics, then this is doubly so.

The purpose of this chapter is to draw together the various strands of the argument presented in the previous chapters and to try to make sense of the broader impact of this protean phenomenon on the mechanisms that underpin modern world politics. As the preceding chapters have shown, while globalization has not radically transformed all walks of international life, it is making its presence felt in sectors of vital importance to the international system. It is transforming the international economy, the conduct of states (both at home and abroad), the form and function of international institutions, the nature of war and the complex business of nationalism and identity. While there may be decisive changes in the role of international institutions or in the likelihood of states to cooperate with one another, it is not immediately clear how these may interact with one another. Moreover, a recurring theme in this book has been that the changes associated with globalization tend to be overstated and their influence often contrary to common expectations. The aim of this chapter is to try to determine how the complex and subtle changes that globalization has brought about in different elements affect the system as a whole.

Rather than attempt to work through every aspect of the international system and determine whether or not globalization has changed its practice – space constraints, to say nothing of the methodological problems such an approach would pose, limit such an effort – the chapter explores this through the notion of international order. International order has traditionally been concerned with states: the primary concern of order is the relations among political entities and only secondarily about orderly or just outcomes for people. This narrow focus has led to significant criticism of this traditional conception. For some, it is morally unacceptable to place the state before people. For others, the international system is populated by such a wealth of actors, such as firms, NGOs and IOs, that an account of the system's operating principles which talks only of states is inadequate. These criticisms are not unreasonable. Yet we must recognize that there is a code of norms, laws and procedures which states have devised to guide their conduct in international society and this broad set of practices and principles, known as international order, form the structural bedrock of world politics. The purpose of focusing on this aspect of world politics is twofold. First, international order is the constitutional basis of the international system. Even though world politics has a host of institutional actors and processes of importance, in legal, material and moral terms the order established by states is of primary importance in shaping how states conceive of their interests and the ways in which they relate with others. Second, it provides an excellent means to gauge the extent to which a decisively transnational phenomenon influences a set of structures that are particularly state-centric. More broadly, for so long as it has attempted to carve out a disciplinary niche for itself, the concept of order has been central to thinking about international relations and thus any reflection on globalization and world politics needs to consider this central issue. The chapter asks two broad questions: is globalization recasting the basis of the international system such that we can begin to discern a new ordering principle at work? How does globalization relate to the ideas of international order and the institutions of world politics which flow from them?

In sum, the chapter argues that although globalization has not fundamentally recast the basic structures of international relations, it is becoming increasingly clear that the orthodox notion of international order is increasingly untenable. The disjuncture between notions of international order and the reality of world politics is not only of academic interest, it has real consequences for the effective functioning of the institutions and rules that flow from this conception of order.

International Order and World Politics

The idea of order has been central to the discipline of international relations. The study of world politics began as a self-consciously irenic project which sought to uncover and promote the basis of order in a system lacking a central authority (Schmidt, 1998). The horrors of the First World War had shown that traditional approaches to the maintenance of international relations – through aristocrats conducting secret diplomacy with a keen eye on the workings of the balance of power – were unsuited to conditions of modern warfare. Approaches to alliances and invocations of the balance of power required the use of force to make them effective. The problem was that industrialization had made warfare a business of such all-encompassing destruction that using force to underwrite the rules of the system had become politically, morally and economically unfeasible. This 'new' social science sought to devise and implement a novel and more effective means to structure the international relations of states.

While the scope of the study of world politics has broadened greatly in recent years, the idea of order, even if not so named, lies at the heart of much scholarship. For example, liberal institutionalists are interested in the way in which international organizations can promote orderly relations among states by building trust and improving information flows between states. Realists are concerned with the effects of power distribution and the way in which its transformation supports or disturbs international order and critical theorists are interested in the ways in which specific interests are served by representing order as natural or pre-ordained. The creation, management and understanding of orderly relations among political entities which exist in a condition of anarchy is at the heart of the study of world politics.

While order is central to so much of the discipline, its meaning is often less than clear. Most commonly, the term is used to refer to the basic character of relations at the international level. In this sense, the term acts as a classificatory schema, such as the bipolar order of the Cold War or the unipolar order of the current system. Order can also be used to describe the broader pattern of power distribution, as well as the character of relations among the states. For example, following the end of the Cold War some commentators felt that international order was entering a new phase in which international problems would be resolved in a more cooperative fashion. George H.W. Bush's much quoted – and often derided – 'new world order' was an attempt to describe these changes. The substance of the transformation referred not only to the shifts in power, but also to ostensible changes in the way in which international relations would be conducted. When scholars write of Wilson's 'new diplomacy' as an effort to craft a new order after the First World War they are deploying this version of the concept. Order therefore describes the characteristic elements of the system, in terms of the dominant powers, alliances and institutions, as well as the nature of conduct among states.

In the scholarly literature, however, order is more usually understood as having an analytic dimension. As a description of the system and its mode of conduct, it is a useful starting point. The real interest lies in order understood as a mechanism or property of the international system itself. Bull's study of order in world politics is perhaps the most prominent and influential exposition of this approach. He famously defines it as 'a pattern of activity that sustains the elementary or primary goals of the society of states, or international society' (Bull, 1977: 9). Order is both the pattern of activity and the process which perpetuates the conduct of international relations between states so as to foster the existence of a society of states. In response to the anarchy begotten by sovereignty, states have developed the means to ensure a basic pattern of relations to guide their interactions. For Bull, the pattern of relations suffices to create a basic sense of society. This means that sovereign equals recognize that they have a minimal set of common interests and values which works to bind them, most of the time, to the core rules and norms. In this sense, the social dimension of international society is the common interest of states in retaining the system of relations which provides them with a moral and material predominance. Order is the means through which the divergent interests of political communities can be mediated to ensure the survival of the states and their system of social relations. In this view, international order is created and sustained by the balance of power, the management function of the great powers, international law, the communication system of modern diplomacy and, ultimately, in the conduct of war. Bull's anarchical society is a state-centric interpretation of international order. Indeed, he clearly distinguishes between international order and world order, the former relating to states and the latter to the social conditions of humanity. In sum, for Bull, and for those of the 'English School' which are associated with this approach, order exists to maintain and perpetuate the international system of sovereign states and does so by establishing rules and modes of behaviour in which physical violence is not the first but the last resort when disagreement among equals arises (e.g. Wheeler, 2000; see generally, Bellamy, 2005)

This orthodox conception is not without its critics. Some of these criticisms are fairly obvious. Bull's version of international order neglects the vital role played by economic factors in international affairs, it gives moral priority to states ahead of individuals and it is premised on an artificial division between the domestic political realm and international society. In one of the most perceptive assessments of the idea of order in world politics, Keene points out that this orthodox conception is based on a flawed understanding of both the origins of the modern order and its function (2002). From this view, the chief problem with the orthodox account is that it overlooks entirely the role of European empires, and the way in which they were politically administered, in the creation of the modern world. In portraying international order as a benign expansion of European ideas of statehood and sovereignty across the globe, one neglects the true history of the political development of the majority of the planet which directly shaped the practices of the contemporary international political system.

The traditional history of the notion of international order ignores the fact that while European states did adhere to the norms of international society – sovereign equality and non-interference – in their relations with one another, they did not extend this treatment to those they felt did not adhere to the 'standards of civilization' (Gong, 1984). International order, for European states, was about managing the differences which emerged between different societies and cultures. But if one's culture was not deemed to be 'civilized' then there was no need for the niceties of toleration. Keene's key point is that implicit in the purpose of international order is the advancement of a way of life that was codified in the language of 'civilization' (2002). Order is thus not only about managing the vagaries of an anarchical society, it is about extending and protecting a specific conception of how domestic society should be organized. This is a view which underlines the linkage between domestic political structures and those which operate at the international level.

In contrast to orthodox understandings, approaches to order which derive from what has been described as a 'constitutive tradition' take a somewhat different perspective (see Halliday, 1994: 94–123). The formation and functioning of international order, viewed from the orthodox perspective, has little to do with the vagaries of domestic life. The problem is that the norms and values which order underpins do not emerge spontaneously from the ether. Rather they have specific histories and embody values and interests which should be taken into consideration. It is from this perspective that a constitutive approach begins. This view sees international order as constituted of a blend of domestic and international factors that work to advance particular interests and specific conceptions of how social life should be organized.

The account of international order set out by Raymond Aron is typical of such an approach. He argues that orderly relations in the international system are not simply the product of mechanisms such as the balance of power and international law. Instead, he emphasizes that the principles on which domestic political systems are built – their conceptions of policy, appropriate forms of behaviour and the legitimate goals of state policy – are fundamental to the nature of any international order (Aron, 1966). Specifically, he argues that the nature and function of international order is the result of the similarities or differences in domestic organizational type; the principles which determine legitimate behaviour and the values which determine and justify state action (Aron, 1966: 104). International laws and the balance of power are influenced by norms and values that derive from domestic conditions. The constitutive approach emphasizes the domestic social foundation of the international system and is thus a particularly useful approach to our concerns here.

The concept of order in world politics appears to mean quite different things depending on the context of use: it is a description of the distribution of power in the system for some, while for others it is the means through which the system is managed. Some see this lack of consensus as symptomatic of the tradition of thought about order itself (see Rengger, 2000). But the question of order is, at heart, a question about the character of the international system and indeed modern life. Whatever one's views about its purpose or its ethical constitution, the question of order derives from the particular economic, political and moral problems which the structure of world politics throws up. The creation of order is ultimately a product of the need to cope with the peculiarities of the modern international system. One may be of the view that order emerges spontaneously from the self-interested actions of states, such as those traditionalists who see the balance of power as akin to market forces. Equally, one may think that the benign description of international order is used to mask the ways in which the rules of the international system facilitate the exploitation of the poor. However conceived, order is the product of efforts to try to find an acceptable existence in the modern international system. These efforts involve both technical and normative dimensions, such as mechanisms to avoid war or to advance a particular conception of justice whether explicitly stated or not.

Order, as something so central to the workings of modern world politics, is therefore an appropriate means to consider the impact of globalization. More directly, it is the central governing feature of the international system and one focused on the traditional notions of state power, sovereignty and territoriality. As such it should be particularly susceptible to the kinds of change that many have claimed in the name of globalization.

Globalization and the Constituent Elements of Order

The orthodox depiction of order – exemplified by Bull's description of an 'anarchical society'– whereby rules guide the conduct of states and are enforced by the five core institutions – does not appear to do justice to the nature and character of the international system that exists in the early years of the 21st century. The mechanisms which regulate the relations between states, the growing importance of the place of the individual in international legal principles, the declining relevance of the idea of 'great powers' in an era of American hyper-power and the importance of economics to international affairs, makes Bull's vision of international society seem almost quaint. Since 1945, world politics has witnessed a huge growth in the range of institutions and mechanisms which are specifically designed to foster international order. This, alongside the expansion of the international system to some 191 sovereign states, the huge growth in the sheer size of the world economy as well as the considerable growth in human population, has created a complex array of institutions, norms, rules and procedures that try to deal with the problems inherent in an international system structured around principles of sovereignty and territoriality on top of the old system of order.

Having provided a background to conceptions of order we need to clarify the notion of international order used here. The view taken in this chapter derives from the constitutive tradition and sees the concept of international order as involving four distinct aspects: a set of fundamental actors and constitutional principles; rules which govern conduct; the distribution of power; and the normative ends which the order serves. The first describes the central units of political authority and the principles which endow them with these properties. The international system is a state system in which the principle of sovereignty determines that all states are considered to be formally equal and have the final authority over their territory. The current order is a political system that defines this authority in territorial terms. This principle reflects not only the moral dominance of the idea of statehood but also the material capacities of states to reinforce this moral centrality. The dominant position of the state is embedded in domestic society through the ideology of nationalism, and has led to a corollary norm of national self-determination becoming increasingly accepted at the international level even while it sits uneasily with existing borders and boundaries. The second aspect of order involves the set of rules which have been devised to cope with the consequences of the fundamental features of the system. This consists of a number of elements. The first are basic rules intended to guide conduct and the institutions that codify and monitor these rules. The second element is the set of principles which underpin these that determine the legitimacy, or otherwise, of action.

This is the managerial element of the international system which consists of international law, the rules of diplomacy, international norms, such as non-interference and self-determination, and international institutions. Its purpose is to cope with the consequences of the anarchical structure of the international system and is most commonly associated with conceptions of international order.

The third element of international order is the distribution of power across the system. Managerial accounts of order can neglect the effects of power, while critics point out that the rules of the game are often shaped by the powerful to serve their own interests. International order in any particular circumstance consists of a constellation of military, economic and moral powers. Holders of moral power are able to shape rules in their favour, for example set the rules of trade and investment that are skewed toward their interests. They are also able to influence conceptions of justice and legitimacy that reflect their interests and values. The fourth element consists of the normative ends which the order advances. The values which ultimately provide the system with a meaningful purchase on political action form a fundamental component of any order. In a system in which states have moral priority, for example, *raison d'état* has political sufficiency. In a system in which moral weight is vested in the individual or a conception of individual rights, then *raison d'état* does not have the moral or political finality it would have in a system where the state trumps all. Thus the normative ends consist of conceptions of justice and rights that are anchored in the specific subjects of those conceptions, such as states, classes, tribes or individuals. The normative focus of the present system is decidedly unclear.

None of the core elements of order are fixed, they are malleable and subject to shifts in environment and circumstance. The second and third aspects are most susceptible to changes that reflect shifting values, declining fortunes and broader transformations in the character of international life. While the fundamental features and the normative ends are themselves subject to modification and transformation, it is the more variable distribution of power and the mechanisms intended to cope with the challenges of the system which are the most common sites for transformation, and the most likely places for globalization to have an influence in the structure of the international system, particularly at this early stage in proceedings.

In the face of the propounded challenges to sovereignty, the weakening position of the state, the growth in importance, scope and power of international organizations, the rise of private sources of authority and the like, there are some grounds for thinking that something about the international system has changed. So what does the international system look like under conditions of globalization? Has there been any significant transformation of the structure of international society?

At the risk of near tautology, the international system is a state system. At the most fundamental level, therefore, the state acts as the primary constituent of international order. Although the state has undergone some important changes in its domestic and international behaviour, it has not had its place at the centre of international political and legal order supplanted. The principle of sovereignty retains its dominance in this system although its practice is varied. Rather than endorsing the view that globalization erodes state sovereignty, the experience thus far supports those who argue that the principle is malleable and adaptable. While it is true that globalization is making the absolutism of sovereignty appear untenable, it is clear that the absolutist views of sovereignty, which critics hold as the measure against which contemporary standards are thought to fall short, do not accurately depict its practice (see Krasner, 1999). For example, membership of the WTO is thought to be indicative of states handing over their sovereign powers in return for the contractual guarantees that are believed to be politically necessary in order to accrue the economic benefits of a liberal trading regime. Sovereignty is, in this view, a commodity traded for economic advantage. Yet the principle of sovereignty is not a commodity, it is a relational principle of authority and power and the commitment to behave along certain lines does not compromise the basic principle of final authority.

Debate on the status of sovereignty is still considerable (e.g. see *Political Studies*, 1999). This is due to the widely differing ways in which it is experienced and exercised across the world. The sovereignty of the PRC is quite different in form and function from the sovereignty of Belgium or the Democratic Republic of Congo (DRC). The PRC places a high political priority on sovereignty which it sees as vital both to guaranteeing its independence in international society and to justifying CCP rule at home. For

Belgium, the exercise of sovereignty includes handing over certain powers to the EU while maintaining juridical sovereignty in the international system. For the DRC, sovereignty is a means to keep the world at bay and, at times, is a cloak to justify the kleptocratic ways of the ruling elite. It is this divergent experience of sovereignty that makes firm judgements about its status difficult. That said, the contemporary experience does not support either those who argue that globalization is killing sovereignty, nor does it give much succour to the conservative view that nothing has changed. Rather, sovereignty appears to be firmly entrenched as the underlying principle of the contemporary international order but it is subject to subtle and varied shifts in interpretation and practice. This has been best articulated by Sørenson who makes a distinction between the constitutive and regulative dimensions of sovereignty (1999). He argues that sovereignty exists as a basic rule of the system which provides for the formal independence of peoples, states and territories. But this formal independence is played out in varying ways depending on differences in its regulative aspects. The particular practice of formal sovereign independence varies as states embrace different means to advance their aims, some of which lead to cooperation and others lead to autarky. In this sense globalization is a set of transnational forces to which states will respond differently through the regulative dimension of sovereignty.

The key feature of the modern idea of sovereignty is mutual recognition of authority over territory. This idea is entirely compatible with cooperative action among states and such action does not necessarily compromise the status of the mutual recognition of authority. Indeed one might argue that the international exercise of sovereign power in a cooperative way can entrench or, in some cases, enhance the sovereignty of the state, even if it ties its hands in particular policy areas. For example, China's accession to the WTO is thought not only to deliver the benefits of trade but acts to signal China's acceptance of the norms of the international system, thus contributing both to its broader foreign policy aims and to the legitimacy of CCP rule (see Hempson-Jones, 2005). International order under conditions of globalization is still a state-based order in which the idea of sovereignty has the central place. Globalization serves to underline two important points. First, we need to recognize that sovereignty has always been played out in a more sophisticated fashion than is traditionally thought. The absolutism of sovereignty as an idea has never been matched with an absolutism in practice. Moreover, it shows that the underlying constitutional notion of sovereignty can coexist with differing modes of application. Second, it emphasizes that the social conditions in which states find themselves are more complex than they have been and that statist approaches to managing external challenges may not be the most appropriate way to advance their interests. Even as the state retains its dominance in practice and as an idea, the circumstances of its existence may not warrant this primary place, or at least demand a rethinking of strategies and approaches. In some of the novel approaches of European integration, some argue, one can see this process at work (e.g. Wallace, 1999).

Nationalism is the second important feature of the contemporary order and facilitates the domestic social foundations of the international state system. For some, international society is built on the social bedrock of nationalism (Mayall, 1990). Without nationalism, states and sovereignty would require brute coercion, or some other means of managing collective identity, to ensure their domestic acceptance. Globalization has not eroded the national idea nor diminished its capacity to act as the sociological glue between state and society. Indeed in some respects, it has reinforced its position. National ideas are clearly more powerful when there is an increased awareness of political, cultural and social differences (however constructed and arbitrary these may be). Moreover, globalization provides those who advance nationalist ambitions with a wide array of opportunities to advance their aims. While the forces of globalization might appear to be driving a cosmopolitan sense among some, they also put a political premium on the national idea in domestic society. The social dislocation that globalized economic systems have fostered, the increasing awareness of lines of difference and the resonance that these have, are reinforcing the power of nationalism. But while nationalism is a statist political form, and nationalism serves as a conduit which drives globalization to reinforce the state (even while many of its forces might otherwise be propelling alternative institutions or conceptions of political authority), the relationship is somewhat uneasy. The tension derives from the discrepant ways in which globalization and nationalism interact. There are three different ways in which globalization enhances nationalist power, but it does so in a way that can be destabilizing to international order. First, it can lead to fragmentation as sub-state nations agitate for change and globalization provides a means to advance and press claims that have significant geopolitical consequences. Second, it could be the motive force for a significant backlash against globalization. Nationalism is the most likely source of pressure that would bring the present era of globalization to an end. It is the only force which presently has the capacity to override the interests and linkages which have been created by globalization's economic integration. Third, globalization also fosters a cosmopolitan sensibility that weakens the power and capacity of nationalism. While we see globalization as strengthening nationalism this should not be confused with the argument that it acts as a means that will only reinforce the existing order in world politics.

Globalization has increased awareness of the economic dimensions of international power, and not only as a means to acquire military capacity and the trappings of geopolitical importance. Where in the past international order was only concerned with questions of political and strategic significance, globalization insists that economic factors need to be more explicitly brought into the structures of international order. Although many tend to think that globalization represents the victory of markets over states, the reality is more complex. Markets are indeed powerful and firms have a considerable command over resources but states retain a dominant position, although their behaviour in international society is increasingly influenced by an economic sensibility. Globalization involves a broad ranging consensus toward policies that generally favour markets and openness and has encouraged states to shift their approaches to governance and authority. But this has not resulted in an exclusive focus on global multilateral cooperation or economic governance. Instead a complex array of bilateral, regional and global multilateral approaches have emerged as the means through which states are trying to advance their particular interests. This derives from a more fundamental point: the integration of the global economy through globalization serves the broader interests of states, it does not weaken or undermine them. It increases prosperity and hence enhances the fiscal capacities of states, but it means also that states need to adopt novel and agile strategies to capitalize on these opportunities. Globalization does not simply strengthen states in the traditional way nor does it mean all states will automatically benefit. But for those able to respond effectively, there is considerable potential to strengthen state capacity and influence. As such, most states are according economic interests a high priority and particularly they are conceiving of these interests as predicated on participation in global networks. In turn this is driving efforts to provide order through formal cooperation and institutionalization, but it also means that national interests are increasingly subject to global pressures.

There are two caveats to this argument. First, these strategies do not necessarily drive support for existing global multilateral efforts, and they are contingent on the continuation of the current consensus about the benefits of openness and the appropriate strategies to advance state interests. Second, strategies of cooperation and coordination do not equal state decline nor the death of sovereignty. Rather, they are novel means to advance statist interests in which sovereignty is subject to a greater regulative pluralism. The place of states and sovereignty has been changed and their modes of behaviour have been importantly influenced by globalization, but their significance has not been dislodged. Most crucially, the forms of cooperation and collaboration that have emerged thus far have been conceived and organized in strictly statist terms. Whether at the WTO or in the finance ministers' meetings under G20 auspices, states still act to establish new approaches and continue to think of their policy challenges in statist terms. Ultimately, globalization reinforces the view that economic matters, and the norms, rules and institutions that structure global economic relations, are fundamental to the character of international order.

What influence has globalization had on the supplementary rules of the international system and the institutions which embody them? Globalization has been closely associated with the growth in power and influence of international institutions and organizations. These organizations, many thought, would be ideally placed not only to increase their influence, but potentially to become more important players in world politics as globalization shows up the functional limitations of a state-based system of order. Yet, existing institutions are a long way from realizing this potential. Clearly in some spheres globalization has provided institutions with an increased capacity to influence states and to shape the character of international outcomes. The WTO's dispute resolution mechanism and the European Commission are two such examples. Institutions have improved their structural influence in the system – states are increasingly willing to participate in formal institutions to advance their interests and to be bound by the rules and requirements of such groupings. In this sense, international order under conditions of globalization is being increasingly institutionalized. However, while states are willing to accede to institutionalization it does not follow that they are entirely willing to defer to institutions in all circumstances. A great number of institutions are suffering precisely because states are not willing to transform an interest in cooperation into more substantive policy determinations. The primary source of these problems lies in their structural characteristics. The lingering power of states puts marked limits on the ways in which collective action can be advanced, and indeed it constrains the conception of the nature of problems which need to be solved. While institutions are increasing their role in international order, they are doing so as the agents of states or as supplements to them.

The increasing role of institutions in world politics reflects a subtle but important shift in the normative purposes of international order. Within the UN and the EU, as well as in the corpus of international law, there is a growing emphasis on a social conception of the purpose of international order. That is, in the past, order was about managing the system to allow states to determine their own fates as they saw fit. In both the increasing importance of institutions, as well as the rules that they embody, managing the consequences of anarchy now involves explicit attempts to advance specific social outcomes. These include proscriptions on particular forms of state behaviour that are thought to be so egregious as to override the principle of sovereign authority (such as genocide), a set of individual rights that states have a duty to uphold and the redistribution of resources to the least well-off. The rules and institutions of international order have a dimension which advances normative ends that are not only associated with states but also with individuals irrespective of their state of origin and with certain economic outcomes. Some of these views predate globalization – the UN's conception of human rights has its origins somewhat earlier than the current phase. But globalization is reinforcing the structural position of institutions and rules which advance normative goals that are at odds with the traditional statist focus of the system. Of course, the acceptance of norms and rules has not permanently achieved these outcomes, but globalization is contributing to an important shift in the purpose of international order, one which does not sit easily with many existing practices and conceptions.

War, and the use of force as an instrument of foreign policy more generally, is the other aspect of international order considered in this book. Traditionally understood, war is not a function of the collapse of international order, rather it is an extreme way in which order could be upheld. The balance of power, the management of great powers and the practice of diplomacy were intended to cope with diverging interests among states. If these could not be reconciled through peaceful means, order could ultimately be imposed by war. The conditions of globalization have led to a clear shift in the role that war plays. In part, globalization has enhanced a tendency that had emerged in earlier times, a trend that involves a growing moral rejection of the legitimacy of the use of force and a recognition of its limited utility in the nuclear age. The order-creating function of war derived from the fact that force was deemed to be a legitimate means to resolve disputes. This legitimacy has been curtailed as globalization has tied state interests in such a way that, in the vast majority of circumstances, makes the use of force unfeasible if not completely counterproductive. Globalization also contributes to this tendency through increasing the political salience of our awareness of the suffering of others and a recognition that it is in our interests, due to the connections of globalization, to take action in response to these problems. On the one hand globalization is narrowing the circumstances in which force can used to resolve disputes or as a tool of foreign policy, but on the other it is increasing the chances that force will be used to resolve humanitarian crises and other complex emergencies. While threats to a state's vital national interests or security have always been thought to be reasonable causes for the use of force, today human rights and democracy have been added to the list of conditions in which, under certain circumstances, force can be used. Indeed for some (although they are in a minority) these new circumstances do not only allow force, they mandate its use. This should not be confused with an assertion that war is obsolete or that militaries have been transformed from war-fighters to the avengers of human rights abuse. Under conditions of globalization the role of war in the workings of international order has become, at once, less important and more.

To summarize, globalization has not revolutionized the structure and functions of international order. While it has presaged important changes, such as the growth in importance of economic relations, the increase in significance of collaboration and institutions and shifts in the use of force, the fundamental character of world politics does not appear to have been changed. Indeed, globalization appears to be entrenching aspects of the existing order. It is enhancing the power and purchase of nationalism in domestic politics and culture. Globalization is also working to further strengthen the idea of the state even while globalization's economic and cultural processes reveal the limitations of statist conceptions of politics and economics. This involves strengthening the appeal of the state as the only institution through which political communities can find meaning in an ever more complex and disorienting world. Third, states are having aspects of their material position enhanced. Globalization is enhancing the taxation revenues of states, at least of those which are adapting to these new circumstances; it is allowing the state greater and more sophisticated domination of society because the increased vulnerability that it brings forces people to turn to the state for enhanced security. This does not mean that all states are better off under globalization, rather it refers to the general way in which globalization provides states with new opportunities to enhance their power and capacity even while it diminishes the range and efficacy of old approaches. Whether in the war against terror or support for export industry, globalization is not only not weakening the state it is also strengthening its hand. It may be said that globalization is bringing with it changes that ought to presage a transformation in the structures of international order – environmental challenges and infectious diseases are only the most obvious developments that present significant incentives for change – yet the idea of political community is not evolving with these demands. While globalization is influencing various components of the current order, when taken together they do not yet aggregate out to a substantive restructuring of the constitutional basis of world politics.

Still an Anarchical Society?

Bull's examination of order famously depicts the international system as an anarchical society. This intuitively oxymoronic label conveys the idea that sociable relations among states exist in spite of the anarchy which one might have assumed precluded such a possibility. Does this view still have purchase given the changes in world politics? The short answer is no. We do not still live in Bull's anarchical society. This conclusion does not, however, derive from a belief that globalization is recasting all the institutions which structure the processes of world politics. Rather, it is because Bull's conception of an anarchical society is ultimately an inadequate description of the system of modern international relations and the limitations of his version of international order are brought into stark relief by globalization. While Bull's account has much to recommend it – it is a much richer interpretation of the character of world politics than the arid rationalist theories that are prevalent in the US – there are a number of shortcomings that globalization makes particularly clear. At a basic level, the institutions which are said to underwrite international society have no place for economic relations and international institutions. These are two of the most important aspects of contemporary world politics whose significance has been enhanced by globalization. The complex networks of the global economy, its systems of trade, finance and production link states and societies in such a way as to have a clear impact upon the aims of states as well as the means they use to pursue these ambitions. One cannot understand the nature of contemporary US–China relations without coming to terms with their complex economic interdependencies. The US relies on China buying treasury bonds to finance its twin deficits, and China relies on the US market for its exports. Thus any political rivalry is riven with these economic twists. Equally, institutions have become central to the system. Even if the US is hostile to the UN it cannot ignore its existence entirely. At the very least it is forced to go through the charade of consultation before taking action, such as in Iraq. The membership of institutions defines so many states' approaches to vital issues that analysis of any sphere of world politics, even from the most statist point of view, must take them into account. More importantly, central to the notion of international society is the view that it is the product of a set of common interests and values which bind it together. Globalization has made clear that any conception of the common interests and values of 21st century world politics must include a high value placed on the smooth functioning of the global economy. No state contests that the stable functioning of the global capitalist economy is in its interest, nor do any states of size, or indeed any meaningful group of states, challenge the fundamental basis of the contemporary economic order.

The idea that globalization is changing the structure of the international system says more about the peculiarities of our ideas about the international system than it does about globalization. The processes of globalization that have been explored in this book are largely the product of relatively recent developments. The financial integration that is so characteristic of the current period dates from the breakdown of the Bretton Woods monetary regime and the rise of international financial markets in the 1970s. Containerization, which has facilitated a great deal of international trade, was a product of the 1960s and the information technology revolution first emerged in the late 1970s. Regionalism – a process central to many experiences of global change – while having earlier experiences in the 1950s and 1960s, became a more deeply rooted process in the 1980s. In contrast to this, the globalization of the international political system dates from 1945 and the decolonization process which created, for the first time, a genuinely global system of international politics. Within 15 years of the UN's foundation in 1945, the membership had nearly doubled from 51 to 99. The economic and cultural globalization that we consider to be the core of the broader process is in many respects catching up with the political programme.

Prior to 1945 the international system was dominated by norms and rules which structured the relations among the wealthy European states and which also justified the dominance of imperialism. These ideas were no longer tenable, both politically and practically, after 1945 and the European powers were obligated to extend the basic norms of the system across the globe. Thus an international system of states in which the entire population of the planet and virtually all of its dry surface is part of a single political system is historically rather new. The globalization of the international state system, while creating significant barriers to the workings of a single global market economy, has also done much to facilitate its incarnation. This new system applied European principles of sovereignty and statehood to all, regardless of race or levels of 'civilization'. At first glance, then, one might say that the orthodox account of order is largely in line with the contemporary situation, although it might need to pay more attention to the brutal means through which international society was expanded and to give more recognition to the genuine novelty of a universal egalitarian international order. So what is the problem? While it was based on European traditions of inter-state conduct, from the outset the new system of world politics

accepted as foundational concepts important conceptions of individual rights, and of state conduct, that reflected a decisive shift in the
normative purpose of the legal and political order from that which
underpinned the pre-existing European system.

The embrace of both old-fashioned conceptions of sovereign
equality and non-interference and new visions of the purpose of
international order is an inconsistency to say the least. As Keene
notes, the world now 'possesses a single global structure of political
and legal order but it is riven by contradictions because we have not
resolved the fundamental modern dichotomy about what order in
world politics is for' (2002: 143). Is the purpose of order to advance
state interests as defined and conceived only by the state or is it
intended to advance and protect a particular conception of acceptable social conduct? This question of what is acceptable conduct,
which drives so much tension in the current order, has become more
pressing due to globalization. The connections among societies, the
growing awareness of a cosmopolitan sensibility and the vested
interests one has in conduct beyond one's own borders due to
economic linkages has exacerbated the tensions inherent in the
contemporary order. Globalization not only reveals more starkly
the political tension which lies at the heart of the modern international system but also has distinctly increased the costs, both social
and economic, in those circumstances where these tensions create
conflict.

The rules and institutions of the international system are an
attempt to cope with the demands that arise from political, cultural
and social differences among peoples. The system is predicated on the
belief that political communities have a moral equality – articulated
in the notion of sovereign equality – and that this should be
respected. Political communities should be free to determine their
fate as they choose. Yet the system is also based on a growing set of
rules that place minimal standards of conduct for political communities. Globalization is working to make peoples across these
communities increasingly aware of one another and is thus exposing
these competing foundational principles of modern international
order to ever greater political, economic and moral pressure.
Globalization is not changing the current system, but highlighting
its structural limitations. Moreover, it is establishing social circumstances under which these contradictions may not be sustainable over
the longer run.

World Politics in the 21st Century

The Cold War in many ways masked the incipient globalization process, or at least the political dimensions of globalization, which was set in train in the ashes of the Second World War. Indeed some claim that one can attribute the collapse of the USSR to globalization. This may well be the case, at least inasmuch as it was unable to cope either with the domestic requirements of a large and complex industrial society or with the international competition which its revolutionary ideology had demanded. The collapse of the USSR led to the incorporation of Russia and the successor states into the global economy and largely completed the structural process of economic globalization. This allowed both the strengths and weaknesses of the post-war institutions and norms to be more plainly visible. The post-war system established an international order that is comprised of states and it continues to reflect their continued dominance of the moral and material realm. Yet one can ask very real questions about the fit between states and the tasks that they discharge under conditions of globalization. Might the world economy be better served by some kind of global economic regulatory body which sets rules for economic interaction? Could human rights be more effectively enforced if the responsibility for their protection were taken out of the hands of the deeply compromised state system? An international military force could be deployed to prevent genocide and to resolve conflicts around the world without the complications which state interests provide. A transnational redistributive system could ensure that resources are directed from the wealthy to the poor, overriding the narrow interests of states and domestic groupings. Globalization seems to insist that these kind of radical changes are increasingly needed.

One of the reasons that so many felt that globalization was going to herald an era of 'multilateral governance', and thus greatly enhance the strength and influence of international institutions and organizations, was the logical fit that they were thought to have with its material circumstances. Globalization reveals starkly the consequences of a territorially based system of exclusive political authority. It shows all too clearly that decisions in one state have consequences for many others beyond the state's borders. Institutions were thought to be able to overcome these limitations and exercise some form of global or transnational governance. The problem, of course, is that states are not especially interested in being overruled. It may be the case that trade policy should be in the hands of a technocratic transnational elite or that global courts should administer justice on those who have transgressed international law. But states and their citizens are not convinced of this logic. Among the many problems with these sorts of notions is the question of legitimacy and voice. In whose name would these groups act? Humanity has a neat rhetorical ring, but it lacks a mobilization capacity that is all too evident. There is a large gap between the institutions and norms of the modern international system – in which states still have the preponderance of material and political power – and the changing conditions of modern life to which globalization is contributing. Europe is often set out as a vanguard example of action where circumstances have driven the construction of new and ostensibly more appropriate political institutions. Yet the considerable disquiet that presently exists within the EU about its role and purpose derives to a large part from the inability of elites to match the institutionalization of politics with appropriate social norms and values. States have been remarkably successful at this, but new versions of political systems, no matter how rationally appropriate they may be to global conditions, show a decided inability to turn this functional fit into broader societal affiliation and support. The European experience lends support to the view that globalization demands a resolution to the 'fundamental dichotomy' of international order, but its experience suggests that this is no closer than it has ever been.

The idea that globalization is heralding a post-Westphalian global order is misplaced. Apart from doing what we can to avoid yet another post-prefixed label, it is out of place because the idea of a Westphalian order is not a particularly useful way of understanding the conditions of modern world politics. The world that was created in 1945, and to which the current order is the logical heir, is a long way from the 17th century Wars of Religion (see Teschke, 2003). World politics is still a state-centred game and, although globalization is changing the material circumstances in which states find themselves, the ideas and norms of international order, and the institutions these beget, have yet to be transformed to match these circumstances. The complex networks of production and exchange that criss-cross the world and draw state interests ever closer do not provide sufficient force to be a stable basis for a peaceful international system nor do they promote a politically tenable restructuring of the current system. Globalization's greatest contribution to the current order is the value premium it places on openness. Yet in spite of this (or indeed because of it), states are increasingly wary of elements of openness. For example, there is widespread scepticism about unregulated population movements and indeed states are growing increasingly leery of immigration in general. While globalization is contributing to a cosmopolitan sensibility it is equally driving a rise in nationalism which not only risks its own future, but is a sobering lesson in the contradictory tendencies of this complex phenomenon. The ideas that govern conduct in world politics appear unable to keep pace with the reality they represent. The state-based conception of modern politics, at both the domestic and international level, still predominates. Its hand has been enhanced by globalization even while these transnational flows show the very real limits of states and statist approaches to political and economic life. Until such time as the ideational and material dominance of statist conceptions of politics change – and there appears little in contemporary globalization that will bring this about – world politics will continue to be a game in which the tensions between a cosmopolitan conception of interests and obligations and a statist conception of politics will play themselves out in predictably depressing ways.

Conclusion: Globalization, World Politics and the 21st Century

Scholars of international relations have a particular urge to publish prognostications of the global order which claim to have distilled the essence of the deeper patterns and processes of international affairs. The rewards to their careers of getting it right, or indeed getting it wrong but in a sufficiently high profile fashion, can be considerable. In times of obvious change this temptation is particularly strong. As the Berlin Wall crumbled and the Soviet Union collapsed an intellectual vacuum emerged. Where ideas of bipolar stability, ideological confrontation and an era of Cold War once held sway there was uncertainty and thus opportunity for the ambitious to make their mark (e.g. Fukuyama, 1989; Huntington, 1993; Kegley and Raymond, 1994; Kennedy, 1993; Mearsheimer, 1990). Theorists and policy-savants argued about whether history had come to an end or whether conflict, the perennial condition of human existence, would be driven by cultural and religious differences rather than interests or ideology. At the century's end it was still not clear what pattern world politics would follow. The Cold War was very much in the past, but no obvious shape had emerged to replace it as a touchstone for policy-makers and scholars. Traditional great power rivalries were not part of the scene, the global economy was galloping at a tremendous pace and, with the exception of a few outlying conflicts and skirmishes, some kind of *pax Americana* seemed to be holding things together. Yet there was no clear consensus as to why this was the case. Were institutions making states cooperate? Was the hegemonic power of the US underwriting systemic stability? Was this simply an interregnum between periods of great power rivalry? Perhaps it had something to do with the claims about globalization that had become so prominent across the social sciences.

211

The absence of consensus about the underlying character of world politics was, and in many ways still is, the feature of the study of world politics. Globalization's sudden appearance as a profound force and putative source of change has only added to the academic disorder. Uncertainty about how to interpret China's growing economic and political power and the consolidation of European integration was compounded by the appearance of a wide-ranging phenomenon which many highly regarded sociologists and social theorists had declared was ushering in a brave new world of globality where space and time were being compressed with profound consequences for all. For many, arguments about the optimal way of getting states to cooperate seemed trivial in comparison with the proposition that sovereignty was on its last legs or that global production and financial networks were bringing states to their knees. Globalization became an important part of the contestation that had become central to studies of world politics. While scholars place a differing weight on its power and significance, it has become key to many debates about world politics, although its influence over the various sub-species of world politics varies considerably. For example, studies of foreign policy-making, considerations of ethics and justice and unorthodox approaches to security have tended to make more detailed assessments of globalization than, for example, mainstream IR theory. Although globalization was thought to be important, it has not been systematically integrated into existing theoretical analyses of international relations nor has it become a central problematic of the discipline.

If world politics is not clearly defined by great power conflict or ideological rivalry, what are its key features and how does the discussion offered in this book influence this tableau? First, the current international system is distinguished by the universality of its system of economic relations. Resource allocation is not evenly distributed and global linkages involve much closer relations among the wealthy developed states than between the rich and the poor. But the vast majority of the states and societies of the planet are members of the system and, importantly, there are no meaningful states which stand outside the system nor are there any significant efforts to provide an alternative to the capitalist means through which it distributes resources. Second, the world now has a genuinely global inter-state system that is governed by principles of sovereignty and legal equality. This state of affairs is a lot newer than many realize and to have the entire population of the planet participating in a properly global system of political relations built on broadly accepted norms and rules is historically unprecedented. Third, the contemporary system is dominated by the military, economic and political power of the United States. Never in modern history has one state been so predominant and has so clearly outstripped all others in almost all measures of influence (Brooks and Wohlforth, 2002; Kennedy, 2002). This overwhelming power is a function of a wide range of developments and it may not last, but the contemporary world is one in which American power is not only unrivalled, it is not even close to being matched. Fourth, the system currently has a number of major states whose power and influence is rapidly increasing. China, Russia and India are three geographically and demographically significant powers which are undergoing rapid economic growth that will dramatically transform the political, economic and cultural balance of world politics. If for the past two hundred years the centre of the world's gravity has been the North Atlantic on whose sides firstly European and latterly American power has resided, then that centre is clearly beginning to shift to Asia. It is in this context – one of a global economic and political system with a power structure that is in flux – that globalization is being played out. In part, globalization is a product of the broader character of the international system. Globalization helps bind elements of the system together, but, as this book has shown, it also reveals structural fault lines and throws up challenges of its own. In this sense it deserves to be considered as a fifth key characteristic of the contemporary world. Taken together, these five elements constitute a distinctive and complex setting for world politics.

In this basic sense it is uncontroversial to say that globalization matters to world politics and this observation is reflected in the syllabuses of most university courses on international relations and its cognate subjects. In such course, students are introduced to states, sovereignty, international order, security, realism, liberalism, Marxism, and constructivism. They will also examine the nature of war and conflict, the role of institutions, regionalism, the global economy, the environment, human rights, international law and, of course, globalization. This is because, whether viewed from an empirical or a theoretical point of view, it is very hard to examine contemporary world politics without talking about globalization. Yet as any undergraduate grappling with an introductory class on International

Relations can attest, working out how globalization sits within (or across) the international system can be particularly challenging. Most of the core literature comes from outside the discipline and thus its frame of reference can be hard to integrate into the paradigms of international relations. Scholte's notion of supraterritoriality (2000) and Waltz's conception of international system (1979) operate on quite different understandings of world politics. Moreover, the absence of any clear attempt to consider the impact of globalization on the broader institutions and processes of world politics makes clarification particularly challenging. Students and scholars of world politics know that globalization is important, the problem is that there is no clear statement about the way in which it matters nor indeed any real consensus on the nature of the international order which currently predominates.

I have tried in this book to resolve at least part of this problem by making an attempt to provide a systematic assessment of globalization's interaction with key features of the international system. I have argued that although globalization is a significant part of world politics, it is not the most important feature and is not yet a source of radical change to the fundamental institutions and practices of the system. Moreover, we have seen that globalization is playing itself out in unexpected and contradictory ways. For example, rather than strengthening the hand of international institutions, globalization is undermining their capacity to influence events. Instead of hollowing out the state it is, in some cases, reinforcing its power. At the outset, the book had two basic purposes. The first was to provide an overview of and reflection on the globalization debate. The sprawling nature of globalization and the equally extensive debate that had grown up around it had caused no small amount of confusion and I have attempted to make some sense of that debate. The second purpose was to assess the nature and extent of changes that globalization had wrought on the structures, norms and institutions of world politics. The book therefore has a number of conclusions that relate to each to these distinct, though related, aims.

Globalization Today

The book offers a reflection on globalization and world politics and provides not only insights into the state of contemporary world politics, and the place of globalization in its structures and institutions, it affords a distinctive perspective on globalization itself. Perhaps the most obvious starting point is to note that the experiences of recent years have put paid to some of the more over-blown claims made by many in the first flush of globalization. Modernity has not been surpassed by 'globality'. While globalization has contributed to a speeding up of some interactions and has reduced the significance of some of the costs that geographic constraints impose in a range of sectors – most notably in the realms of finance and production – the idea that the rise of 'supra-territoriality', or some other compression of space and time, is fundamentally restructuring social life is not especially compelling. This is particularly so from a world politics perspective. Indeed globalization seems to be exacerbating some of the problems of modernity that have been central to the dynamics of world politics, such as the inequalities that derive from the structure of the capitalist economy and the processes of nationalism. Yet while recent developments have made clear that much of what was written about globalization has been over-hyped, there have been important shifts in social practices due to the transformations associated with globalization – from the forms of identity to the strategies of states – and to dismiss the idea is to ignore an important part of modern world politics. So how can one make some theoretical sense of globalization? The first recommendation of this study is to counsel against the construction of grand theories of globalization. The argument advanced here has taken a fairly constrained consequentialist conception because efforts to build over-arching theories of globalization are of little substantive help. In part this a function of the sheer scale and complexity of the wide range of processes that constitute the broader trend. Just as expansive theories of nationalism, modernity and war tend to have more wrong with them than they have right, so maximalist approaches to globalization tend to obscure more than they reveal. Put more directly, globalization is best understood in the context of the specific sector of social experience that one is trying to comprehend. Instead of seeking to build macro theories that are applicable in all sectors and under all conditions it is perhaps more useful to limit the focus of globalization, its nature and impact, to the particular sector one is trying to grasp. This constraint is urged not only in the name of practicality, but also because it appears that globalization does not make sense as a social phenomenon abstracted from its particular circumstances. As a label for a broad-ranging trend it is reasonable, but beyond that, trying to tie together all of its disparate threads into a neat analytic package not only frustrates, it takes us away from the very important task of ascertaining how the increase in rate and speed of the movement of goods, capital, people and knowledge is influencing specific aspects of social life. When attempting the difficult task of trying to adjudicate among existing approaches, one key method to begin to make sense of the debate is to constrain the conception and application of ideas associated with globalization to the specific aspect of the social realm in which one is interested.

The assessment of globalization's interaction with the international system shows that the phenomenon is a deeply contradictory creature. Rather than the unified, homogenizing process that was the popularized in much early work, both critical and supportive, globalization pulls social affairs in quite different and often unexpected directions. Instead of pushing political authority up to the more 'sensible' plane of supranational global governance, it is acting to help stymie some of these efforts. While it forces states to transform their behaviour and to reduce their scope for action in some spheres, it strengthens their hands in others. The global economy is perhaps the best example of this. Globalization acts to draw the world ever closer as the costs of trade and investment are reduced. Yet as it unifies the international system through global economic interaction it distributes resources in a highly uneven way. Indeed, it is this unevenness and inequality which threatens to be a force which could bring the processes of globalization to an end. Third, globalization is a contingent phenomenon. Although politicians and some scholars use an almost elemental language to capture its influence and its dynamic (it is like the weather or gravity), there is nothing natural or inevitable about it. The increasing interactions among and across states and societies are made possible by a raft of policy choices, ideological preferences as well as geopolitical and security circumstances. The conditions which have allowed globalization to emerge are themselves subject to change. A transformation in the geopolitical circumstances of world politics or a shift in ideological preferences will have a significant impact on globalization in general and the way in which it influences the international system in particular. To think that globalization has bound the interests of states and societies so as to make any move away from contemporary

levels of integration and openness is to misunderstand the fundamental character of this process.

The sharpest line of differentiation in the globalization debate is
between those who dispute whether globalization is a positive or
negative force. For many mainstream economists, this is a no-
brainer. Globalization promotes growth and growth is good for
everyone, most especially the poor. On the other hand, a wide-
ranging group argues that in some sectors globalization has a
decidedly malignant impact. Growth can make some of the poor
worse off and exacerbate global inequality. For others, globalization
is thought to be harmful to the environment, to be eroding
democracy and undermining the rights of workers. So, is globalization a positive or negative force? One of the sources of this dispute
lies in the differing standards and measures that each side adopts.
When considering whether globalization is good for the poor,
conclusions depend on whether one is considering aggregate global
data, country-by-country figures or other competing measurement
methods (such as how one measures inequality). In some respects,
these debates will always be with us because ongoing methodological
shortcomings mean that unambiguous 'objective' answers to these
questions will not arrive any time soon. In general it appears that
perceptions of globalization's consequences derive from one's belief
about its basic character (see Aisbett, 2005). Critics of globalization
share a perception that the phenomenon involves power moving
upward and away from those they feel are suffering because of its
transformation. Supporters, on the other hand, see globalization as a
force which distributes resources more widely and hence provides
opportunities to enhance wealth and power to a greater degree than
previously. In short, this dispute is as much about different perceptions of globalization as it is about globalization's 'true' consequences. While the issues raised in this book are not focused explicitly
on these issues they do allow us to make several points in this regard.
First, as globalization is not undermining the state, complaints about
its negative consequences that are directed in this fashion are short of
the mark. It may be that many states are deregulating labour markets
or lowering taxation rates to enhance their competitiveness, but these
are choices of and by states, and thus concern about the social
consequences of these changes should be directed at politicians and
policy elites and not blamed on globalization. Second, this book has
shown that globalization does not simply involve a clear-cut

concentration of power by the well-off at the expense of those without power. It operates in a much more contradictory way. For example, many are concerned that firms are the unquestioned beneficiaries of globalization. Yet, while some firms are benefiting from the process, the marked increase in competitive pressure on a wider range of firms – the result of more and more sectors becoming exposed to international competition – means that many also lose out, as do their workers and shareholders. This is not to say that concerns raised about concentrations of wealth and power by some firms and states are misplaced. Rather it is to emphasize that the processes which produce such a concentration create a range of other consequences – such as cheaper food or national trade dependence – which can play themselves out in unexpected ways.

One of the most common questions asked of globalization is whether it provides greater benefits than costs. In trying to answer this question there is considerable temptation to draw up a ledger-style account in which one tots up the benefits (such as rising GDP) and sets them alongside the costs (reduced capacity for statist economic policy) and then determine some overall balance. This is a popular approach among supporters and critics alike. For the supporters, the benefits are said to include reduced costs and improved quality of goods to consumers, rising living standards for the poor, a greater dynamism about economic relations and other positive macro-level transformations that they feel accrue from the openness and integration that globalization brings (e.g. Legrain, 2002; Wolf, 2004). In their minds, the benefits clearly outweigh the transition costs borne by workers whose industries are no longer competitive, increased environmental pollution or the loss of some aspects of local culture. On the other hand, critics tend to argue that firms benefit at the cost of states, that capital benefits at the cost of labour, that the West gains to the detriment of the rest of the world and that the rich benefit disproportionately while the poor pay for these gains, both within and between states (e.g. Anderson and Cavanagh, 2000; Klein, 2000; Monbiot, 2003). From this view the ledger is heavily skewed toward the costs and whatever benefits do accrue are tainted by a dubious morality. Notwithstanding the problem that balance sheets of this kind cannot really be objectively drawn up because of wildly differing measurements, there is a much larger problem that results from irreconcilably different standards. Any cost–benefit analysis will always reflect the underlying value placed on a given sphere because it is impossible to devise common standards across the entire range of sectors influenced by globalization that will allow reasonable assessment along these lines.

Yet there is still a need, both instinctive and analytic, to make some sort of broader judgment as to the impact of globalization. How can one do this and avoid the problems of measurement and differentials in relative worth? One way is indicated in this study. As seen in the various chapters, the impact of globalization is rarely linear or intuitive: it strengthens institutions we might have expected to have been weakened and undermines others that appear well placed to take advantage of new conditions. It is simply wrong to conclude that firms benefit at the cost of states or that capital benefits at the cost of labour. One can always find firms that have not been able to compete and capital that has lost out. Ultimately success or failure under conditions of globalization depends on the capacity of a given group or institution to optimize the opportunities that the changes bring and on its ability to minimize or absorb the costs. China has, so far, been particularly successful at managing its relationship with global markets and investors and has been able to drive a remarkable economic growth program by harnessing the possibilities of globalization and coping with the costs. Yet it is not clear that its political structures will be able to cope with the consequences of this development. Globalization may yet have the final say. This view, that costs and benefits are determined by institutional response capacity, draws attention to the fact that states have an important role to play in the way in which globalization develops. They do this by coping with the transition costs of globalization, by preparing groups (whether firms, workers or society more generally) for the challenges that globalization will pose and by setting the institutional and regulatory framework through which globalization will be played out. Finally, while broadly normative judgments are hard to make, it seems that globalization has a tendency to amplify the advantages and disadvantages it brings. Thus, if one gets the settings right then the benefits can be large, while if one gets them wrong the impact can be disastrous.

Globalization is clearly adding an energy to the global economy, but it is not undermining any of the dominant political structures of the international system. This has consequences for the perception of its worth. More particularly, it means that the injustices of the international economic system that result from its structural characteristics will continue. The rules of trade that favour wealthy producers are unlikely to be radically transformed. Moreover, the way in which membership of international society endows despots with the legal infrastructure for corruption and abuse is continuing to be facilitated. If anything, aid and other programmes of global governance which work through the existing systems of international order will serve to entrench the notion that globalization is unjust. In this sense, perceptions of worth derive not from the changes it has wrought, but from what has not been transformed. In short, globalization does not have an inherent quality, whether positive or negative. Rather it is a set of changes that alters the environment in which states and societies operate. Its capacity to provide benefits, or impose further costs, is thus dependent on the way in which those states and societies respond. There can be no doubt that there is tremendous economic, political and social possibility in the changes associated with globalization, but this potential will not necessarily move only in one way. Rather its capacity to improve the lives of many millions, or not, is contingent on how we respond to these new circumstances, to the kinds of rules and institutions we create and the underlying values that these represent and reinforce.

To summarize, this book draws the following conclusions about globalization. First, it is most usefully thought of as a context-specific social phenomenon and not as a stand-alone exogenous force. Second, globalization is a highly uneven and contradictory phenomenon. Third, thus far it has not had a significant impact on the social structures of world politics, but it continues to drive important lower-level changes among actors, particularly in the way they conceive of their preferences and in the strategies they use to advance them.

Globalization and World Politics

The second purpose of the book is to assess the implications of the changes associated with globalization for the workings and structures of the international system. The intention was to try to provide an assessment of the current state of the system, and particularly those elements where globalization is thought to be especially influential so that those who have to deal with its changes – students, scholars and policy-makers – can have a better sense of what they are up against. In its most basic sense, this book has sought to show that globalization has not and is not likely to fundamentally reconfigure the nature of the international system in the short to medium term. To draw on the classic distinction, globalization has not brought about a fundamental transformation of the nature of the international system but its character has undergone some important though subtle shifts.

This is most evident in the way in which globalization is making increasingly clear the shortcomings of the existing system. From the tensions between the underlying normative purpose of international order to the manifest inadequacy of the sovereign state system to be able to provide the sort of authoritative rule making and enforcement that a genuinely global economy requires, globalization increasingly reveals the fissures that are created when a system of territorially defined legally equal political entities is overlaid with a global set of networks of resource, capital and knowledge distribution. Related to this, globalization shows that many of the concepts we have developed to make sense of the international system are increasingly out of step with the world they are trying to understand and explain. Globalization shows that the formal distinction between domestic and international spheres, one that is premised on the belief that there is a decisively different logic of political and economic action in each, makes little sense. Equally, it shows that orthodox conceptions of sovereignty – a view which sees it as a resource of the state which globalization either reinforces or undermines – are of little use. Sovereignty is a relational principle whose malleability is a function of the differing ways in which states and others put it into practice. To see sovereignty as an idea being eroded by transnational or global forces is to misunderstand the character of this cornerpiece of modern world politics.

Globalization has also changed the relative significance of the central actors in several important ways. First, and most obviously, globalization enhances the role, influence and capacity of non-state actors at the global level. One need look only at the role of private financial institutions to get some sense of this change. The Asian financial crisis of 1997–98 was triggered by private financial institutions. They also help states finance their budgets through the purchase of bonds and the extension of credit and through this can act to discipline state policy choice. This expansion of important actors in the system is not only the purview of finance and economics. Globalization provides the opportunity for small and weak states, as well as non-state actors such as criminal organizations and terrorist groups, to significantly increase their influence on the strategic environment. The global networks afford increased access to weaponry and opportunities to organize and conduct strategic operations at great distance with remarkable effect. Globalization also provides an increasing range of targets as the vulnerability of states and societies has become greater. To be sure, states maintain their position as the most important actors in the system, but they are influenced to a greater extent than ever before by the relative increase in power and influence of non-state actors.

The expansion in range and influence of actors has produced a shift in the character of international relations. States have not lost power to institutions, nor are MNCs the new masters of the global universe. Reductions in the costs of the movement of goods, people, capital and knowledge have meant that states, firms, NGOs and institutions must adjust the way they conduct their relations with one another, if only subtly. Globalization thus supports the view of those pluralists who have long argued that relations among actors in the system should not be defined only by conflict. Rather, globalization has led many actors to recognize that coordination and cooperation is vital to their interests. Thus, while competition among states has not disappeared, foreign policy no longer starts from a zero-sum conception of state interaction. Moreover, states recognize that non-state actors, such as NGOs, firms and international institutions, play an important role in advancing their interests. As such the interaction among actors is characterized by a pragmatism which reflects the growing importance of non-state sources of power. This should not be understood as representing a world in which states rationally pursue their interests in a cooperative fashion and sensibly deploy pareto-optimal policy approaches. Statist and nationalist conceptions of interests still intervene in this landscape and at times seem to thrive under these conditions. Rather the point is simply that states increasingly recognize that their fates are interlinked and that non-state actors are of increasing importance. How they respond to this varies, as does the extent to which a recognition of interests leads to policies which optimally pursue their interests.

Related to the subtle shift in the character of international relations are changes in the strategies that actors undertake to advance their interests. Most obviously this refers to the increasing willingness of states to cooperate. But this does not mean simply a turn to the global and the multilateral. Rather, states are looking to a wide range of means through which they can seek to influence their increasingly complex environment. One can see this tendency most clearly in bilateral trade agreements and regional political and economic groupings. Whether through efforts such as the Chiang Mai Initiative or the expansion of the Southern African Development Community, states are undertaking novel strategies to deal with the changed circumstances that globalization presents. But these shifts are not all cooperative. The foreign policy preferences of George W. Bush's US presidency show how globalization's challenges have prompted a much less cooperative approach to security than in the recent past. Globalization is heralding a range of changes, firstly in the way states define their interests, and secondly in the means through which they seek to advance these interests. But it is not driving a singular homogenized and predictable response.

Finally, globalization has most tangibly influenced the context of world politics by making states and societies increasingly vulnerable to a wider range of threats. These include global economic forces, such as rising oil prices or volatile financial markets, which in themselves are nothing particularly new. But globalization has increased the extent, reach, and scope of these vulnerabilities and has expanded the number of states and societies which are so vulnerable. Of course states and societies are not equally exposed to these problems, but without global financial markets and their associated massive movements of short-term capital then economic vulnerability would be considerably less significant. Globalization has also shifted the nature of threat perceptions among societies and states. While the transmission of contagious diseases has always accompanied human interaction, the speed and rate of human movements means that diseases such as SARS or pandemic influenza can be spread around the world faster than ever before. Equally, globalization has made states recognize that non-traditional challenges, such as unregulated population movement, criminal organizations and economic instability, provide decisive security threats. Again, these are not new developments as such, but there is a new perception that they are fundamental challenges, not only to human well-being, but also to the basic existence of the state–society complex. Globalization has made states and societies more vulnerable and has made them perceive that they face severe existential threat because of these vulnerabilities.

In summary, globalization is implicated in key changes to the setting of the international system. It is not the motive force for a conceptual or institutional revolution, but it has wrought some clear shifts in important areas. World politics is now a more complex place. It is populated by a wider array of actors, with diverging interests and power capacities, than ever before. While interests are increasingly interlinked, the insecurities that globalization breeds, both the social cohesion within states and the international security environment between them, act to mitigate the benefits that might accrue from this apparent harmonization. The international system's underlying structures and principles are still dominating the business of international order but they are increasingly at odds with the social reality that they are trying to navigate. This discrepancy appears to be growing in recent years and is perhaps the greatest challenge that globalization poses to the current structure of world politics.

Globalization and Transformation

At present, globalization has not brought about significant structural change to world politics but it is not to say that things will forever remain as they are. For one thing a sufficient number and range of small changes can aggregate out to much more substantial transformation. The conclusions noted above can be read as early indicators that a broader shift may be forthcoming. The changes associated with globalization do have within them the potential to bring about some broader significant transformations of the fundamental structures of world politics. There are at least three plausible scenarios in which one can see such an outcome. The first scenario involves globalization working to make the shortcomings of the current system politically untenable, thus generating significant systemic change. The linkages which globalization creates between states and societies will exacerbate the shortcomings of the existing system – such as the way in which states block more effective cooperation to combat climate change – to the point where the system ceases to function. It is impossible to ascertain quite what processes might actually bring about change – whether to do with the environment or financial crisis – but this scenario involves a collective recognition by key actors that it is in their interests to reconfigure the rules of the game to better cope with changing circumstances. The second scenario involves a growth in anti-systemic political action and violence producing radical transformation of a different kind. Here, one can plausibly imagine the inequalities and injustices which are perceived to result from globalization providing fuel for radical political movements to try to overturn their systemic origins. In the brutalities of Islamist terrorism one sees a leading edge of such trends. This is not to say that al Qa'eda is about to turn the international system on its head, rather that anti-systemic violence, and more importantly the responses to that violence, could very plausibly contribute to a radical transformation of the international system.

A third, and perhaps most plausible, possibility is that globalization reveals the limits of the existing system, understood in both ethical and efficiency terms, yet its contradictory impulses do not trigger systemic revolution but reaction and a backlash. This 'end of globalization' scenario involves states reaffirming their dominant place but through much greater control of cross-border transactions in which the openness of the current system is replaced with closure and tight regulation of movements of goods, capital, people and knowledge. This is a scenario in which the dislocation and insecurity that globalization breeds, and the inability of existing institutions to cope with its changes, leads not to reform to find better and more appropriate institutions, but a closure of the global chapter.

One cannot know with any certainty what the future has in store, for history has a particular talent for surprise. This book began by noting that many were convinced that globalization was to be the motive force for wide-ranging transformation. The argument presented here has shown that one should be cautious about the extent and character of change. Yet it is important to keep contemporary assessment balanced by a sense of the revolutionary potential that the changes associated with globalization may still have. The current structure of world politics does not have an air of settled stability about it, indeed, it is hard to imagine the structure of the current order muddling along for any great length of time. It is difficult to ascertain what direction it will take, but one suspects that it will necessitate something dramatic, possibly cataclysmic, to produce a more decisive shape to world affairs, and that the process of globalization will be central to this change. The primary message of this book is that globalization matters for world politics but not in the way that many claim or might have thought. The constituent elements that comprise this complex phenomenon are important, not only to the grand processes of the international system, but also to the day-to-day realities of people everywhere. The challenge that students of world politics face, and one which is made the more acute by globalization, is to understand the way in which these two spheres – the global and the everyday – intersect and shape one another. For it is this relationship – how global circumstances affect the life chances of political communities in a tangible way – that will be the most important in determining the extent to which globalization will contribute to a more peaceful or more dangerous international system in the coming century.

References

Abbott, K. W. and Snidal, D. (1998) 'Why States Act through Formal International Organizations', *Journal of Conflict Resolution*, 42(1): 3–32.

Abrahamian, E. (1993) *Khomeinism: Essays on the Islamic Republic* (Berkeley, CA: University of California Press).

Abu-Lughod, J. (1989) *Before European Hegemony: The World System, 1250–1350* (Oxford: Oxford University Press).

Aghion, P. and Williamson, J. G. (1998) *Growth, Inequality and Globalization: Theory, History and Policy* (Cambridge: Cambridge University Press).

Aisbett, E. (2005) *Why are the Critics so Convinced that Globalization is Bad for the Poor?*, NBER Working Paper Number 11066 (Washington, DC: NBER).

Albrow, M. (1996) *The Global Age: State and Society Beyond Modernity* (Cambridge: Polity).

Amin, S. (1997) *Capitalism in the Age of Globalization* (London: Zed Books).

Anderson, B. (1983) *Imagined Communities* (London: Verso).

Anderson, B. (1998) *The Spectre of Comparisons: Nationalism, Southeast Asia and the World* (London: Verso).

Anderson, S. and Cavanagh, J. (2000) *The Top 200: The Rise of Corporate Global Power* Washington, DC: Institute for Policy Studies, http://www.ips-dc.org/reports/top200text.htm.

Angell, N. (1933) *The Great Illusion 1933* (London: William Heinemann).

Annan, K. A. (2000) *We the Peoples: The Role of the United Nations in the 21st Century* (New York: United Nations).

Appadurai, A. (1990) 'Disjuncture and Difference in the Global Cultural Economy' *Theory, Culture and Society*, 7: 295–310.

Appadurai, A. (1996) *Modernity at Large: Cultural Dimensions of Globalization* (Minneapolis: University of Minnesota Press).

Appadurai, A. (2000) 'The Grounds of the Nation-State: Identity, Violence and Territory', in K. Goldmann, U. Hannerz and C. Westin (eds), *Nationalism and Internationalism in the Post-Cold War Era* (London: Routledge), 129–42.

Aron, R. (1966) *Peace and War: A Theory of International Relations* (New York: Doubleday) [first pub. 1964].

ASEAN (2005) *Joint Statement of the Thirty Seventh ASEAN Economic Ministers' Meeting*, Vientiane, ASEAN Secretariat, September, http://www.aseansec.org/17778.htm.

Avant, D. D. (2005) *Market for Force: The Consequences for Privatizing Security* (Cambridge: Cambridge University Press).

Axford, B. (1995) *The Global System: Economics, Politics and Culture* (Cambridge: Polity).

Bairoch, P. (1993) *Economics and World History: Myths and Paradoxes* (London: Harvester Wheatsheaf).

Bairoch, P. and Kozul-Wright, R. (1998) 'Globalization Myths: Some Historical Reflections on Integration, Industrialization and Growth in the World Economy', in R. Kozul-Wright and R. Rowthorn (eds), *Transnational Corporations and the Global Economy* (Basingstoke: Macmillan–UNU–WIDER).

Baldwin, D. A. (ed.) (1993) *Neorealism and Neoliberalism* (New York: Columbia University Press).

Baldwin, R. E. and Martin, P. (1999) *Two Waves of Globalization: Superficial Similarities, Fundamental Differences*, NBER Working Paper No. 6904 (Washington, DC: NBER).

Barber, B. J. (1995) *Jihad vs. McWorld* (New York: Times Books).

Barnett, M. N. and Finnemore, M. (1999) 'The Politics, Power and Pathologies of International Organizations', *International Organization*, 53(4): 699–732.

Barnett, M. N. and Finnemore, M. (2004) *Rules for the World: International Organizations in World Politics* (Ithaca, NY: Cornell University Press).

Bauman, Z. (1998) *Globalization: The Human Consequences* (Cambridge: Polity).

Bayly, C. A. (2004) *The Birth of the Modern World, 1780–1914: Global Connections and Comparisons* (Oxford: Blackwell).

Beck, U. (1999) *World Risk Society* (Cambridge: Polity).

Beck, U. (2000) *What is Globalization?* (Cambridge: Polity).

Bellamy, A. J. (ed.) (2005) *International Society and its Critics* (Oxford: Oxford University Press).

Bennison, A. K. (2002) 'Muslim Universalism and Western Globalization', in A. G. Hopkins (ed.), *Globalization in World History* (London: Pimlico), 74–97.

Berdal, M. (2005) 'Beyond Greed and Grievance – and Not Too Soon...', *Review of International Studies*, 31(4): 687–98.

Berdal, M. and Malone, D. (eds) (2000) *Greed and Grievance: Economic Agenda in Civil Wars* (Boulder, CO: Lynne Rienner), 91–111.

Berger, S. and Dore, R. (eds) (1996) *National Diversity and Global Capitalism* (Ithaca, NY: Cornell University Press).

Berridge, G. R. (2005) *Diplomacy: Theory and Practice*, 2nd edn (Basingstoke: Palgrave Macmillan).

Bhagwati, J. (2004) *In Defence of Globalization* (Oxford: Oxford University Press and Council on Foreign Relations).

Bildt, C. (2000) 'Force and Diplomacy', *Survival*, 42(1): 2000.

Bisley, N. (2004) *The End of the Cold War and the Causes of Soviet Collapse* (Basingstoke: Palgrave Macmillan).

Bisley, N. (2006) 'Enhancing America's Alliances in a Changing Asia-Pacific', *Journal of East Asian Affairs*, 20(2).

Bisley, N. (2007) 'Great Powers and the International System: Between Unilateralism and Multilateralism', in C. A. Snyder (ed.), *Contemporary Security and Strategy*, 2nd edn (Basingstoke: Palgrave Macmillan).

Blustein, P. (2003) *The Chastening: Inside the Crisis that Rocked the Global Financial System and Humbled the IMF* (New York: Public Affairs).

Bordo, M. D, Eichengreen, B. and Irwin, D. A. (1999) *Is Globalization Today Really Different Than Globalization a Hundred Years Ago?*, NBER Working Paper 7195 (Washington DC: National Bureau of Economic Research).

Bornstein, M. (ed.) (1994) *Comparative Economic Systems: Models and Cases*, 7th edn (Homewood, IL: Irwin).

Boyer, R. and Drache, D. (eds) (1996) *States Against Markets: The Limits of Globalization* (London: Routledge).

Brooks, S. G. and Wohlforth, W. (2002) 'American Primacy in Perspective', *Foreign Affairs*, July/August.

Brown, C. (2002) *Sovereignty, Rights and Justice: International Political Theory Today* (Cambridge: Polity).

Brown, C. (2004) 'Do Great Powers Have Great Responsibilities? Great Powers and Moral Agency', *Global Society*, 18(1).

Bueno de Mesquita, B. and Root, H. L. (eds) (2000) *Governing for Prosperity* (New Haven, CT: Yale University Press).

Bull, H. (1977) *The Anarchical Society: A Study of Order in World Politics* (London: Macmillan).

Burton, J. W. (1990) *Conflict: Resolution and Prevention* (New York: St. Martin's Press).

Buzan, B. and Little, R. (2000) *International Systems in World History: Remaking the Study of International Relations* (Oxford: Oxford University Press).

Cable, V. (1999) *Globalization and Global Governance* (London: RIIA).

Callinicos, A. *et al.* (1994) *Marxism and the New Imperialism* (London: Bookmarks).

Camilleri, J. A. and Falk, J. (1992) *The End of Sovereignty? The Politics of a Shrinking and Fragmenting World* (Aldershot: Edward Elgar).

Campbell, K. (2002) 'Globalization's First War?', *The Washington Quarterly*, 25(1).

Carr, E. H. (1945) *Nationalism and After* (London: Macmillan).

Casson, M. (ed.) (1992) *International Business and Global Integration* (Basingstoke: Macmillan).

Castells, M. (1996) *The Rise of the Network Society* (Oxford: Blackwell).

Castells, M. (1997) *The Power of Identity* (Oxford: Blackwell).

Castells, M. (1998) *End of Millennium* (Oxford: Blackwell).

Castles, S. and Miller, M. J. (1998) *The Age of Migration: International Population Movements in the Modern World*, 2nd edn (Basingstoke: Macmillan).

Cerny, P. G. (1995) 'Globalization and the Changing Logic of Collective Action', *International Organization*, 49(4).

Cerny, P. G. (1997) 'Paradoxes of the Competition State: The Dynamics of Political Globalization', *Government and Opposition*, 32(2): 251–74.

Cha, V. D. (2000) 'Globalization and the Study of International Security', *Journal of Peace Research*, 37(3): 391–403.

Chaudhuri, K. N. (1990) *Asia Before Europe: Economy and Civilization of the Indian Ocean from the Rise of Islam to 1750* (Cambridge: Cambridge University Press).

Chussodovsky, M. (1997) *Globalization of Poverty: The Impact of IMF and World Bank Reforms* (London: Zed).

Clark, G. and Feenstra, R. C. (2003) 'Technology in the Great Divergence', in M. D. Bordo, A. M. Taylor and J. G. Williamson (eds), *Globalization in Historical Perspective* (Chicago: University of Chicago Press), 277–314.

Clark, I. (1999) *Globalization and International Relations Theory* (Oxford: Oxford University Press).

Clausewitz, C. von (1976) *On War*, ed. and trans. by Michael Howard and Peter Paret (Princeton, NJ: Princeton University Press).

Cleaver, T. (2002) *Understanding the World Economy*, 2nd edn (London: Routledge).

Cohen, B. J. (ed.) (2004) *International Monetary Relations in the New Global Economy* (Cheltenham: Edward Elgar).

Coker, C. (2001) *Humane Warfare* (London: Routledge).

Collier, P. (2000) 'Doing Well out of War: An Economic Perspective', in M. Berdal and D. Malone (eds), *Greed and Grievance: Economic Agenda in Civil Wars* (Boulder, CO: Lynne Rienner), 91–111.

Connor, W. (1994) *Ethnonationalism: The Quest for Understanding* (Princeton: Princeton University Press).

Cooper, R. N. (ed.) (1989) *Can Nations Agree?* (Washington DC: Brookings Institution Press).

Craig, P. and de Búrca, G. (2003) *EU Law: Texts, Cases and Materials* (Oxford: Oxford University Press).

Cronin, A. K. (2002) 'Behind the Curve: Globalization and International Terrorism', *International Security*, 27(3): 30–58.

Cutler, A. C, Haufler, V. and Porter, T. (1999) *Private Authority and International Affairs* (Albany, NY: State University of New York Press).

Day, G. and Thompson, A. (2004) *Theorizing Nationalism* (Basingstoke: Palgrave Macmillan).

de Graaff, B. (2005) 'The Wars in the Former Yugoslavia in the 1990s: Bringing the State Back In', in I. Duyvesteyn and J. Angstrom (eds), *Rethinking the Nature of War* (London: Frank Cass), 159–79.

Delanty, G. and O'Mahony, P. (2002) *Nationalism and Social Theory* (London: Sage).

Denemark, R. A., Friedman, J., Gills, B. K. and Modelski, G. (eds) (2000) *World System History: The Social Science of Long-Term Change* (London: Routledge).

Dicken, P. (1992) *Global Shift: The Internationalization of Economic Activity*, 2nd edn (London: Chapman & Hall).

Doremus, P. N., Keller, W. W., Pauly, L. W. and Reich, S. (1998) *The Myth of the Global Corporation* (Princeton: Princeton University Press).

Doyle, M. (1983) 'Kant, Liberal Legacies and Foreign Affairs', *Philosophy and Public Affairs*, 12(3): 205–35.

Drahos, P. and Braithwaite, P. (2000) *Global Business Regulation* (Cambridge: Cambridge University Press).

Duffield, M. R. (2000) 'Globalization, Transborder Trade and War Economies', in M. Berdal and D. Malone (eds), *Greed and Grievance: Economic Agenda in Civil Wars* (Boulder, CO: Lynne Rienner).

Dunning, J. H. (1981) *International Production and the Multinational Enterprise* (London: Allen & Unwin).

Dunning, J. H. (1993) *Multinational Enterprise and the Global Economy* (Wokingham: Addison-Wesley).

Dupont, A. (2001) *East Asia Imperilled: Transnational Challenges to Security* (Cambridge: Cambridge University Press).

Easterly, W. (2001) *The Elusive Quest for Growth: Economists' Adventures and Misadventures in the Tropics* (Cambridge, MA: MIT Press).

Economides, S. and Wilson, P. (2001) *The Economic Factor in International Relations* (London: I.B. Tauris).

Economist (2005a) 'The Great Thrift Shift', 22 September.

Economist (2005b) 'Tired of globalization', 3 November.

Eichengreen, B. (1996) *Globalizing Capital: A History of the International Monetary System* (Princeton, NJ: Princeton University Press).

Eichengreen, B. (2003) *Capital Flows and Crisis* (Cambridge, MA: MIT Press).

Elliott, L. (2003) 'ASEAN and Environmental Cooperation: Norms, Interests and Identity', *Pacific Review*, 16(1): 29–52.

Emmers, R. (2003) *Cooperative Security and the Balance of Power in ASEAN and the ARF* (London: Routledge).

European Commission (2000a) *The Budget of the European Union: How is Your Money Spent?* (Brussels: European Commission).

European Commission (2000b) *How Europeans See Themselves: Looking Through the Mirror with Opinion Surveys* (Brussels: European Commission).

Falk, R. (1999) *Predatory Globalization: A Critique* (Cambridge: Polity).

Featherstone, M. (1990) *Global Culture: Nationalism, Globalization and Modernity* (London: Sage).

Featherstone, M., Lash, S. and Robertson, R. (eds) (1995) *Global Modernities* (London: Sage).

Feenstra, R. C. (1998) 'Integration of Trade and Disintegration of Production in the Global Economy', *Journal of Economic Perspectives*, 12(4): 31–50.

Ferguson, N. (2002) *Empire: The Rise and Demise of the British World Order and the Lessons for Global Power* (London: Basic Books).

Ferguson, N. (2005) 'Sinking Globalization', *Foreign Affairs*, March–April.

Ferguson, N. (2006) *The War of the World: History's Age of Hatred* (London: Allen Lane).

Fieldhouse, D. K. (1999) *The West and the Third World* (Oxford: Blackwell).

Finnemore, M. (2003) *The Purpose of Intervention: Changing Beliefs about the Use of Force* (Ithaca, NY: Cornell University Press).

Fisher, S. (2000) 'On the Need for an International Lender of Last Resort', paper presented to the American Economic Association and the American

Finance Association, 3 January 1999 (Washington, DC: IMF), http://www.imf.org/external/np/speeches/1999/010399.htm.

Foreman-Peck, J. (ed.) (1998) *Historical Foundations of Globalization* (Cheltenham: Edward Elgar).

Forrester, V. (1999) *The Economic Horror* (Cambridge: Polity).

Fortune (2006) 'The *Fortune* Global 500', July, http://money.cnn.com/magazines/fortune/global500/2006/index.html.

Frank, A. G. and Gills, B. K. (eds) (1993) *The World System: Five Hundred Years or Five Thousand?* (London: Routledge).

Frankel, J. A. (1993) *On Exchange Rates* (Cambridge, MA: MIT Press).

Freedman, L. (1998) *The Revolution in Strategic Affairs*, Adelphi Paper No. 318 (Oxford: Oxford University Press–IISS).

Frieden, J. A. (2006) *Global Capitalism: Its Rise and Fall in the Twentieth Century* (New York: W.W. Norton).

Friedman, T. L. (1999) *The Lexus and the Olive Tree* (New York: Farrar, Strauss & Giroux).

Friedman, T. L. (2005) *The World is Flat: A Brief History of the Twenty-First Century* (New York: Farrar, Strauss & Giroux).

Fukuyama, F. (1989) 'The End of History?', *The National Interest*, 16 (Summer).

Garrett, G. (1998) 'Global Markets and National Politics: Collision Course or Virtuous Circle', *International Organization*, 52(4): 787– 824.

Garrett, G. (2000) 'Globalization and National Autonomy', in N. Woods (ed.), *The Political Economy of Globalization* (Basingstoke: Macmillan – now Palgrave Macmillan).

Gelber, H. G. (1997) *Sovereignty through Interdependence* (London: Kluwer Law International).

Gellner, E. (1983) *Nations and Nationalism* (Oxford: Blackwell).

Germain, R. D. (ed.) (2000) *Globalization and its Critics: Perspectives from Political Economy* (Basingstoke: Macmillan – now Palgrave Macmillan).

Germain, R. D. (2001) 'Global Financial Governance the Problem of Inclusion', *Global Governance*, 7(4): 411–27.

Giddens, A. (1990) *The Consequences of Modernity* (Cambridge: Polity).

Giddens, A. (1994) *Beyond Left and Right: The Future of Radical Politics* (Cambridge: Polity).

Giddens, A. (1999) *Runaway World: How Globalization is Reshaping our Lives* (London: Profile).

Gilpin, R. (2001) *Global Political Economy: Understanding the International Economic Order* (Princeton, NJ: Princeton University Press).

Gilpin, R. (2002) *The Challenge of Global Capitalism: The World Economy in the 21st Century* (Princeton, NJ: Princeton University Press).

Gong, G. (1984) *The Standard of Civilization in International Society* (Oxford: Clarendon Press).

Goodhart, C. (1988) *The History of Central Banks* (Cambridge, MA: MIT Press).

Goulding, M. (2003) *Peacemongers* (Baltimore, MD: Johns Hopkins University Press).

Gray, C. H. (1997) *Postmodern War: The New Politics of Conflict* (London: Routledge).

Gray, C. S. (1999) 'Clausewitz Rules, OK with GPS', *Review of International Studies*, 29(5): 161–82.

Gray, C. S. (2002) *Strategy for Chaos: Revolutions in Military Affairs and the Evidence of History* (London: Frank Cass).

Gray, C. S. (2005) *Strategic Surprise* (Carlisle, PA: US Army War College).

Gray, J. (1998) *False Dawn: The Delusions of Global Capitalism* (London: Granta).

Greider, W. (1997) *One World, Ready or Not: The Manic Logic of Global Capitalism* (New York: Simon & Schuster).

Guéhenno, J.-M. (1995) *The End of the Nation State* (Minneapolis, MN: University of Minnesota Press).

Guéhenno, J.-M. (1998) 'The Impact of Globalization on Strategy', *Survival*, 40(4): 5–19.

Guibernau, M. (1999) *Nations without States: Political Communities in a Global Age* (Cambridge: Polity).

Guibernau, M. (2001) 'Globalization and the Nation-State', in M. Guibernau and J. Hutchinson (eds), *Understanding Nationalism* (Cambridge: Polity).

Hall, J. (1986) (ed.) *States in History* (Oxford: Blackwell).

Hall, P. and Soskice, D. (eds) (2001) *Varieties of Capitalism: The Institutional Foundations of Comparative Advantage* (Oxford: Oxford University Press).

Hall, R. B. and Biersteker, T. J. (eds) (2002) *The Emergence of Private Authority in Global Governance* (Cambridge: Cambridge University Press).

Halliday, F. (1994) *Rethinking International Relations* (Basingstoke: Macmillan – now Palgrave Macmillan).

Halliday, F. (1999) *Revolution and World Politics: The Rise and Fall of the Sixth Great Power* (Basingstoke: Macmillan – now Palgrave Macmillan).

Halliday, F. (2000) 'Global Governance: Prospects and Problems', *Citizenship Studies*, 4(1).

Hammarlund, P. A. (2005) *Liberal Internationalism and the Decline of the State: The Thought of Richard Cobden, David Mitrany and Kenichi Ohmae* (Basingstoke: Palgrave Macmillan).

Hannerz, U. (1996) *Transnational Connections: Culture, People, Places* (London: Routledge).

Hardt, M. and Negri, A. (2000) *Empire* (Cambridge, MA: Harvard University Press).

Harley, C. K. (1996) *The Integration of the World Economy, 1850–1914* (Cheltenham: Edward Elgar).

Harvey, D. (1989) *The Condition of Postmodernity* (Oxford: Blackwell).

Harvey, D. (2003) *The New Imperialism* (Oxford: Oxford University Press).

Hay, C. (2004) 'Globalization's Impact on States', in J. Ravenhill (ed.), *Global Political Economy* (Oxford: Oxford University Press), 235–62.

Hay, C. (2006) 'What's Globalization Got to Do With It? Economic Interdependence and the Future of European Welfare States', *Government and Opposition*, 41(1): 1–22.

Hay, C. and Marsh, D. (2000) 'Introduction: Demystifying Globalization', in C. Hay and D. Marsh (eds), *Demystifying Globalization* (Basingstoke: Macmillan – now Palgrave Macmillan).

Hayes, C. J. H. (1948) *The Historical Evolution of Modern Nationalism* (New York: Macmillan).

He, B. (2004) 'East Asian Ideas of Regionalism: A Normative Critique', *Australian Journal of International Affairs*, 58(1): 105–25

Held, D. (2003) 'Cosmopolitanism: Globalization Tames?', *Review of International Studies*, 29(4): 465–80.

Held, D., Barnett, A. and Henderson, C. (eds) (2005) *Debating Globalization* (Cambridge: Polity).

Held, D., McGrew, A., Goldblatt, D. and Perraton, J. (1999) *Global Transformations* (Cambridge: Polity).

Hempson-Jones, J. (2005) 'The Evolution of China's Engagement with International Governmental Organizations: Toward a Liberal Foreign Policy?', *Asian Survey*, 45(5): 702–21.

Henning, C. R. (2002) *East Asian Financial Cooperation* (Washington DC: Institute for International Economics).

Hertel, S. (2003) 'The Private Side of Global Governance', *Journal of International Affairs*, 57(1): 41–54.

Hertz, N. (2001) *The Silent Takeover: Global Capitalism and the Death of Democracy* (London: Heinemann).

Hill, C. (2003) *The Changing Politics of Foreign Policy* (Basingstoke: Palgrave Macmillan).

Hinsley, F. H. (1973) *Nationalism and the International System* (London: Hodder & Stoughton).

Hirst, P. (1997) 'The Global Economy: Myths and Realities', *International Affairs*, 73(3).

Hirst, P. and Thompson, G. (1996) *Globalization in Question* (Cambridge: Polity).

Hobsbawm, E. (1990) *Nations and Nationalism since 1780* (Cambridge: Cambridge University Press).

Hobson, J. M. (2003) 'Disappearing Taxes of the "Race to the Middle"? Fiscal Policy in the OECD', in L. Weiss (ed.), *States in the Global Economy: Bringing Domestic Institutions Back In* (Cambridge: Cambridge University Press), 37–57.

Hoekman, B. M. and Kostecki, M. M. (2001) *The Political Economy of the World Trading System: The WTO and Beyond* (Oxford: Oxford University Press).

Hoffman, S. (2002) 'Clash of Globalizations', *Foreign Affairs*, 81(4).

Holsti, K. J. (1996) *The State, War and the State of War* (Cambridge: Cambridge University Press).

Holton, R. J. (1998) *Globalization and the Nation-State* (Basingstoke: Macmillan – now Palgrave Macmillan).

Hoogvelt, A. (1997) *Globalization and the Post-colonial World* (Basingstoke: Macmillan – now Palgrave Macmillan).

Hopkins, A. G. (ed.) (2002) *Globalization in World History* (London: Pimlico).

Horsman, M. and Marshall, A. (1994) *After the Nation-State* (New York: HarperCollins).

Howard, M. (1983) *The Causes of War and Other Essays* (London: Temple Smith).

Hoyt, K. and Brooks, S. G. (2004) 'A Double Edged Sword: Globalization and Biosecurity', *International Security*, 28(3): 123–48.

Hufbauer, G. C. (2003) 'Looking 30 years Ahead in Global Governance', in H. Siebert (ed.), *Global Governance: An Architecture for the World Economy* (Berlin: Springer), 245–69.

Hughes, C. (1997) 'Globalization and Nationalism: Squaring the Circle in Chinese International Relations Theory', *Millennium: Journal of International Studies*, 26(1): 103–24.

Huntington, S. P. (1993) 'The Clash of Civilizations?', *Foreign Affairs*, 72(3).

Huntington, S. P. (1996) *The Clash of Civilizations and the Remaking of World Order* (New York: Simon & Schuster).

Hurrell, A. and Fawcett, L. (eds) (1995) *Regionalism in World Politics Regional Organization and International Order* (Oxford: Oxford University Press).

ICISS (International Commission on Intervention and State Sovereignty) (2001) *The Responsibility to Protect: Report of the International Commission on Intervention and State Sovereignty*, Ottawa.

Ignatieff, M. (1994) *Blood and Belonging: Journeys into the New Nationalism* (London: Vintage).

IISS (International Institute for Strategic Studies) (2005) *The Military Balance, 2005–06* (London: Taylor & Francis).

IISS (International Institute for Strategic Studies) (2006) *Armed Conflict Database* (London: IISS and Taylor & Francis), http://www.iiss.org/publications/armed-conflict-database.

Ikenberry, G. J. (2001) *After Victory: Institutions, Strategic Restraint and the Rebuilding of Order after Major Wars* (Princeton, NJ: Princeton University Press).

Jackson, J. H. (1998) *The World Trading System: Law and Policy of International Economic Relations*, 2nd edn (Cambridge, MA: MIT Press).

Jacquin-Berdal, D., Oros, A. and Verweij, M. (eds) (1998) *Culture in World Politics* (Basingstoke: Macmillan – now Palgrave Macmillan in association with *Millennium*).

James, H. (2001) *The End of Globalization: Lessons from the Great Depression* (Cambridge, MA: Harvard University Press).

Jentleson, B. (1999) *Opportunities Missed, Opportunities Seized: Preventive Diplomacy in the Post-Cold War World* (Lanham, MD: Rowman & Littlefield).

Jones, R. J. B. (2000) *A World Turned Upside Down? Globalization and the Future of the State* (Manchester: Manchester University Press).

Jonsson, C. and Langhorne, R. T. B. (2004) *Diplomacy*, 3 vols (London: Sage).

Josselin, D. and Wallace, W. (eds) (2001) *Non-state Actors in World Politics* (Basingstoke: Palgrave Macmillan).

Kaiser, K. (2003) 'The New NATO', *Asia-Pacific Review*, 10(1): 64–71.

Kaldor, M. (1999) *New and Old Wars: Organized Violence in a Global Era* (Cambridge: Polity).

Kaldor, M. (2004) 'Nationalism and Globalization', *Nations and Nationalism*, 10(1/2): 161–77.

Kalyvas, S. N. (2001) '"New" and "Old" Civil War: A Valid Distinction?', *World Politics*, 54(1): 99–118.

Kaplan, R. D. (2000) *The Coming Anarchy: Shattering the Dreams of the Post-Cold War World* (New York: Random House).

Karns, M. P. and Mingst, K. A. (2004) *International Organizations: The Politics and Processes of Global Governance* (Boulder, CO: Lynne Rienner).

Kaul, I., Grunberg, I. and Stern, M. A. (eds) (1999) *Global Public Goods: International Cooperation in the 21st Century* (Oxford: Oxford University Press).

Keane, J. (2003) *Global Civil Society?* (Cambridge: Cambridge University Press).

Kedourie, E. (1966) *Nationalism*, 3rd edn (London: Hutchison).

Keen, D. (1998) *The Economic Functions of Violence in Civil Wars*, Adelphi Paper No. 320 (Oxford: Oxford University Press–IISS).

Keene, E. (2002) *Beyond the Anarchical Society* (Cambridge: Cambridge University Press).

Kegley, C. W. (ed.) (1995) *Controversies in International Relations: Realism and the Neoliberal Challenge* (New York: St. Martin's Press).

Kegley, C. W. and Raymond, G. A. (1994) *A Multipolar Peace? Great Power Politics in the Twenty First Century* (New York: St. Martin's Press).

Kennedy, P. (1993) *Preparing for the Twenty First Century* (New York: HarperCollins).

Kennedy, P. (2002) 'The Greatest Superpower Ever', *New Perspectives Quarterly*, 19.

Keohane, R. O. (1984) *After Hegemony: Cooperation and Discord in the World Political Economy* (Princeton, NJ: Princeton University Press).

Keohane, R. O. (1989) *International Institutions and State Power: Essays in International Relations Theory* (Boulder, CO: Westview).

Keohane, R. O. (2002) *Power and Governance in a Partially Globalized World* (London: Routledge).

Keohane, R. O. and Nye, J. S. (eds) (1972) *Transnational Relations and World Politics* (Cambridge, MA: Harvard University Press).

Keohane, R. O. and Nye, J. S. (1977) *Power and Interdependence: World Politics in Transition* (Boston, MA: Little, Brown).

Keohane, R. O. and Nye, J. S. (eds) (2000) 'Globalization: What's New? What's Not? (And So What?)', *Foreign Policy* (Spring): 104–19.

Keynes, J. M. (1920) *The Economic Consequences of the Peace* (New York: Harcourt, Brace & Howe).

Kindleberger, C. P. (1969) *American Business Abroad: Six Lectures on Foreign Direct Investment* (New Haven, CT: Yale University Press).

King, M. R. (2001) 'Who Triggered the Asian Financial Crisis', *Review of International Political Economy*, 8(3): 438–66.

Kitson, M. and Michie, J. (1995) 'Trade and Growth: A Historical Perspective', in J. Michie and J. G. Smith (eds), *Managing the Global Economy* (Oxford: Oxford University Press).

Klein, N. (2000) *No Logo: No Space, No Choice, No Jobs* (London: Flamingo).

Knox, M. and Murray, W. (eds) (2001) *The Dynamics of Military Revolution, 1300–2050* (Cambridge: Cambridge University Press).

Kobrin, S. J. (2002) 'Economic Governance in an Electronically Networked Global Economy', in R. B. Hall and T. J. Biersteker (eds), *The Emergence of Private Authority in Global Governance* (Cambridge: Cambridge University Press), 43–75.

Kofman, E. and Youngs, G. (eds) (1996) *Globalization: Theory and Practice* (London: Pinter).

Kohn, H. (1958 [1944]) *The Idea of Nationalism: A Study of its Origins and Background* (London: Macmillan).

Korten, D. C. (2001) *When Corporations Rule the World* (San Francisco: Berrett-Koehler Publishers).

Krahmann, E. (2003) 'National, Regional and Global Governance: One Phenomenon or Many?', *Global Governance*, 9(3): 323–57.

Krasner, S. D. (1993) 'Economic Interdependence and Independent Statehood', in R. H. Jackson and A. James (eds), *States in a Changing World* (Oxford: Oxford University Press).

Krasner, S. D. (1999) *Sovereignty: Organized Hypocrisy* (Ithaca, NY: Cornell University Press).

Krueger, A. O. (2000) 'Trading Phobias: Governments, NGOs and the Multilateral System', John Bonython Lecture.

Krugman, P. R. (1995) 'Growing World Trade: Causes and Consequences', *Brookings Papers on Economic Activity*, 1: 327–62.

Krugman, P. R. and Obstfeld, M. (2003) *International Economics: Theory and Practice*, 6th edn (Boston, MA: Addison-Wesley).

Lapid, Y. and Kratochwil, F. (eds) (1996) *The Return of Culture and Identity in IR Theory* (Boulder, CO: Lynne Rienner).

Latham, A. J. H. (1978) *The International Economy and the Undeveloped World: 1865–1914* (London: Croom Helm).

Latham, R. (1997) *The Liberal Moment: Modernity, Security and the Making of the Post-war Order* (New York: Columbia University Press).

Latouche, S. (1996) *The Westernization of the World: The Significance, Scope and Limits of the Drive Towards Global Uniformity* (Cambridge: Polity).

Leadbetter, C. (2002) *Up the Down Escalator: Why the Global Pessimists are Wrong* (London: Viking).

Legrain, P. (2002) *Open World: The Truth About Globalization* (London: Abacus).

Leonard, M. (2000) *Going Public: Diplomacy in the Information Age* (London: Foreign Policy Centre).

Levinson, M. (2006) *The Box: How the Shipping Container Made the World Smaller and the World Economy Bigger* (Princeton, NJ: Princeton University Press).

Lévy, B.-H. (2004) *War, Evil and the End of History* (London: Duckworth).

Lieven, A. (2004) *America Right or Wrong: An Anatomy of American Nationalism* (Oxford: Oxford University Press).

Linklater, A. (1998) *The Transformation of Political Community: Ethical Foundations of the Post-Westphalian Order* (Cambridge: Polity).

Lipschutz, R. (ed.) (1995) *On Security* (New York: Columbia University Press).

Lock, P. (1998) 'Military Downsizing and Growth in the Security in the Security Industry in Sub-Saharan Africa', *Strategic Analysis*, 22(9): 1393–426.

Long, D. and Wilson, P. (1995) *The Thinkers of the Twenty Years' Crisis: Inter-war Idealism Reassessed* (Oxford: Clarendon).

Luard, E. (1988) *The Blunted Sword: The Erosion of Military Power in Modern World Politics* (London: I.B. Tauris).

Luard, E. (1990) *The Globalization of Politics: The Change Focus of Political Action in the Modern World* (London: Macmillan – now Basingstoke: Palgrave Macmillan).

Lukacs, J. (2005) 'Foreword', in K. Ungváry, *The Siege of Budapest: One Hundred Days in World War II* (New Haven, CT: Yale University Press), xiii–xxiv.

MacDonald, D. B. (2002) *Balkan Holocausts? Serbian and Croatian Victim-centred Propaganda and the War in Yugoslavia* (Manchester: Manchester University Press).

Maddison, A. (2001) *The World Economy: A Millennial Perspective* (Paris: OECD).

Maghroori, R. and Ramberg, B. (1982) *Globalism versus Realism: International Relations' Third Great Debate* (Boulder, CO: Westview).

Mallaby, S. (2005) 'Saving the World Bank', *Foreign Affairs*, 84(3).

Malone, D. M. (2004) 'Conclusion', in D. M. Malone (ed.), *The UN Security Council: From the Cold War to the 21st Century* (Boulder, CO: Lynne Rienner), 617–49.

Mandel, R. (2002) *Armies Without States: The Privatization of Security* (Boulder, CO: Lynne Rienner).

Mandelbaum, M. (1998) 'Is Major War Obsolete?', *Survival*, 40(4): 20–38.

Mann, M. (1993) *Sources of Social Power Vol. II: The Rise of Classes and Nation-States, 1760–1914* (Cambridge: Cambridge University Press).

Mann, M. (1997) 'Has Globalization Ended the Rise and Rise of the Nation-State?', *Review of International Political Economy*, 4(3): 472–96.

Mansfield, E. D. and Milner, H. (1999) 'The New Wave of Regionalism', *International Organization*, 53(3): 589–627.

Martin, L. L and Simmons, B. A. (1998) 'Theories and Empirical Studies of International Institutions', *International Organization*, 52(4): 729–57.

Mayall, J. (1990) *National and International Society* (Cambridge: Cambridge University Press).

McGrew, A. (2005) 'Globalization and Global Politics', in J. Baylis and S. Smith (eds), *The Globalization of World Politics*, 3rd edn (Oxford: Oxford University Press).

McGrew, A. and Lewis, P. (eds) (1992) *Global Politics: Globalization and the Nation-State* (Cambridge: Polity).

McNeill, W. H. (1963) *The Rise of the West: A History of the Human Community* (Chicago: University of Chicago Press).

Mearsheimer, J. J. (1990) 'Back to the Future: Instability in Europe After the Cold War', *International Security*, 15(1): 5–50.

Mearsheimer, J. J (1994) 'The False Promise of International Institutions', *International Security*, 19(3): 5–50.

Mearsheimer, J. J (2001) *The Tragedy of Great Power Politics* (New York: W.W. Norton).

Micklethwait, J. and Wooldridge, J. (2000) *A Future Perfect: The Challenge and Hidden Promise of Globalization* (London: William Heinemann).

Millennium: Journal of International Studies (1999) Special Issue, 'Territorialities, Identities and Movement in International Relations', 28(3)

Milner, H. V. (2005) 'Globalization, Development and International Institutions: Normative and Positive Perspectives', *Perspectives on Politics* , 3(4): 833–54.

Modelksi, G. (1972) *Principles of World Politics* (New York: Free Press).

Monbiot, G. (2003) *The Age of Consent: A Manifesto for a New World Order* (London: Flamingo).

Moore, M. (ed.) (1998) *National Self-Determination and Secession* (Oxford: Oxford University Press).

Moran, T. (1999) *Foreign Direct Investment and Development: The New Policy Agenda for Developing Countries and Economies in Transition* (Washington, DC: Institute for International Economics).

Moravscik, A. (1998) *The Choice for Europe: Social Purpose and State Power from Messina to Maastricht* (Ithaca, NY: Cornell University Press).

Motyl, A. J. (1999) *Revolutions, Nations, Empires: Conceptual Limits and Theoretical Possibilities* (New York: Columbia University Press).

Mudde, C. (2004) 'The Populist Zeitgeist', *Government and Opposition*, 39(4): 541–63.

Mueller, J. (1989) *Retreat from Doomsday: The Obsolescence of Major War* (New York: Basic Books).

Musah, A.-F. and Fayemi, J. K. (eds) (2000) *Mercenaries: An African Security Dilemma* (London: Pluto Press).

Muthien, B. and Taylor, I. (2002) 'The Return of the Dogs of War? The Privatization of Security in Africa', in R. B. Hall and T. J. Biersteker (eds), *The Emergence of Private Authority in Global Governance* (Cambridge: Cambridge University Press), 183–99.

Nederveen Pieterse, J. (2004) *Globalization and Culture: Global Melange* (Lanham, MD: Rowman & Littlefield).

Noble, G. W. and Ravenhill, J. (eds) (2000) *The Asian Financial Crisis and the Architecture of Global Finance* (Cambridge: Cambridge University Press).

Norberg, J. (2001) *In Defence of Global Capitalism* (Stockholm: Timbro).

Nyland, C. and Smyth, R. (2004) 'Australian Roadmaps to Globalism: Explaining the Shift from Multilateralism to Imperial Preference', in G. Davies and C. Nyland (eds), *Globalization in the Asian Region: Impacts and Consequences* (Cheltenham: Edward Elgar).

O'Brien, P. (1984) 'Europe and the World Economy', in H. Bull and A. Watson (eds), *The Expansion of International Society* (Oxford: Clarendon Press), 43–60.

O'Brien, R. and Williams, M. (2004) *Global Political Economy: Evolution and Dynamics* (Basingstoke: Palgrave Macmillan).

O'Hanlon, M. E. (2000) *Technological Change and the Future of Warfare* (Washington, DC: Brookings Institution Press).

O'Rourke, K. H. and Williamson, J. G. (1999) *Globalization and History: The Evolution of a Nineteenth Century Atlantic Economy* (Cambridge, MA: MIT Press).

Obstfeld, M. (1998) 'The Global Capital Market: Benefactor or Menace?', *Journal of Economic Perspectives* 12(4): 9–30.

Obstfeld, M. and Taylor, A. M. (2003) 'Globalization and Capital Markets', in M. D. Bordo, A. M. Taylor and J. G. Williamson (eds), *Globalization in Historical Perspective* (Chicago: University of Chicago Press), 121–83.

OECD (Organization for Economic Cooperation and Development) (1999) *Post-Uruguay Round Tariff Regimes: Achievements and Outlooks* (Paris: OECD).

OECD (Organization for Economic Cooperation and Development) (2006) *Main Economic Indicators* (Paris: OECD), http://www.oecd.org/document/54/0,2340,en_2649_33715_15569334_1_1_1_1,00.html.

Ohmae, K. (1990) *The Borderless World: Power and Strategy in the Interlinked World* (New York: Collins).

Ohmae, K. (1995) *The End of the Nation-State: The Rise of Regional Economies* (New York: Free Press).

OMB (Office of Management and Budget) (2005) *Historical Tables: Budget of the US Government, Financial Year 2006* (Washington, DC: US Government Printing Offices).

Østergaard-Nielsen, E. (2001) 'Diasporas in World Politics', in D. Josselin and W. Wallace (eds), *Non-state Actors in World Politics* (Basingstoke: Palgrave Macmillan).

Ostry, S. (2003) 'What Are the Necessary Ingredients for the World Trading Order', in H. Siebert (ed.), *Global Governance: An Architecture for the World Economy* (Berlin: Springer), 123–47.

Owen-Vandersluis, S. and Yeros, P. (2000) *Poverty in World Politics: Whose Global Era?* (Basingstoke: Macmillan – now Palgrave Macmillan).

Özkirimli, U. (2005) *Contemporary Debates on Nationalism: A Critical Engagement* (Basingstoke: Palgrave Macmillan).

Pelton, R. Y. (2006) *Licensed to Kill: Hired Guns in the War on Terror* (New York: Crown).

Pogge, T. W. (2002) *World Poverty and Human Rights: Cosmopolitan Responsibilities and Reforms* (Cambridge: Polity).

Political Studies (1999) Special Issue 'Sovereignty at the Millennium', 47(3).

Pomeranz, K. and Topik, S. (2006) *The World that Trade Created: Society, Culture and the World Economy, from 1400 to the Present* (Armonk, NY: M.E. Sharpe).

Potts, L. (1990) *The World Labour Market: A History of Migration* (London: Zed Books).

Preston, P. (1996) *Development Theory: An Introduction* (Oxford: Blackwell).

Ravenhill, J. (2000) 'APEC Adrift: Implications for Economic Regionalism in the Asia-Pacific', *Pacific Review*, 13(2): 319–33.

Reich, R. (1991) *The Work of Nations: Preparing Ourselves for 21st Century Capitalism* (New York: Knopf).

Rengger, N. J. (2000) *International Relations, Political Theory and the Problem of Order* (London: Routledge).

Rhodes, R. A. W. (1996) 'The New Governance: Governing without Government', *Political Studies*, 44(4).

Risse, T., Ropp, S. C. and Sikkink, K. (eds) (1999) *The Power of Human Rights: International Norms and Domestic Change* (Cambridge: Cambridge University Press).

Roberts, A. (1996) 'From San Francisco to Sarajevo: The UN and the Use of Force', *Survival*, 37(4): 7–28.

Roberts, A. (2004) 'The Use of Force', in D. M. Malone (ed.), *The UN Security Council: From the Cold War to the 21st Century* (Boulder, CO: Lynne Rienner), 133–52.

Roberts, A. (2006) *The Wonga Coup: The New Scramble for Africa* (London: Profile Book).

Robertson, R. (1992) *Globalization Social Theory and Cultural Change* (London: Sage).

Rodrik, D. (1996) 'Why do More Open Economies have Bigger Governments?', NBER Working Paper.

Rodrik, D. (1997) *Has Globalization Gone Too Far?* (Washington, DC: Institute for International Economics).

Rodrik, D. (1998) 'The Debate About Globalization: How to Move Forward by Looking Backward', Conference Paper on the Future of the International Trading System (Washington, DC: Institute for International Economics).

Rosecrance, R. (1999) *The Rise of the Virtual State: Wealth and Power in the Coming Century* (New York: Basic Books).

Rosenau, J. N. (1990) *Turbulence in World Politics: A Theory of Change and Continuity* (Princeton, NJ: Princeton University Press).

Rosenau, J. N. (1997) 'Governance and Democracy in a Globalizing World', in D. Archibugi, D. Held and M. Köhler (eds), *Re-imagining Political Community: Studies in Cosmopolitan Democracy* (Cambridge: Polity).

Rosenau, J. N. and Czempiel, E.-O. (eds) (1992) *Governance without Government: Order and Change in World Politics* (Cambridge: Cambridge University Press).

Rosenberg, J. (2000) *The Follies of Globalization Theory: Polemical Essays* (London: Verso).

Rosenberg, J. (2005) 'Globalization Theory: A Post Mortem', *International Politics*, 42(1): 2–74.

Ruggie, J. G. (ed.) (1993) *Multilateralism Matters: The Theory and Praxis of an Institutional Form* (New York: Columbia University Press).

Ruggie, J. G. (2003) 'The United Nations and Globalization: Patterns and Limits of Institutional Adaptation', *Global Governance*, 9(3): 301–23.

Rugman, A. M. (2000) *The End of Globalization* (London: Random House).

Rugman, A. M. (2005) *The Regional Multinationals: MNEs and 'Global' Strategic Management* (Oxford: Oxford University Press).

Ruigrok, W. and van Tulder, R. (1995) *The Logic of International Restructuring* (London: Routledge).

Sachs, J. and Warner, A. (1995) 'Economic Reform and the Process of Global Integration', *Brookings Papers on Economic Activity*, 1(1): 1–118.

Sally, R. (2000) 'Has Globalization Gone too Far?', *Government and Opposition*, 35(2).

Sambanis, N. (2001) 'Do Ethnic and Non-ethnic Civil Wars Have the Same Causes: A Theoretical and Empirical Inquiry', *Journal of Conflict Resolution*, 45(3): 259–82.

Sandler, T. (1997) *Global Challenges: An Approach to Environmental, Political and Economic Problems* (Cambridge: Cambridge University Press).

Sandler, T. (2004) *Global Collective Action* (Cambridge: Cambridge University Press).

Sassen, S. (1998) *Globalization and its Discontents* (New York: New Books).

Sassen, S. (1999) 'Embedding the Global in the National: Implications for the Role of the State', in D. A. Smith, D. J. Solinger and S. C. Topik (eds), *States and Sovereignty in the Global Economy* (London: Routledge).

Sassen, S. (2002) 'The State and Globalization', in R. B. Hall and T. J. Biersteker (eds), *The Emergence of Private Authority in Global Governance* (Cambridge: Cambridge University Press), 91–112.

Schirm, S. A. (2002) *Globalization and the New Regionalism: Global Markets, Domestic Politics and Regional Cooperation* (Cambridge: Polity).

Schmidt, B. C. (1998) *The Political Discourse of Anarchy: A Disciplinary History of International Relations* (Albany, NY: SUNY Press).

Scholte, J. A. (1993) *International Relations of Social Change* (Buckingham: Open University Press).

Scholte, J. A. (1997) 'Global Capitalism and the State', *International Affairs*, 73(3).

Scholte, J. A. (2000) *Globalization: A Critical Introduction* (Basingstoke: Palgrave Macmillan).

Scholte, J. A. (2005) *Globalization: A Critical Introduction*, 2nd edn (Basingstoke: Palgrave Macmillan).

Schwartz, H. M. (2000) *States versus Markets: The Emergence of a Global Economy*, 2nd edn (Basingstoke: Palgrave Macmillan).

Segal, A. (1993) *An Atlas of International Migration* (London: Hans Zell).

Shanks, C., Jacobson, H. and Kaplan, J. (1996) 'Inertia and Change in the Constellation of Inter-Governmental Organizations, 1981–92', *International Organization*, 50(4): 593–627.

Shaw, M. (1997) 'The State of Globalization: Towards a Theory of State Transformation', *Review of International Political Economy*, 4(3): 497–513.

Sinclair, T. J. (2000) 'Reinventing Authority: Embedded Knowledge Networks and the New Global Finance', *Environment and Planning C: Government and Policy*, 18(4): 487–502.

Sinclair, T. J. (2001) 'The Infrastructure of Global Governance: Quasi-Regulatory Mechanism and the New Global Finance', *Global Governance*, 7(4): 441–52.

Singer, P. W. (2002) 'Corporate Warriors: The Rise of Privatized Military Industry and its Ramifications for International Security', *International Security*, 26(3): 186–220.

Singer, P. W. (2003) *Corporate Warriors: The Rise of the Privatized Military Industry* (Ithaca, NY: Cornell University Press).

Slaughter, A.-M. (2004) *A New World Order* (Princeton, NJ: Princeton University Press).

Smith, A. D. (1995) *Nations and Nationalism in a Global Era* (Cambridge: Polity).

Smith, A. D. (1998) *Nationalism and Modernism* (London: Routledge).

Smith, A. D. (2001) *Nationalism* (Cambridge: Polity).

Sørenson, G. (1999) 'Sovereignty: Change and Continuity in a Fundamental Institution', *Political Studies*, 47(3): 590–604.

Sørenson, G. (2003) *The Transformation of the State* (Basingstoke: Palgrave Macmillan).

Soros, G. (2002) *George Soros on Globalization* (New York: Public Affairs).

Stevis, D. and Mumme, S. (2000) 'Rules and Politics in International Integration: Environmental Regulation in NAFTA and the EU', *Environmental Politics*, 9(4): 20–42.

Stiglitz, J. E. (2002) *Globalization and its Discontents* (New York: Norton).

Stiglitz, J. E. (2006) *Making Globalization Work: The Next Steps to Global Justice* (New York: Norton).

Stopford, J. and Strange, S. (1991) *Rival States, Rival Firms* (Cambridge: Cambridge University Press).

Strange, S. (1996) *The Retreat of the State: The Diffusion of Power in the World Economy* (Cambridge: Cambridge University Press).

Talbott, S. (1997) 'Globalization and Diplomacy: A Practitioner's Perspective', *Foreign Policy*, Fall.

Tanzi, V. and Schuknecht, L. (2000) *Public Spending in the 20th Century: A Global Perspective* (Cambridge: Cambridge University Press).

Taylor, A. M. (1996) *International Capital Mobility in History: The Savings-Investment Relationship*, NBER Working Paper No. 5743.

Teschke, B. (2003) *The Myth of 1648: Class, Geopolitics and the Making of Modern International Relations* (London: Verso).

Thacker, S. C. (1999) 'The High Politics of IMF Lending', *World Politics*, 52(1): 38–75.

Thirlwell, M. P. (2005) *The New Terms of Trade*, Lowy Institute Paper 07 (Sydney: Lowy Institute for International Policy).

Thompson, H. (2006) 'The Modern State and its Adversaries', *Government and Opposition*, 41(1): 23–39.

Thucydides (1972) *History of the Peloponnesian War*, rev. edn (London: Penguin).

Tilly, C. (1990) *Coercion, Capital and European States, AD 990–1990* (Oxford: Blackwell).

Towsend, M. E. (1941) *European Colonial Expansion Since 1871* (Chicago: Lippincott).

UNCTAD (United Nations Conference on Trade and Development) (2005) *World Investment Report, 2005* (New York: United Nations).

UNDP (United Nations Development Programme) (1999) *United Nations Development Report* (New York: United Nations).

Van Creveld, M. (1991) *The Transformation of War* (New York: Free Press).

Van Creveld, M. (1999) *The Rise and Fall of the State* (Cambridge: Cambridge University Press).

Vaubel, R. (1996) 'Bureaucracy at the IMF and the World Bank: A Comparison of the Evidence', *The World Economy*, 19(2): 195–210.

Vernon, R. (1971) *Sovereignty at Bay: The Multinational Spread of US Enterprises* (London: Longman).

Vreeland, J. (2003) *The IMF and Economic Development* (Cambridge: Cambridge University Press).

Wallace, W. (1999) 'The Sharing of Sovereignty: The European Paradox', *Political Studies*, 47(3): 503–21.

Wallerstein, I. M. (1974) *The Modern World System Vol. 1* (New York: Academic Press).

Walt, S. (1996) *Revolution and War* (Ithaca, NY: Cornell University Press).

Walter, A. (1991) *World Power and World Money: The Role of Hegemony and International Monetary Order* (London: Harvester).

Waltz, K. N. (1959) *Man, the State and War: A Theoretical Analysis* (New York: Columbia University Press).

Waltz, K. N. (1979) *Theory of International Politics* (Boston: Addison-Wesley).

Waltz, K. N. (1993) 'The Emerging Structure of International Politics', *International Security*, 18(2): 44–79.

Wang, G. (ed.) (1997) *Global History and Migrations* (Boulder, CO: Westview).

Waters, M. (1995) *Globalization* (London: Routledge).

Weinstein, M. M. and Charnovitz, S. (2001) 'The Greening of the WTO', *Foreign Affairs*, 80(6): 147–56.

Weiss, L. (1998) *The Myth of the Powerless State: Governing the Economy in a Global Era* (Cambridge: Polity).

Weiss, L. (2003a) 'Introduction: Bringing Domestic Institutions Back in', in L. Weiss (ed.), *States in the Global Economy: Bringing Domestic Institutions Back in* (Cambridge: Cambridge University Press).

Weiss, L. (2003b) 'Is the State Being Transformed by Globalization?', L. Weiss (ed.), *States in the Global Economy: Bringing Domestic Institutions Back in* (Cambridge: Cambridge University Press), 293–317.

Weiss, L. (2003c) 'Guiding Globalization in East Asia: New Roles for Old Developmental States', in L. Weiss (ed.), *States in the Global Economy: Bringing Domestic Institutions Back In* (Cambridge: Cambridge University Press), 245–70.

Weiss, L. (2005) 'Global Governance, National Strategies: How Industrialized States Make Room to Move Under the WTO', *Review of International Political Economy*, 12(5): 723–49.

Welsh, J. M. (ed.) (2004) *Humanitarian Intervention and International Relations* (Oxford: Oxford University Press).

Wheeler, N. J. (2000) *Saving Strangers: Humanitarian Intervention in International Society* (Oxford: Oxford University Press).

Wilensky, H. L. (2002) *Rich Democracies: Political Economy, Public Policy and Performance* (Berkeley, CA: University of California Press).

Williams, M. (2005) 'Globalization and Civil Society', in J. Ravenhill (ed.), *Global Political Economy* (Oxford: Oxford University Press), 345–69.

Williams, P. (2002) 'Transnational Organized Crime and the State', in R. B. Hall and T. J. Biersteker (eds), *The Emergence of Private Authority in Global Governance* (Cambridge: Cambridge University Press), 161–82.

Williamson, J. G. (1998) 'Globalization, Labor Markets and Policy Backlash in the Past', *Journal of Economic Perspectives*, 12(4): 51–72.

Wolf, M. (2004) *Why Globalization Works* (New Haven, CT: Yale University Press).

Woods, N. (2000a) 'The Political Economy of Globalization', in N. Woods (ed.), *The Political Economy of Globalization* (Basingstoke: Palgrave Macmillan), 1–19.

Woods, N. (2000b) 'The Challenge to International Institutions', in N. Woods (ed.), *The Political Economy of Globalization* (Basingstoke: Palgrave Macmillan), 202–23.

World Bank (2002) *Globalization, Growth and Poverty: Building an Inclusive World Economy* (New York: World Bank/Oxford University Press).

Wriston, W. (1992) *The Twilight of Sovereignty* (New York: Scribner).

WTO (World Trade Organization) (2001) *Doha WTO Ministerial Declaration*, WT/MIN(01)/DEC/1 (Geneva: WTO), http://www.wto.org/english/thewto_e/minist_e/min01_e/mindecl_e.htm.

WTO (World Trade Organization) (2005) *International Trade Statistics, 2005* (Geneva: WTO).

Yahuda, M. (1996) *The International Politics of the Asia-Pacific, 1945–1995* (London: Routledge).

Yergin, D. A. and Stanislaw, J. (1998) *The Commanding Heights: The Battle Between Government and the Marketplace that is Remaking the Modern World* (New York: Simon & Schuster).

Young, O. R. (1994) *International Governance: Protecting the Environment in a Stateless Society* (Ithaca, NY: Cornell University Press).

Zevin, R. (1992) 'Are World Financial Markets More Open? If So, Why and With What Effects?', in T. Banuri and J. B. Schor (eds), *Financial Openness and National Autonomy: Opportunities and Constraints* (Oxford: Oxford University Press).

Zhao, S. (2000), 'Chinese Nationalism and its International Limits', *Political Science Quarterly*, 115(1): 1–33.

Zolberg, A. (1997) 'Global Movements, Global Walls: Responses to Migration, 1885–1925', in G. Wang (ed.), *Global History and Migrations* (Boulder, CO: Westview).

Zürn, M. (2004) 'Global Governance and Legitimacy Problems', *Government and Opposition*, 39(2): 260–87.

Index

246